THE RACE AROUND
THE WORLD

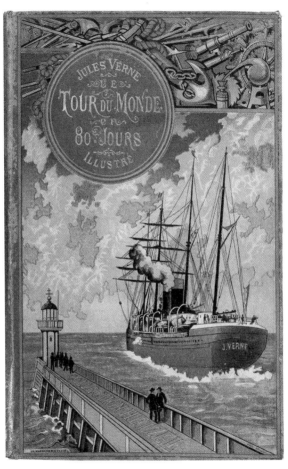

The cover of a French edition of the novel Around the World in 80 Days *by Jules Verne that inspired Bly and Bisland*

The Lakeside Classics

THE RACE AROUND
THE WORLD

by Nellie Bly and Elizabeth Bisland

EDITED BY

MATTHEW GOODMAN

The Lakeside Press

R. R. DONNELLEY & SONS COMPANY

December 2015

PUBLISHER'S PREFACE

As you enjoy the holiday season, we are pleased to bring to you the stories of two intrepid young women who, more than one hundred years ago, found themselves celebrating Christmas and New Year's half a world away from their friends and family.

In 1889, Nellie Bly, one of the first women investigative reporters, convinced her newspaper, *The World,* to send her on a trip around the globe in an effort to beat the fictional record of Phileas Fogg, hero of Jules Verne's highly popular novel *Around the World in Eighty Days. Cosmopolitan Magazine*, determined not to be bested in the circulation competition, simultaneously sent its literary critic, Elizabeth Bisland, in the opposite direction to race both Fogg and Bly.

Upon returning home, the women wrote fascinating accounts of their experiences and of the world as seen through the eyes of two young women similar in many respects but also very different in their perspectives.

Both Bly and Bisland were in their twenties; both were from families who had become impoverished. Both had broken into journalism through local newspapers and then had moved to New York, where each woman supported herself by writing for commercial publications. Neither had previously traveled beyond North America.

Yet, in many respects, they couldn't have been more different. Bly was a Northerner from the mill towns of Pennsylvania; Bisland was a Southern belle raised on a decaying plantation in Louisiana. Bly was a brash investigative reporter; Bisland was an intellectual literary critic. Bly sought the adventure and notoriety of the journey; Bisland was initially shocked by the idea and appalled by the fame it brought her. Bly was an American chauvinist; Bisland an Anglophile. Bly wrote in a brusque style for the masses; Bisland wrote in florid prose, peppered with literary allusions and quotations.

For this 113th edition of the Lakeside Classic series, we have abridged and merged their narratives using Bisland's device of "stages," presenting first Bly's and then Bisland's account. As a reader, you may choose to read them in the sequence we have created or skip through the book, reading each author's narrative individually.

It has been our good fortune that Matthew Goodman, historian and author, agreed to serve as the Historical Editor of this volume. His introduction sets context for the story; his epilogue tells what happened after their life-changing voyages. For those interested in learning more, we highly recommend Goodman's *New York Times* best-selling history *Eighty Days: Nellie Bly and Elizabeth Bisland's History-Making Race Around the World* (Ballantine Books, 2013).

WHEN WE JOIN NELLIE BLY and Elizabeth Bisland on their adventures traversing the globe, we are transported to a time and place in stark contrast to our world today.

Consider the communications of the time: In 1889, the telegraph was the technological Internet of its day. Print publications were the primary medium of news and information around the world. The telephone was in its infancy (invented in 1876), and the first intercontinental phone call was more than twenty-five years in the future (1915). The most efficient communications available to both reporters were a combination of brief cable messages sent from ports and railway stations, and substantial handwritten reports sent by steamship and railroad. As a result, the published stories detailed places each reporter had left several weeks earlier.

It may be difficult for any of us today to fully appreciate the courage and fortitude it must have required for these women to make such a leap into the unknown—unchaperoned (shocking at the time), and entirely unconnected—except for the ability to send home the occasional cable or posted mail. As we are drawn into their detailed accounts, their tales bring into sharp contrast key differences between their daily life and ours today—especially in the manner and pace with which we communicate, and the way organizations work internationally.

Imagine if the full range of RR Donnelley's present-day offerings had been available as the authors undertook their journeys. Our capabilities could create, produce, manage, optimize, and distribute vivid content throughout the course of their travels. We could deliver synchronized, customized content to target audiences across multiple formats—how, where, and when they wanted it. There could be a dedicated website designed to immerse us in the journey as it unfolded, bringing their stories to life through interactive maps, videos of interviews with characters met along the way, historical background articles, and stunning photography of people, towns, and scenic vistas. At journey's end, beautiful books could be printed and distributed to truly capture the excitement of the experience and create a lasting, tangible memoir.

RR Donnelley has grown by continuing to diversify its offerings and maintain a rigorous commitment to product innovation and development. We have become a *leading integrated communication services provider.* In 2015, we continue to enhance our capabilities in creative development and design, content management, digital and print production, supply chain management, business process outsourcing, logistics, and more.

Today, RR Donnelley has more than 65,000 employees, working across 39 countries on five continents, in 14 different time zones. The company now operates in more than 500 locations, providing local service while leveraging the economic, geographic, and technological advantages of a global organization. As we continue to expand our offerings, we deploy our comprehensive resources all over the world in order to best fulfill our customers' evolving communications needs.

For example, in Poland, we complete intricate kitting and custom packaging for some of the world's most well-known brands. In our Singapore operations, we have a quality-compliant facility where we are packaging medical diagnostic devices for use in the management of life-changing conditions. And, in China, we design and produce sophisticated packaging for smart phones and tablets distributed all over the world.

Imagine if Ms. Bly and Ms. Bisland would have had today's tools! When they *hand-wrote* their notes, they could not have envisioned the manner and speed with which millions of pieces of information would be customized, targeted, and delivered in the future. For instance, customers in international life-sciences businesses have highly complex, exacting regional and local requirements impacting their communications across the globe. They trust RR Donnelley's vast operations to reliably deliver efficient one-company convenience for varied products and services such as prescription-drug instruction sheets, packaging, kitting, supply-chain management, and logistics.

Today's financial services industry also must move massive amounts of complex, confidential communications at lightning speed. RR Donnelley's fast and intuitive Venue® virtual data room solution manages more than 150 million pages of sensitive information for more than 600,000 financial services users around the globe. In fact, our Venue solution has earned an impressive track record with the deal-making community and has powered the 10 largest U.S. merger and acquisition deals of the last decade.

Not everything can move virtually, however, and that's when our customers turn to RR Donnelley Logistics Services. We offer a full range of print, mail, and general freight solutions, including managing international outbound mail delivery to more than 150 countries through our global postal and logistics network. Customers can rely on the comprehensive resources that are available only from one of the largest print and mail logistics providers in the United States.

As a global enterprise, we acutely understand the importance of using the right language as an essential part of the cultural adaptation of communication. RR Donnelley designs, creates, and distributes communications across a variety of channels to help our customers speak in as many as 140 languages and dialects. Our Language Solutions group is now one of the largest linguistic service providers in the world and has translated more than 550 million words in the past year. These dedicated and experienced translation teams offer a wide range of multilingual communication solutions for domestic and global corporations in a variety of industries.

When the media publications sponsored Bly's and Bisland's tours, they were motivated by publicity to generate sales more than by an interest in highlighting multiculturalism. As modern-day global brands work to develop an emotional connection to their audience in many cities, regions, or countries, their communications must be appropriate to each location and culture to gain maximum acceptance in target communities. Our production teams in India work in connection with our numerous creative studios worldwide to adapt our customers' branded collateral across digital and print formats and to provide adjustments to details such as clothing styles and garment colors, as well as overall context, to help customers maintain their brand integrity and to fit appropriately into cultures throughout the world.

The stories in *The Race Around the World* underscore how vast our world is and how much "smaller" it has become by virtue of technological advancements. RR Donnelley has a long history of combining creativity with engineering to gain a competitive advantage through innovation. Our research and development hub with more than 100 engineers and imaging scientists in Grand Island, New York, fosters new technologies to improve and invent better methods to enable *our* customers to reach *their* customers.

With a global portfolio of more than seven hundred patents, we continue to develop and deliver pioneering, industry-changing communication solutions that merge print and digital technologies. In fact, RR Donnelley ranked forty-seventh on the 2015 *InformationWeek* Elite 100 list, one of the industry's most prestigious rankings designed to honor the most innovative organizations applying information technology in creative and unconventional ways.

Whether combining traditional print with augmented reality experiences for our customers' audiences, or providing manufacturers with enhanced

RFID sensor data through the supply chain and product lifecycle, RR Donnelley continues to demonstrate that its future is a combination of print *and* digital.

While we are proud of our many industry- and customer-bestowed awards, nothing is more important than the safety of our employees throughout the world. In the past year, more than 130 RR Donnelley facilities completed more than one year or one million hours without a recordable injury or missed day, and an additional 82 facilities worked an entire year without experiencing a single recordable injury. We continue our endeavor to achieve more zero-injury milestones.

At home or abroad, everyone at RR Donnelley remains focused on the opportunities to better serve our customers, and we work every day to earn the trust that is placed in us. Operating with integrity and the highest ethical conduct is the cornerstone of RR Donnelley company values.

While Nellie Bly and Elizabeth Bisland were astute observers of the communities they visited, everywhere we operate we become a part of the community around us. At RR Donnelley, we value diversity and inclusion and want to be good corporate citizens of the places in which we live and work. In many areas, our employees are volunteering in education, environmental, and other community-service projects. We take these actions not because they are in our job descriptions, but simply because we care and we want to create positive results in the world.

As the year draws to a close, we are deeply grateful to our customers for giving us the opportunity to serve them, to our many stakeholders for their ongoing support, and to our employees for the countless ways in which they deliver the very best our industry has to offer.

We wish you all a joyous and peaceful holiday season, and all the best for a happy and safe New Year.

THE PUBLISHER
December 2015

Contents

Contents

ILLUSTRATIONS

Illustrations

HISTORICAL INTRODUCTION

ON THE MORNING of November 14, 1889, a dark-haired young reporter who called herself Nellie Bly[1] set out by steamship from Hoboken, New Jersey, on a race around the world.

Her real name, in fact, was Elizabeth Cochrane; "Nellie Bly" was a pen name given her five years earlier by an editor of the *Pittsburg Dispatch*[2] after the popular Stephen Foster song of the time. At the time of the race, Bly was twenty-five years old—though she claimed to be twenty-three—and for the past two years she had been a reporter for *The World* of New York, the largest and most influential newspaper of its time. No female reporter before her had ever seemed quite so audacious, so willing to risk personal safety in pursuit of a story. In her first exposé for *The World,* Bly had feigned insanity so that she might report firsthand on the mistreatment of the female patients of the Blackwell's Island Insane Asylum; she spent ten days on Blackwell's Island, and the articles she wrote upon her release from the asylum created a sensation, leading to a grand-jury investigation and, ultimately, correction of long-standing abuses.

At *The World* Bly often went undercover to experience firsthand the subjects about which she wrote. Answering an advertisement that had appeared in the paper, she assumed the role of a new mother and applied to an agency that would, for a small fee, sell her unwanted baby for her. She got herself hired in a paper-box factory, where young women worked all day for low pay in an unventilated room reeking of glue. In one of her most ambitious exposés, she posed as the wife of a seller of patent medicines who hoped to kill a bill coming up for consideration by an assembly committee; she visited the hotel-room offices of Edward R. Phelps, the "Lobby King" of Albany, who assured her that for as little as one thousand dollars he could purchase the votes of a majority of the committee members. After *The World* published Bly's article about her meeting with Phelps, public condemnation of the Lobby King's corrupt influence was so sharp and immediate that within the week Phelps fled Albany: the King, crowed *The World*, had been "driven from his throne."

It is difficult to overstate just how unusual this was. Of the 12,308 Americans listed as journalists in the 1880 U.S. Census, only 288—just over 2 percent—were women. The number whose writing appeared in the news sections of the newspaper, as Nellie Bly's did in *The World*, was far smaller still; nearly all of them wrote instead for what was called "the women's page." By the 1880s, many American newspapers, recognizing that women were an as-yet untapped market, had established a separate page featuring articles devoted to the topics about which women were thought to be most interested: fashion, shopping, recipes, homemaking, child rearing, and the doings of high society. The articles were not only directed at women but were overwhelmingly written by them; male editors justified the reliance on female contributors to fill this section by explaining that it was where their natural aptitude lay—as, for instance, the editor of the *New York Telegram*, who once pointed out that in reporting on society functions, "A man must examine minutely a woman's costume in order to describe it, where a woman would take the whole thing in at a glance."

It simply would not do to ask a woman to perform the tasks routinely asked of male reporters—to travel by herself at night, and in all kinds of weather; to pursue stories wherever they led, into tenements and dance halls and barrooms and gambling dens; to consort with criminals and policemen alike; to be present at riots and strikes and fires and other municipal disturbances; to uncover the lies spoken and misdeeds committed by men who held positions of power. For a woman to engage in such behavior was not only risky, it was also improper, undignified, and unseemly: in a word, unladylike.

Nellie Bly, for her part, did all she could to resist being confined to the women's page; as she would later write, she was "too impatient to work along at the usual duties assigned women on newspapers." When her editor at the *Pittsburg Dispatch* assigned her to the women's page, Bly quit and decamped for New York. At *The World* she maintained a grueling work pace, often turning out a new adventure every week. In addition to her investigative pieces, Bly brought her readers along as she partook of all the variety the city had to offer. She played cornet in a marching band and made friends with the women of a Wild West show. She learned to ice skate and to fence, to ride a bicycle and to dance ballet. She trained with the boxing champion John L. Sullivan; she visited with a remarkable deaf, mute, and blind nine-year-old girl by the name of Helen Keller. Before long Bly had become so popular that her name appeared not only in the bylines of her stories—in itself an achievement for the time—but in the headlines as well: "Nellie Bly on the Wing," "Nellie Bly as a Mesmerist," "Nellie Bly a Prisoner."

In 1889, though, she undertook the most sensational adventure of all: an attempt to set the record for the fastest trip around the world. Sixteen years earlier, the French author Jules Verne[3] had imagined that such a trip could be accomplished in eighty days; Nellie Bly hoped to do it in seventy-five.

In 1889, at the age of sixty-one, Jules Verne was arguably the most famous novelist in the world; he was certainly the most successful practitioner of the literary genre that would come to be known as science fiction, but which in the late nineteenth century was more often called "scientific romance." His novels, among them *A Journey to the Center of the Earth* and *Twenty Thousand Leagues Under the Sea*, took readers on fantastic trips to undreamed-of places, anticipating twentieth-century technologies such as the rocket ship and the nuclear submarine. The most popular of all his novels, however, went no farther than around the world, and involved only technologies—primarily the steamship and the steam locomotive—available to anyone with enough money for a ticket.

That book, of course, was *Around the World in Eighty Days.*[4] It tells the story of a hyper-rational Englishman named Phileas Fogg[5] who, after an argument with whist-mates at his London social club, wagers his life's fortune on the proposition that he can travel around the world in only eighty days. The idea for the novel seems to have been born in the summer of 1871, when Jules Verne, sitting in a Paris café, noticed a newspaper advertisement for a tourist trip around the world being organized by the British travel agent Thomas Cook. That previously unthinkable notion—that not just a single country or continent but the entire globe might be the subject of a tourist excursion—was itself traceable to the opening of the Suez Canal in November of 1869, which established for the first time a direct

*An imaginative rendering of the fictional Phileas Fogg,
the hero of Verne's novel*

water route between Europe and Asia. In conjunction with the new transatlantic railroad in the United States (completed just six months earlier), the opening of the canal meant that a traveler could now pursue a more-or-less direct path around the world via train and steamship, on a line across the Northern Hemisphere that stretched from Europe through Asia and North America and then back around to Europe. The inevitable next question was how quickly such a trip might be completed, and though no one could yet say for sure, speculation began to center on a period of eighty days.

Verne's novel first appeared at the end of 1872 as a serialization in the Parisian newspaper *Le Temps* and subsequently, as *Around the World in Eighty Days*, in English and American newspapers. Appearing in book form in 1873, it quickly became the most beloved of all Verne's novels, selling more than a hundred thousand copies in France during his lifetime and hundreds of thousands of copies in translation around the world.

Still, for all its success, no one had actually tried to replicate Phileas Fogg's feat—in a sense, to turn fiction into fact—before Nellie Bly walked into the offices of *The World* in 1888 and proposed to her editors that she do it.

Needless to say, reaction to Bly's idea in the *World* offices was uniformly unenthusiastic. "There is no use talking about it," George Turner, the paper's business manager, told her firmly. "No one but a man can do this."

In the first place, Turner explained, she was a woman and, therefore, would require a protector to travel with her. The *World* couldn't very well have a young female reporter wandering across the farthest reaches of the globe without a chaperone; it was far too dangerous. And even if it *was* possible for her to travel unaccompanied, as a female traveler she would require so many bags—probably a dozen trunks or more—that she would be never be able to make the rapid changes that this sort of lightning trip would require.

Bly left that day having at least obtained the promise that if the paper was to send anyone racing around the world, it would be her. For the next year the idea was hardly discussed, as Bly and her editors moved on to other stories.

At the time, *The World* had ascended to the very top of the highly competitive world of New York daily newspapers, which included, among others, *The Tribune*, *The Herald*, *The Sun*, and *The Times*. Joseph Pulitzer,[6] a Hungarian Jewish immigrant who had made a fortune in the St. Louis newspaper business, had purchased *The World* from the Wall Street financier Jay Gould in 1883. Immediately he began to revamp the paper to appeal to the city's working-class and immigrant population,

Joseph Pulitzer, publisher of Bly's newspaper, The World

featuring a greater number of crime stories, local-interest stories, and investigations of political corruption and police brutality, as well as an editorial line that advocated a sharply graduated income tax, opposed monopolies, and supported the rights of labor unions to organize. The results were nothing short of sensational: when Pulitzer bought *The World* in 1883, the paper's circulation stood at 15,770; within two years it had increased tenfold, to 153,213.

Almost at once *The World*'s newfound influence was dramatically demonstrated on the national stage. For seven years, from 1877 to 1884, the American fundraising committee for the Statue of Liberty had been trying to raise $100,000 to build the granite pedestal on which the statue would stand; however, little progress had been made until Joseph Pulitzer issued an appeal for funds in the pages of *The World*. From the paper's working-class readers came an outpouring of support, and within five months the $100,000 had been raised—80 percent of it from donations of less than a dollar.

By 1889, however, *The World*'s circulation had begun to falter, and the paper's editors began to look for a sensational story—one that would rivet the public's attention, and not just for a day or two, but for months on end. That was when it was decided to take Nellie Bly up on her proposal to race around the world. The paper's editor in chief, John

Cockerill,[7] summoned Bly to his office. "Can you start around the world day after tomorrow?" he asked.

"I can start this minute," she replied.

Bly decided that she would take but a single bag into which she would pack everything she would need for a two-and-a-half-month trip around the world. Being able to carry her own bag would help prevent any delays that might arise from the incompetence or interference of porters and customs officials; no less important, it would give the lie to the notion that a female traveler inevitably requires numerous suitcases for any long journey. For her single carrying bag Nellie Bly chose a leather gripsack measuring, at its bottom, sixteen by seven inches.[8] In that small bag she managed to pack a lightweight silk bodice, two traveling caps, three veils, a pair of slippers, a complete set of toiletries, an inkstand, pens, pencils, paper, pins, needles and thread, a dressing gown, a tennis blazer, a flask and drinking cup, several changes of underwear (flannel for cold weather, silk for hot), handkerchiefs, and a jar of cold cream. In a light shoulder strap she would carry a silk waterproof, her only concession to rainy weather. With these few provisions she felt confident that she could meet whatever conditions she might encounter along the way. "If one is traveling simply for the sake of traveling," Bly liked to say, "and not for the purpose of impressing fellow travel-

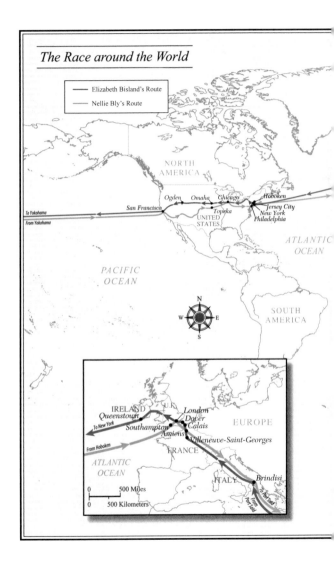

The Race around the World

Elizabeth Bisland's Route
Nellie Bly's Route

NORTH AMERICA

Ogden Omaha Chicago Hoboken
San Francisco Topeka Jersey City
UNITED New York
STATES Philadelphia

To Yokohama
From Yokohama

ATLANTIC OCEAN

PACIFIC OCEAN

SOUTH AMERICA

IRELAND
Queenstown London
U.K. Dover
To New York Southampton Calais
Amiens Villeneuve-Saint-Georges EUROPE

From Hoboken
FRANCE

ATLANTIC OCEAN

ITALY Brindisi
To Red Sea

0   500 Miles
0   500 Kilometers

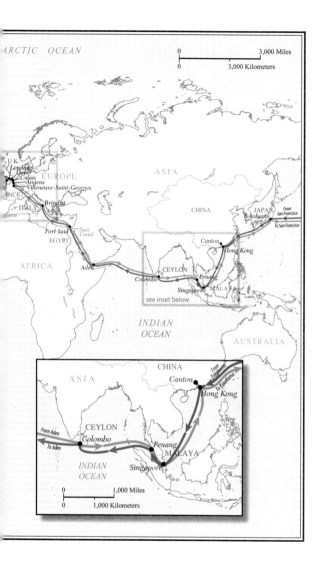

ers, the problem of baggage becomes a very simple one."

To serve as her traveling dress she chose a two-piece garment of dark-blue broadcloth trimmed with camel's hair. For warmth she took a long black-and-white plaid Scotch ulster coat, with twin rows of buttons running down the front, that covered her from neck to ankles; and rather than the hat and veil worn by most of the fashionable oceangoing women of the time, she wore a jaunty wool ghillie cap—the English-style cap later worn by Sherlock Holmes in the movies. The blue dress, the plaid ulster, the ghillie cap: to outward appearances it was not an especially remarkable outfit, but before long it would become the most famous one in all the world.

On the front page of *The World* for November 14, 1889, a map stretching across five columns of type showed "The Lines of Travel to be Followed by The World's Flying Representative." The line began in New York, extended across the Atlantic Ocean to England, moved down through Europe to the Mediterranean, continued south through the Suez Canal to the Arabian Sea along the northeast coast of Africa, then shifted eastward past Ceylon [Sri Lanka] and up to Hong Kong and Japan, crossed the Pacific Ocean to San Francisco, and then concluded through the northern part of the United States back to New York.

Among the New Yorkers who read *The World*'s announcement of Bly's trip was the publisher of a high-toned monthly magazine called *The Cosmopolitan*.[9] John Brisben Walker[10] had come to New York from the West, where he had already made and lost fortunes in wheat and alfalfa, and was presently amassing a third in magazine publishing. He understood at once the publicity value of *The World*'s scheme, even as it occurred to him that a world traveler might do better by heading west rather than east as Bly was planning to do. (Walker had spent years living in China, and he believed that the westerly direction of the prevailing winds across the South China Sea would cost Bly between three and four days.) At once an idea suggested itself: *The Cosmopolitan* would sponsor its own competitor in the around-the-world race, traveling in the opposite direction. Of course, *The Cosmopolitan*'s circumnavigator would have to be, like Bly, a young woman—there was a pleasing symmetry to the notion, and in any case, a man racing against a woman would never win anyone's sympathy—and she would have to leave at once, if she was to have any chance at all of returning to New York before Nellie Bly. After a quick conference at the office with his business manager, Walker sent him off to a travel agency to prepare an itinerary and dispatched a messenger to Elizabeth Bisland's apartment, only a few blocks away in Murray Hill.

Elizabeth Bisland[11] was twenty-eight years old, and after nearly a decade of freelance writing had recently obtained a job on the staff of *The Cosmopolitan*, for which she wrote a monthly review of recently published books entitled "In the Library." Born into a Louisiana plantation family ruined by the Civil War and its aftermath, at the age of twenty she had moved to New Orleans and then, a few years later, to New York, where she contributed to a variety of magazines and was regularly referred to as the most beautiful woman in metropolitan journalism. Bisland was tall, with large dark eyes and pale skin, and spoke in a low, gentle voice. She reveled in gracious hospitality and smart conversation, both of which were regularly on display in the literary salon that she hosted in the little apartment she shared with her sister on Fourth Avenue, where members of New York's creative set, writers and painters and actors, gathered to discuss the artistic issues of the day. Bisland herself was well aware that feminine beauty was useful but fleeting ("After the period of sex-attraction has passed," she once wrote, "women have no power in America"), and she took pride in the fact that she had arrived in New York with only fifty dollars in her pocket and that the thousands of dollars now in her bank account had come by virtue of her own pen. Capable of working for eighteen hours at a stretch, she wrote book reviews, essays, feature articles, and poetry in the classical vein. She was a believer, more than anything, in the joys of literature, which she had first experienced as a girl in ancient volumes of Shakespeare and Cervantes that she had found in the library of her family's plantation house. (She taught herself French while she churned butter so that she might read Rousseau's *Confessions* in the original—a book, as it turned out, that she hated.) She cared nothing for fame, and indeed found the prospect of it distasteful. So when Walker proposed that she race Nellie Bly around the world, she initially told him no. However, Walker was not a man who was easily dissuaded, and at last Bisland relented.[12] Six hours later, she was on a New York Central Line train bound for Chicago.

On the surface the two women, Nellie Bly and Elizabeth Bisland, were about as different as could be: one woman a northerner, the other from the South; one a scrappy, hard-driving crusader, the other priding herself on her gentility; one seeking out the most sensational of news stories, the other preferring novels and poetry and disdaining most newspaper writing as "a wild, crooked, shrieking hodge-podge." Elizabeth Bisland hosted tea parties; Nellie Bly was known to frequent O'Rourke's saloon on the Bowery. But each of them was acutely conscious of the unequal position of women in America. Each had grown up without much money and had come to New York to make a place for herself in big-city journalism, achieving a hard-won success in what was still, unquestionably, a man's world. More than anything else, of course, the two women were to be linked forever by unique shared experience: partners, in a sense, in a vast project that for months would captivate the United States, and much of the world besides.

Accounts of the race appeared seemingly everywhere, in every town large enough to support a newspaper. "The entire press of the country is discussing the trip," observed *The Journalist*, the industry's trade magazine. From the nation's capital, *The World*'s distinguished correspondent Frank G. Carpenter reported that "Nellie Bly's trip around the world excites great interest in Washington. It is one of the common subjects of conversation in the cloakrooms of the House and Senate, in the hotels and at dinners. Miss Bly's course is commented upon, and not a few prominent men try to figure out where she is from day to day."

Bly's and Bisland's progress, of course, could be charted thanks to the invention of the telegraph—the Victorian-era technology that, much like the Internet today, was transforming the world by its power to allow nearly instantaneous communication across vast distances. Indeed, this was the time period when newspapers began appearing with names such as *The Telegram* or *The Daily Telegraph*, the word having come to be synonymous in the public mind with the speediest possible gathering of news. Throughout the trip Bly and Bisland sent regular reports of their progress via Western Union offices located at ports and railroad stations around the globe.

Though Bly and Bisland could cable home brief messages, more substantial written reports had to be delivered by the traditional method of letters carried by steamship and railroad. Thus, for the duration of the trip, newspaper readers learned almost daily about each woman's progress; published articles, however, only brought news of places the reporter had left three or more weeks earlier.

On the morning of Friday, November 29, 1889, fifteen days after Bly departed from Hoboken, *The World* printed a small advertisement announcing "The Nellie Bly Guessing Match," which would commence the following Sunday. The next day a full article, headlined A GUESS THAT WILL PAY, revealed that *The World* would be furnishing a free first-class trip to Europe—including a week each in London and Paris—to the person who came closest to guessing Nellie Bly's finishing time in days, hours, minutes, and seconds. Anyone could participate in the guessing match, but there was one important stipulation: all guesses had to be recorded on the official coupons that would be printed in Sunday copies of *The World*.[13] Only one guess would be permitted per coupon; those who wanted to submit multiple guesses had to purchase multiple copies of the paper.

"The match will be the biggest thing that New York has ever seen," *The World* gleefully predicted, and indeed by the end of the first day, the paper had received more than one hundred thousand guesses. Within a week of initiating the contest, the paper's weekly circulation had risen by more than three hundred thousand copies, from 2.3 to more than 2.6 million. By the time the contest was over, nearly one million coupons had been submitted. The winning guess was a mere two-fifths of a second off Bly's actual finishing time; the next-closest guess was off by three-fifths of a second—or just one-fifth of a second away from a claim to the prize.

Thanks in large part to *The World*'s constant promotion—or "booming," as it was called in the nineteenth century—by the time Nellie Bly returned home, she was perhaps the most famous woman in the United States. It was an age when American companies were beginning to understand that the image of a famous person could be used to sell products; through advertising the traits generally associated with the person—in Nellie Bly's case, they included pluck, vitality, and courage—they seemed to be transferred to the product and, by extension, to the person using it. So that year women around the country wore Nellie Bly caps and Nellie

Nellie Bly, on the Fly, *an advertising card using Bly's fame
to promote baking soda*

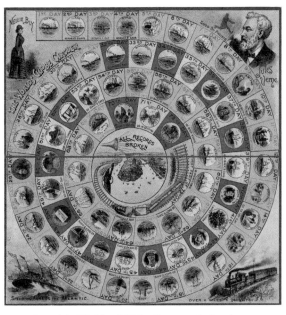

Round the World with Nellie Bly, *a popular board game
based on her journey*

Bly dresses, modeled on the ones she made famous during her trip. Children used the Nellie Bly notebook and carried it to school in a Nellie Bly school bag. At home, one could write on Nellie Bly stationery with the Nellie Bly fountain pen in the light of the Nellie Bly lamp, and afterwards relax with the Nellie Bly photograph album. The W. E. Piaget Company offered a Nellie Bly bonbon box. The George L. Ingerson Company of Syracuse, New York, even sold Nellie Bly Horse Feed.

A series of delicately tinted advertising trade cards, extolling the virtues of numerous products, showed Nellie Bly in her iconic traveling outfit, ubiquitous gripsack in hand, in various whimsical settings—sitting on the crescent moon, standing atop a dragonfly, walking a tightrope between the earth and the moon—each one accompanied by a laudatory verse. The cards promoted everything from coffee to tobacco to spices, from baking soda to Dr. Morse's India Root Pills, which promised fast relief for "biliousness, headache, and constipation."

Probably the most popular product associated with Bly's trip was the board game *Round the World with Nellie Bly*, advertised as "A Novel and Fascinating Game with Plenty of Excitement on Land and Sea." The game came with a spinner and a set of markers; after each spin, the player moved his or her marker forward the corresponding number of spaces, with fate determined by the luck of the spin.

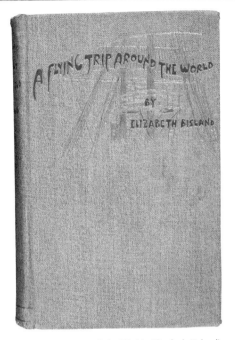

A Flying Trip around the World, *Elizabeth Bisland's
narrative of her voyage*

Thus, on the fifth day one encountered an iceberg
and had to go back to port; on the ninth day one
met Jules Verne and was granted an additional
throw; fair weather on the Pacific sent one ahead
two days; a steamship collision on the sixty-third
day sent one back fifteen days. In reaching the final
space, the player landed at the center of the spiral,

where a trumpet blared *ALL RECORDS BROKEN*, on a Manhattan Island on which the only recognizable structure is the World Building.

After their return home both women published book-length accounts about their respective trips: Nellie Bly's *Around the World in Seventy-two Days* and Elizabeth Bisland's *In Seven Stages: A Flying Trip Around the World*. Not surprisingly, the writing styles were as markedly different as the authors themselves. Bisland was a published poet, and her book is replete with long, lyrical descriptions of the vistas through which she is traveling. "In the night a hoar frost had fallen," she wrote one morning, "that was to snow as sleep is to death; and the pale reaped fields, the sere meadows, and silent uplands were transfigured by the first gleam of day." As she revealed in her book, there was much about the race that Bisland found distasteful. She had no interest in fame and disdained the notoriety that she understood such a sensational endeavor would bring. She was deeply distressed, for instance, at the stream of visitors who came to call at her San Francisco hotel, all of them wanting to get a look at the young circumnavigator; she termed it "an inexpensive freak show." Upon her return she wrote that she wished to live the rest of her life in such a way that her name would never again appear in a newspaper headline.

Still, Elizabeth Bisland eventually came to revel in the trip around the world. Her few days in Japan—where she marveled at the opalescent silks of the kimonos, the latticed glove boxes of the tea houses, the lacquered figures outside the mikado's palace—would turn out to be her favorite of the entire journey, sparking a lifelong fascination with the country; in her later years she would return there twice more, the second time as a sixty-one-year-old widow, when she undertook a seven-month tour of Japan and China, wanting to take one more look at the sights she first saw at age twenty-eight, during her race around the world.

By contrast, Nellie Bly's account of the race is sharp and peppery, filled with amusing anecdotes. She took special pleasure in noting the idiosyncrasies of her fellow ship's passengers: One man crossing the Atlantic aboard the *Augusta Victoria* took his pulse after each meal; another, for some reason, counted the number of steps he took each day. One of the female passengers, Bly discovered, had not gotten undressed since the ship embarked several days earlier. "I am sure we are going down," she explained, "and I am determined to go down dressed."

However, it should also be noted that Bly was not entirely immune from the temptation to embroider certain events to make them even more sensational. In one episode from the last leg of her journey, for instance, Bly's train was speeding east across the continent. Just outside Gallup, New Mexico, railroad men were repairing a bridge that spanned a deep ravine. While the repairs were in progress, the bridge was held up only by jackscrews, without the girders that normally helped to support it. Hearing Bly's train coming, the workmen frantically tried to flag it down before it reached the bridge, but they were too late, and they watched helplessly as it thundered past at fifty miles an hour, over the weakened bridge and safely across to the other side. "The escape is a miraculous one," *The World* marveled in its news account the next day, "and section men who witnessed the train flash past on the frail structure regard the escape as one of the most miraculous in railway history."

The fast run across a rickety bridge would seem dramatic enough in itself, but over time, in Nellie Bly's retelling, it became even more so. In her version of the story, the bridge not only threatened to fall; in this version it actually fell. In her book *Around the World in Seventy-two Days* Bly asserted that "my train had run safely across a bridge which was held in place only by jackscrews, and which fell the moment we were across." Apparently no one seemed to notice or care that the scene had been lifted directly from *Around the World in Eighty Days*, when Phileas Fogg's train races across a ruined bridge in Wyoming. "But hardly had the train passed the river," wrote Jules Verne, "when the bridge, now completely demolished, crashed noisily down into the rapids of Medicine Bow."

Elizabeth Bisland was a loyal employee of *The Cosmopolitan*, and she knew that her colleagues at the magazine were counting on her to win the race. Near the end she undertook a mad dash across Europe, enduring, as she put it in her book, "hunger, lack of sleep, and fatigue" (in the course of two days she found herself aboard a train, a boat, another train, another boat, and still another train) in order to meet a steamship in Queenstown, Ireland, that would bring her to New York ahead of schedule. Still, for her the trip provided an unexpected and unparalleled opportunity to see the world, and she privately harbored a feeling of glee whenever a ship was delayed in port, as it allowed her more time for sightseeing. It is instructive to note that in her book *In Seven Stages: A Flying Trip Around the World*, Bisland always refers to the undertaking as a "trip" or "journey," and never—not even once—as a "race."

For Nellie Bly, on the other hand, it was always a race. Driven, ambitious, and deeply competitive—they were traits that helped her become an excellent investigative reporter—she was constantly worrying about schedules and deadlines, and lived in silent agony whenever one of her ships was delayed; indeed, one cannot help but feel that she would have been happier never to make port at all, thus to have made the circumnavigation in the shortest possible time. On more than one occasion she was heard to utter that she would rather die than return to New York behind time. "More speed!" she would often cry to a ship's engineer. "More speed!"[14]

Bly, however, seems never to have actually gone down to the fire room where workers shoveled the coal that produced that speed; thus she never experienced at firsthand the astonishingly severe conditions inside the fire room, where the temperature often rose to 130 degrees Fahrenheit and above. Nor did Bly ever leave her first-class quarters to investigate the conditions in which the steerage passengers there had to cross the ocean—the very topic about which she had proposed to write for *The World* when she first sought a job on the paper. Throughout the trip Bly's most passionate and concerted attention was devoted not to the world around her, but to her own itinerary.

Bly's reactions to the trip, like Elizabeth Bisland's, were heavily colored by her views of Great Britain. The segment of Americans most resolutely hostile to Britain—working-class northerners, and especially Irish Catholic immigrants—were the very people among whom Bly had long lived and worked; her own paternal grandparents had left Ireland's County Derry and settled in western Pennsylvania in 1804. Bly distrusted the British government and considered the Englishmen among whom she traveled to be arrogant, smug, and condescending, and blind to the privilege that imperial power routinely conferred on its citizens—they could, if they chose to, carry the empire along with them on their travels, as they sailed on English ships, slept in English hotels, and ate English meals, taking little notice of the specific characteristics of the countries through which they traveled. Bly did not like the English,[15] but she did envy them their privilege, and the farther she got from home, the more instinctively patriotic she became. Passing the American Embassy in Canton, China, Bly removed her cap and announced to the rest of the group: "That is the most beautiful flag in the world, and I am ready to whip anyone who says it isn't." Upon her return to the United States, she regaled all who would listen with tales of American superiority: America, she liked to say, was "far ahead" of all other nations, and indeed the only one to which it was worth paying much attention. "There is really not so much for Americans to see in foreign lands," Bly told a reporter while speeding through Kansas. "We've got the best of everything here; we lack in nothing; then when you go over there you must be robbed, you get nothing fit to eat, and you see nothing that America cannot improve upon wonderfully."

Elizabeth Bisland, on the other hand, descended

from a Scottish dry-goods merchant who immigrated to North Carolina shortly before the American Revolution; she was a southerner and an Episcopalian, and, though not wealthy herself, she was by disposition entirely comfortable among aristocrats. In Ceylon, for instance, she would begin a close friendship with Lady Broome, who wrote travel books under the name "Lady Barker." Throughout the trip Bisland reveled in the vigor and virility she perceived in the Englishmen she met, so markedly different from the southern men around whom she had grown up. "It fills my soul with a passion of pride that I, too, am an Anglo-Saxon," Bisland wrote upon her first sight of the cliffs of Dover; disembarking from the ferry, she at last set foot upon what she termed "the mother soil."

Though the two were acutely conscious of the obstacles faced by women in society and wrote often and perceptively on the topic, Nellie Bly and Elizabeth Bisland were, like most of their contemporaries, less clear-sighted about issues of racism and colonialism. Their tendency to refer to people by color—black, yellow, white—although common at the time, grates on the modern reader. Both of their accounts of some races and nationalities are shot through with racial stereotypes. Bly, for instance, reported to her readers that the Chinese were dirty and shabby and invidiously compared them to the clean Japanese. Bisland, similarly, writes condescendingly that the Japanese boatmen of Yokohama are "small, lithe creatures with good-looking yellow countenances, bearing no resemblance to the flat-faced Chinese."

Neither Bly nor Bisland, then, was an entirely reliable observer in the travels through the British Empire. Still, the modern reader cannot fail to take note of the many disquieting sights of their trip: the teeming inner city of Hong Kong, home of more than 160,000 people (an astonishing sixteen hundred people per acre, far denser than even the most crowded blocks of New York's Lower East Side) who live and work in the shadow of British hilltop villas, where officers and traders drink tea and play tennis on backyard courts; the beggars crying for *baksheesh* in Port Said, Egypt; the children of Aden, Yemen, diving for coins tossed by Western tourists into the sea for fun. Without ever quite realizing it, Bly and Bisland, as they sped through the Eastern colonies, provide a vivid and memorable portrait of daily life there at the apex of the British Empire.

The two women raced around the globe on the most powerful and modern forms of transportation yet created, the ocean-going steamship and the steam railroad, sending back messages to waiting editors by means of telegraph lines that had—in the expression of the period—annihilated space and time. From Hong Kong in the east to Ireland in the west, they sailed across the breadth of the British

Empire, their own ships carrying the tea and cotton and opium and other valuable goods that helped sustain the imperial economy. They traveled through a world defined by custom and deformed by class, in every country they visited, and even on the ships and trains they used to get there.

As it turned out, Nellie Bly and Elizabeth Bisland were racing not only around the world; they were racing through the very heart of the Victorian age.

Matthew Goodman
Brooklyn, New York
February 2015

Notes

1. Nellie Bly (1864–1922) was born Elizabeth Jane Cochrane but became a famous investigative journalist under this pseudonym taken from a misspelling of the Stephen Foster song "Nelly Bly." In 1895, Bly married Robert Livingston Seaman and briefly managed his enamelware firm. After its economic failure, she returned to reporting.

2. At the time, Pittsburgh's newspapers spelled the city's name without the final *h*.

3. Jules Verne (1828–1905) was a French author whose highly popular works laid the foundation for modern science fiction.

4. In the original French, *Le tour du monde en quatre-vingts jours.*

5. The hero's first name is often mistakenly rendered as "Phineas." Verne said that his protagonist's last name was a play on the word *fog*, emblematic of the character's London home.

6. Joseph Pulitzer (1847–1911) was a newspaper owner, editor, and publisher. He is best known today for his multimillion-dollar gift to endow coveted prizes in journalism, letters, drama, and music.

7. John Albert Cockerill (1845–96) was the editor of Joseph Pulizers's New York newspaper *The World*. In 1887, he hired Nellie Bly. During his long career, Cockerill also worked for many of the country's other most important papers, including the *Cincinnati Enquirer*, the *Washington Post*, Pulitzer's *St. Louis Post-Dispatch*, and the *New York Herald*.

8. That bag is today on display in the Newseum in Washington, D.C.

9. In later years the magazine would be purchased by Joseph Pulitzer's rival William Randolph Hearst and subsequently assume a very different character; today it is the women's magazine *Cosmopolitan*.

10. John Brisben Walker (1847–1913) was an entrepreneur and journalist.

11. Elizabeth Bisland (1861–1929) was a journalist and author.

12. Walker proposed to bring Bisland on as a full-time employee of *The Cosmopolitan*, amply compensating her for any writing income she might lose while on the trip. It is possible as well that Walker suggested that she would lose her job if she refused his request—all Bisland would ever say about it was that he made "substantial arguments."

13. On December 10, in the face of the overwhelming popularity of the guessing match, *The World* began to include coupons in each day's issue, rather than only on Sundays.

14. Aboard the *Oceanic*, which carried Bly on her return across the Pacific Ocean, the chief engineer ordered a rhyming couplet to be written on the ship's engines: "For Nellie Bly/We'll win or die."

15. This enmity persisted to the very end of her life. Even years later those who had known Bly recalled how cold and distant she became whenever she met an Englishman, and at the *Evening Journal*, the newspaper for which she was working at the time of her death, her secretaries knew better than to send in to her anyone with even the hint of an English accent.

THE RACE AROUND
THE WORLD

Nellie Bly

Elizabeth Bisland

PRELUDE

BLY: THE IDEA

WHAT GAVE ME THE IDEA?

It is sometimes difficult to tell exactly what gives birth to an idea. Ideas are the chief stock in trade of newspaper writers, and generally they are the scarcest stock in market, but they do come occasionally.

This idea came to me one Sunday. I had spent a greater part of the day and half the night vainly trying to fasten on some idea for a newspaper article. But ideas did not come that day, and three o'clock in the morning found me weary and with an aching head, tossing about in my bed. At last tired and provoked at my slowness in finding a subject, something for the week's work, I thought fretfully: "I wish I was at the other end of the earth! And why not?" The thought came: "I need a vacation; why not take a trip around the world?" It is easy to see how one thought followed another. The idea of a trip around the world pleased me, and I added: "If I could do it as quickly as Phileas Fogg did, I should go."

I approached my editor [John Cockerill] rather timidly on the subject. I was afraid that he would think the idea too wild and visionary. "Have you any ideas?" he asked, as I sat down by his desk.

"One," I answered quietly. He sat toying with his

pens, waiting for me to continue, so I blurted out: "I want to go around the world!"

"Well?" he said, inquiringly looking up with a faint smile in his kind eyes.

"I want to go around in eighty days or less. I think I can beat Phileas Fogg's record. May I try it?"

To my dismay he told me that in the office they had thought of this same idea before, and the intention was to send a man. However, he offered me the consolation that he would favor my going, and then we went to talk with the business manager about it.

"It is impossible for you to do it" was the terrible verdict. "In the first place you are a woman and would need a protector, and even if it were possible for you to travel alone, you would need to carry so much baggage that it would detain you in making rapid changes. Besides you speak nothing but English, so there is no use talking about it; no one but a man can do this."

"Very well," I said angrily. "Start the man, and I'll start the same day for some other newspaper and beat him."

"I believe you would," he said slowly. I would not say that this had any influence on their decision, but I do know that before we parted, I was made happy by the promise that if anyone was commissioned to make the trip, I should be that one.

One cold, wet evening, a year after this discussion, I received a little note asking me to come to the office at once. I went in and sat down beside the editor, waiting for him to speak. He looked up from the paper on which he was writing and asked quietly: "Can you start around the world day after tomorrow?"

"I can start this minute," I answered, quickly trying to stop the rapid beating of my heart.

"We did think of starting you on the *City of Paris*[1] tomorrow morning, so as to give you ample time to catch the mail train out of London. There is a chance if the *Augusta Victoria,*[2] which sails the morning afterwards, has rough weather, of your failing to connect with the mail train."

"I will take my chances on the *Augusta Victoria* and save one extra day," I said.

The next morning I went to Ghormley, the fashionable dressmaker, to order a dress. "I want a dress that will stand constant wear for three months," I said. Bringing out several different materials, he threw them in artistic folds over a small table, studying the effect in a pier glass before which he stood. In a few moments he had selected a plain blue broadcloth and a quiet plaid camel's hair as the most durable and suitable combination for a traveling gown.

Before I left, probably one o'clock, I had my first fitting. When I returned at five o'clock for a second fitting, the dress was finished. I considered this promptness and speed a good omen and quite in keeping with the project.

After leaving Ghormley's, I went to a shop and ordered an ulster [a long, loose, rugged overcoat]. Then going to another dressmaker's, I ordered a lighter dress to carry with me to be worn in the land where I would find summer.

I bought one handbag with the determination to confine my baggage to its limit. Packing that bag was the most difficult undertaking of my life; there was so much to go into such little space.

I got everything in at last except the extra dress. Then the question resolved itself into this: I must either add a parcel to my baggage or go around the world in and with one dress. I always hated parcels, so I sacrificed the dress, but I brought out a last summer's silk bodice and, after considerable squeezing, managed to crush it into the handbag.

The evening before I started, I went to the office and was given £200 in English gold and Bank of England notes. The gold I carried in my pocket. The Bank of England notes were placed in a chamois-skin bag which I tied around my neck. Besides this, I took some American gold and paper money to use at different ports as a test to see if American money was known outside of America.

Down in the bottom of my handbag was a special passport, number 247, signed by James G. Blaine, secretary of State. Someone suggested that a

Bly, wearing her checked coat, with Gladstone bag in one hand and ghillie cap in the other, waves goodbye.

revolver would be a good companion piece for the passport, but I had such a strong belief in the world's greeting me as I greeted it, that I refused to arm myself. I knew if my conduct was proper, I should always find men ready to protect me, let them be Americans, English, French, German, or anything else.

It is quite possible to buy tickets in New York for the entire trip, but I thought that I might be compelled to change my route at almost any point, so the only transportation I had provided on leaving New York was my ticket to London.

One never knows the capacity of an ordinary hand-satchel until dire necessity compels the exercise of all one's ingenuity to reduce everything to the smallest possible compass. In mine I was able to pack two traveling caps, three veils, a pair of slippers, a complete outfit of toilet articles, inkstand, pens, pencils, and copy paper, pins, needles and thread, a dressing gown, a tennis blazer, a small flask and a drinking cup, several complete changes of underwear, a liberal supply of handkerchiefs and fresh ruchings,[3] and most bulky and uncompromising of all, a jar of cold cream to keep my face from chapping in the varied climates I should encounter.

That jar of cold cream was the bane of my existence. It seemed to take up more room than everything else in the bag and was always getting into just the place that would keep me from closing the satchel. Over my arm I carried a silk waterproof, the only provision I made against rainy weather. After-experience showed me that I had taken too much rather than too little baggage. At every port where I stopped at I could have bought anything from a ready-made dress down, except possibly at Aden, and as I did not visit the shops there, I cannot speak from knowledge.

The possibilities of having any laundry work done during my rapid progress was one which had troubled me a good deal before starting. I had equipped myself on the theory that only once or twice in my journey would I be able to secure the services of a laundress. I knew that on the railways it would be impossible, but the longest railroad travel was the two days spent between London and Brindisi [Italy], and the four days between San Francisco and New York. On the Atlantic steamers they do no washing. On the Peninsular and Oriental steamers[4]—which everyone calls the P&O boats—between Brindisi and China, the quarter-master turns out each day a wash that would astonish the largest laundry in America. Even if no laundry work was done on the ships, there are at all of the ports where they stop plenty of experts waiting to show what Orientals[5] can do in the washing line. Six hours is ample time for them to perform their labors, and when they make a promise to have work done in a certain time, they are prompt to the

9

minute. Probably it is because they have no use for clothes themselves but appreciate at its full value the money they are to receive for their labor. Their charges, compared with laundry prices in New York, are wonderfully low.

So much for my preparations. It will be seen that if one is traveling simply for the sake of traveling and not for the purpose of impressing one's fellow passengers, the problem of baggage becomes a very simple one. On one occasion—in Hong Kong, where I was asked to an official dinner—I regretted not having an evening dress with me, but the loss of that dinner was a very small matter when compared with the responsibilities and worries I escaped by not having a lot of trunks and boxes to look after.

I F, ON THE 13TH *of November, 1889, some amateur prophet had foretold that I should spend Christmas Day of that year in the Indian Ocean, I hope I should, with the gentleness due a severe case of aberrated predictiveness, have merely called his attention to that passage in the Koran in which it is written, "The Lord loveth a cheerful liar"—and bid him go in peace. Yet I did spend the 25th day of December steaming through the waters that wash the shores of the Indian Empire and did do other things equally preposterous, of which I would not have believed myself capable if forewarned of them.*

On the 14th of November of the aforementioned year, I was awakened at eight o'clock as usual by the maid with the breakfast tray—which also contained the morning papers and a neat pile of notes and letters. I read the papers leisurely, made a calm and uneventful toilet, and the very first intimation I received of the coming thunderbolt out of the serene sky of my existence was a hurried and mysterious request, at half-past ten o'clock, that I would come as soon as possible to the office of the magazine [The Cosmopolitan] *of which I was one of the editors.*

On arriving, the editor and owner [John Brisben Walker] *of the magazine asked if I would leave New York that evening for San Francisco and continue from there around the world, endeavoring to complete the journey in some absurdly inadequate space of time.*

But in the course of half an hour I had become convinced that the editor really wished me to make the attempt, and I had earnestly endeavored to convince him that I meant to do nothing of the sort. To begin with, I didn't wish to. In the second place, guests were coming to my house to tea on the following day; thirdly, I was not prepared in the matter of appropriate garments for such an abrupt departure; and lastly, but most weightily, I foresaw the notoriety that an effort to outdo the feat of Jules Verne's hero was likely to bring upon me, and to this notoriety I most earnestly objected. Though for some years I had been more or less connected with journalism, I had appeared in the papers only as the contributor of unsigned articles, and the amount of distress I experienced when I first saw my name in a headline was so far beyond even my anticipations that I then and there registered a vow—throughout this voyage I had cause to owe much gratitude to journalists for all manner of aid and civility, but I resolved in the future to so endeavor to conduct myself that they would never have reason to put my name in a headline again.

The editor and I having passed the better part of an hour going over this matter, substantial arguments were finally advanced by him which persuaded me to make the experiment of lowering the circumnavigatory record.

The next few hours were busy ones.

To the masculine mind there appears to be some-

thing strangely exhilarating in the thought of a woman being abruptly torn from her home without sufficient time to put her wardrobe in order, and to all the men responsible for this voyage, the most delightful feature apparently of the whole affair was the fact that I should be forced to get ready in five hours for a seventy-five days' voyage around the world. Why this should be so, a woman cannot easily divine. It fails utterly to appeal to her sense of humor. It is one of those hopeless warps in the male mind that my sex no longer attempts to comprehend or to straighten, and, finding it incurable, have learned to bear with and ignore it as far as possible.

I finally managed to get all absolute necessaries of travel into a good-sized steamer trunk, a large Gladstone [light travel] bag, and a shawl-strap, but found, by experience, that my progress would have been in no degree retarded, and my comfort and happiness far better served, by carrying a second and larger box with everything I could possibly have required. I managed the trip on two cloth gowns, half a dozen light bodices, and an evening silk, but might quite as well have carried my entire winter and a large part of my summer wardrobe. Happily I took the precaution of carrying plenty of pins and hairpins.

I remember thinking rapidly on all manner of subjects, telling myself warningly that it would not do to forget anything or make any mistakes, as they could not be rectified. . . . I remember thinking that my new gown fitted very well, and that, though my face was drawn and white with the excitement and fatigues of the day, my new hat was distinctly becoming. . . . Then there were cabs and hurry—kisses—last directions— the bumping of the box on the stair—a big bunch of pink roses (which I felt was a nice complementary touch to my traveling ensemble)—everybody talking at once and giving different advice and directions—the glare of lights—the coffin-like smell of a sleeping car— and I was off for seventy-five days' travel round the globe.

NOTES

1. SS *City of Paris*: a British passenger liner of the Inman Line.

2. SS *Augusta Victoria*: a new passenger steamship of the Hamburg America Line.

3. Ruchings: pleated materials, probably for refreshing her collars and cuffs.

4. Peninsular and Oriental Steamers: (P&O), a British shipping company founded in the 1830s that carried mail, cargo, and passengers from the United Kingdom to ports in Asia and Australia.

5. Orientals: inhabitants of East Asia. Now considered derogatory, especially in her implication that they excelled in doing laundry.

STAGE ONE

Bly: Eastward across the Atlantic

On thursday, november 14, 1889, at 9.40.30 o'clock, I started on my tour around the world.

Those who think that night is the best part of the day and that morning was made for sleep know how uncomfortable they feel when, for some reason, they have to get up with—well, with the milkman.

I turned over several times before I decided to quit my bed. I wondered sleepily why a bed feels so much more luxurious, and a stolen nap that threatens the loss of a train, is so much more sweet than those hours of sleep that are free from duty's call. I dozed off very sweetly over these thoughts to wake with a start, wondering anxiously if there was still time to catch the ship.

I endeavored to take some breakfast, but the hour was too early to make food endurable. The last moment at home came. There was a hasty kiss for the dear ones, and a blind rush downstairs trying to overcome the hard lump in my throat that threatened to make me regret the journey that lay before me.

"Don't worry," I said encouragingly, as I was unable to speak that dreadful word, *goodbye*; "only think of me as having a vacation and the most enjoyable time in my life."

Then to encourage myself, I thought, as I was on

my way to the ship: "It's only a matter of twenty-eight thousand miles, and seventy-five days and four hours, until I shall be back again."

A few friends, who, told of my hurried departure, were there to say goodbye. The morning was bright and beautiful, and everything seemed very pleasant while the boat was still; but when they were warned to go ashore, I began to realize what it meant for me. "Keep up your courage," they said to me while they gave my hand the farewell clasp. I saw the moisture in their eyes, and I tried to smile so that their last recollection of me would be one that would cheer them.

But when the whistle blew and they were on the pier and I was on the *Augusta Victoria*, which was slowly but surely moving away from all I knew, taking me to strange lands and strange people, I felt lost. My head felt dizzy, and my heart felt as if it would burst. Only seventy-five days! Yes, but it seemed an age, and the world lost its roundness and seemed a long distance with no end, and—well, I never turn back.

I looked as long as I could at the people on the pier. I did not feel as happy as I have at other times in life. I had a sentimental longing to take farewell of everything. "I am off," I thought sadly, "and shall I ever get back?"

Intense heat, bitter cold, terrible storms, shipwrecks, fevers, all such agreeable topics had been drummed into me until I felt much as I imagine one would feel if shut in a cave of midnight darkness and told that all sorts of horrors were waiting to gobble one up.

The morning was beautiful, and the bay never looked lovelier. The ship glided out smoothly and quietly, and the people on deck looked for their chairs and rugs and got into comfortable positions, as if determined to enjoy themselves while they could, for they did not know what moment someone would be enjoying themselves at their expense.

When the pilot went off, everybody rushed to the side of the ship to see him go down the little rope ladder. I watched him closely, but he climbed down and into the rowboat that was waiting to carry him to the pilot boat, without giving one glance back to us. It was an old story to him, but I could not help wondering if the ship should go down, whether there would not be some word or glance he would wish he had given.

"You have now started on your trip," someone said to me. "As soon as the pilot goes off and the captain assumes command, then, and only then, our voyage begins, so now you are really started on your tour around the world."

Something in his words turned my thoughts to that demon of the sea—seasickness. Never having taken a sea voyage before, I could expect nothing else than a lively tussle with the disease of the wave.

"Do you get seasick?" I was asked in an interested, friendly way. That was enough; I flew to the railing.

Sick? I looked blindly down, caring little what the wild waves were saying, and gave vent to my feelings.

People are always unfeeling about seasickness. When I wiped the tears from my eyes and turned around, I saw smiles on the face of every passenger. I have noticed that they are always on the same side of the ship when one is taken suddenly, overcome, as it were, with one's own emotions.

The smiles did not bother me, but one man said sneeringly: "And she's going around the world!"

I too joined in the laugh that followed. Silently I marveled at my boldness to attempt such a feat wholly unused, as I was, to sea voyages. Still I did not entertain one doubt as to the result.

Of course I went to luncheon. Everybody did, and almost everybody left very hurriedly. I joined them, or, I don't know, probably I made the start. Anyway, I never saw as many in the dining room at any one time during the rest of the voyage.

When dinner was served, I went in very bravely and took my place on the captain's left. I had a very strong determination to resist my impulses, but yet, in the bottom of my heart was a little faint feeling that I had found something even stronger than my willpower.

Dinner began very pleasantly. The waiters moved

He Meant Well, *a humorous cartoon showing the captain of an ocean liner toasting seasick passengers*

about noiselessly, the band played an overture, Captain [Adolph] Albers, handsome and genial, took his place at the head, and the passengers who were seated at his table began dinner with a relish equaled only by enthusiastic wheelmen when roads are fine. I was the only one at the captain's table who might be called an amateur sailor. I was bitterly conscious of this fact. So were the others.

I might as well confess it: while soup was being served I was lost in painful thoughts and filled with a sickening fear. I felt that everything was just as pleasant as an unexpected gift on Christmas, and I endeavored to listen to the enthusiastic remarks about the music made by my companions, but my thoughts were on a topic that would not bear discussion.

I felt cold, I felt warm; I felt that I should not get hungry if I did not see food for seven days; in fact, I had a great, longing desire not to see it, nor to smell it, nor to eat of it, until I could reach land or a better understanding with myself.

Fish was served, and Captain Albers was in the midst of a good story, when I felt I had more than I could endure.

"Excuse me," I whispered faintly, and then rushed, madly, blindly out. I was assisted to a secluded spot where a little reflection and a little unbridling of pent-up emotion restored me to such a courageous state that I determined to take the captain's advice and return to my unfinished dinner.

"The only way to conquer seasickness is by forcing one's self to eat," the captain said, and I thought the remedy harmless enough to test.

They congratulated me on my return. I had a shamed feeling that I was going to misbehave again, but I tried to hide the fact from them. It came soon, and I disappeared at the same rate of speed as before.

Once again I returned. This time my nerves felt a little unsteady and my belief in my determination was weakening. Hardly had I seated myself when I caught an amused gleam of a steward's eye, which made me bury my face in my handkerchief and choke before I reached the limits of the dining hall.

The bravos with which they kindly greeted my third return to the table almost threatened to make me lose my bearings again. I was glad to know that dinner was just finished, and I had the boldness to say that it was very good!

I went to bed shortly afterwards. No one had made any friends yet, so I concluded sleep would be more enjoyable than sitting in the music hall looking at other passengers engaged in the same first-day-at-sea occupation.

I went to bed shortly after seven o'clock. I had a dim recollection afterwards of waking up enough to drink some tea, but beyond this and the remembrance of some dreadful dreams, I knew nothing until I heard an honest, jolly voice at the door calling to me.

Opening my eyes, I found the stewardess and a lady passenger in my cabin and saw the captain standing at the door.

"We were afraid that you were dead," the captain said when he saw that I was awake.

"I always sleep late in the morning," I said apologetically.

"In the morning!" the captain exclaimed, with a laugh, which was echoed by the others, "It is half-past four in the evening!"

"But never mind," he added consolingly, "as long as you slept well, it will do you good. Now get up and see if you can't eat a big dinner."

I did. I went through every course at dinner without flinching, and stranger still, I slept that night as well as people are commonly supposed to sleep after long exercise in the open air.

The weather was very bad, and the sea was rough, but I enjoyed it. My seasickness had disappeared, but I had a morbid, haunting idea, that although it was gone, it would come again; still I managed to make myself comfortable.

I think it is only natural for travelers to take an innocent pleasure in studying the peculiarities of their fellow companions. We were not out many days until everybody that was able to be about had added a little to their knowledge of those that were not. I will not say that the knowledge acquired in that way is of any benefit, nor would I try to say that those passengers who mingled together did not find one another as interesting and as fit subjects for comment. Nevertheless, it was harmless and it afforded us some amusement.

I remember when I was told that we had among the passengers one man who counted his pulse after every meal, and they were hearty meals, too, for he was free from the disease of the wave, that I waited quite eagerly to have him pointed out so that I might watch him. If it had been my pulse, instead of his own, that he watched so carefully, I could not have been more interested thereafter.

I almost forgot my interest in this one man, when my attention was called to another, who counted the number of steps he took every day. This one in turn became less interesting when I found that one of the women, who had been a great sufferer from seasickness, had not undressed since she left her home in New York.

"I am sure we are all going down," she said one day in a burst of confidence, "and I am determined to go down dressed!"

While at luncheon on the 21st of November, someone called out that we were in sight of land. The way everyone left the table and rushed on deck was surely not surpassed by the companions of Columbus when they discovered America. I cannot give any good reason for it, but I know that I looked at the first point of bleak land with more interest than I would have bestowed on the most beautiful bit of scenery in the world.

We had not been long in sight of land until the decks began to fill with dazed-looking, wan-faced people. It was just as if we had taken on new passengers. We could not realize that they were from New York and had been enjoying a season of seclusion since leaving that port.

Dinner that evening was a very pleasant affair. Extra courses had been prepared in honor of those that were leaving at Southampton. I had not known one of the passengers when I left New York seven days before, but I realized, now that I was so soon to separate from them, that I regretted the parting very much. Had I been traveling with a companion, I should not have felt this so keenly, for naturally then I would have had less time to cultivate the acquaintance of my fellow passengers.

They were all so kind to me that I should have been the most ungrateful of women had I not felt that I was leaving friends behind. Captain Albers had served many years as commander of a ship in Eastern seas, and he cautioned me as to the manner in which I should take care of my health. As the time grew shorter for my stay on the *Augusta Victoria*, some teased me gently as to the outcome of my attempt to beat the record made by a hero of fiction, and I found myself forcing a false gaiety that helped to hide my real fears.

The passengers on the *Augusta Victoria* all stayed up to see us off. We sat on deck talking or nervously walking about until half-past two in the morning. Then someone said the tugboat had come alongside, and we all rushed over to see it. After it was made secure, we went down to the lower deck to see who would come on and to get some news from land.

One man was very much concerned about my making the trip to London alone. He thought as it was so late, or rather so early, that the London correspondent, who was to have met me, would not put in an appearance.

"I shall most certainly leave the ship here and see you safely to London, if no one comes to meet you," he protested, despite my assurances that I felt perfectly able to get along safely without an escort.

More for his sake than my own, I watched the men come on board and tried to pick out the one that had been sent to meet me. Several of them were passing us in a line just as a gentleman made some remark about my trip around the world. A tall young man overheard the remark, and turning at the foot of the stairs, looked down at me with a hesitating smile. "Nellie Bly?" he asked inquiringly.

"Yes," I replied, holding out my hand, which he gave a cordial grasp, meanwhile asking if I had enjoyed my trip and if my baggage was ready to be transferred.

The man who had been so fearful of my traveling to London alone took occasion to draw the correspondent into conversation. Afterwards he came to me and said with the most satisfied look upon his face: "He is all right. If he had not been so, I should have gone to London with you anyway. I can rest satisfied now, for he will take care of you."

I went away with a warm feeling in my heart for that kindly man who would have sacrificed his own comfort to ensure the safety of an unprotected girl.

A few warm hand clasps, and interchanging of good wishes, a little dry feeling in the throat, a little strained pulsation of the heart, a little hurried run down the perpendicular plank to the other passengers who were going to London, and then the tug cast off from the ship, and we drifted away in the dark.

BISLAND: WESTWARD ACROSS THE CONTINENT

THEN NO MORE DISTINCT *impressions until Chicago suddenly steps across my twenty-five-thousand-mile path and it is necessary to change cars. . . . Even this is vague. I remember that through some mistake, there was no one there to meet me as had been arranged—that I wandered about a vast, gloomy, and rather empty station in the care of a friendly conductor—that I sat on a high stool at a counter and quenched internal cravings, caused by lack of dinner, with tea and ham; every mouthful regarded with wan interest by the person who officiated in the echoing lunch hall—that the conductor having bidden me a commiserating adieu, I slid away into the night, very homesick, very cross, and haunted by the bitterest suspicions of the happy results of a tea-and-ham dinner.*

But with that night's sleep, I slept away my stupefaction of amazement, and awoke at daybreak in my right mind, and, pulling up my window curtain, found the sun almost ready to rise.

Now the lifted curtain showed me a New Jerusalem. . . . As if to one who should rise to pray at the moment when God gave his great daily fiat of "Let there be light," there should be vouchsafed a white, luminous foreshadowing of that which it hath not entered into the heart of man to understand. . . . Not the strangely narrow and urban vision of Patmos;[1] no streets or walls, but a limitless Land of Pearl!

. . . Soft undulations, full and tender as the bosom of a sleeping mother, rose and fell far beyond the eye's reach, and melted into the sky. No tree or thicket broke the suave outlines, but where the thin silver veins of the streams slipped through the curves of the plain, slim, leafless willows, hung, like glistening fringes. . . . In the night a hoar frost had fallen that was to snow as sleep is to death; and the pale reaped fields, the sere meadows, and silent uplands were transfigured by the first gleam of day to a mystery and glory of silver and pearl. As the light grew, nacreous tints of milky blue and rose flushed the argent pallor of the land, and when the yellow disk rolled up over the horizon's edge, I traveled for some brief space in a world of intolerable splendor, where innumerable billions of frost crystals flashed back to the sun the reflection of his shining face.

As I passed in my swift circle about the great ball plunging along its planetary paths, many mighty and glorious visions of the coming and passing of light were revealed to me; but none more fair than this with that radiance of youth, whose vast, sweet nature-shadow and simulacrum the dawning is.

. . . In developing my mental Kodak [photo] roll after returning, I found that during this period of the journey most of the views are landscapes, seeing that I was afflicted with peculiarly uninteresting fellow travelers who made poor subjects for snapshots. Across the *aisle from me was a pair of ancient little lovers who numbered some hundred or more years between them, I fancy. They had nested long since; all their fledglings were flown, and, left alone together once more, they were on their way to Los Angeles to spend a second honeymoon among the winter orange blossoms: a pretty, pale afterglow of love.*

That night we were in Council Bluffs, Omaha, and by chance got passage on the new fast mail train, which had been put on as an experiment in time across the continent and was carrying but one sleeper and the general manager's private car.

The pace was tremendous from the start. . . . We began to climb the Great Divide. Trees and shrubs grew rare and more rare, and finally vanished altogether.

. . . Great gray plains lay all about us, covered thinly with a withered, ashen-colored plant, the bitter results of an unequal struggle for existence, and strangely resembling in miniature the gnarled, writhen cedars that cling to wind-scourged coasts. Settlements were few and far between. Scrawny horses picked up a scant living in the desolate upland meadows; and an occasional yellow cur that came out and barked at us as we went by was the only other form of animal life to be seen. From time to time we passed a dwelling, a square cabin of gray unpainted boards, always tightly closed and the dwellers always absent somewhere on business. The only distinct proof I ever saw of the human habi-

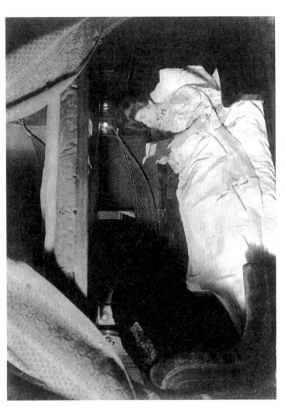

A woman reading in the comfort of a Pullman car

tance of these silent, lonely homes was a tiny pair of butternut trousers fluttering on the clothesline. The minute American citizen who should have occupied these trousers was invisible, and I greatly fear they were perhaps his only pair.

. . . We climbed and climbed, always at tremendous speed, and always the land growing more desolate, and wildly drear, like the cursed site of some prehistoric Sodom, sown with salt. The air shone with a luminous clearness undreamable in coast countries, and at night the stars were huge and fierce.

During the night, our way lay through that still more desolate portion of this dry region named, with simple and expressive literalness, the Badlands; and here again I saw a most wonderful coming of the light. The moon, wan with the dawn, hung directly in the zenith, and on the eastern rim of the ghostly gray plain, under the quivering jewel of the morning star, burned the first vague flush of day. Slowly a dusky amethyst radiance filled the sapphire bowl of the sky, quenching the stars one by one as it rose, and when the sun showed over the world's edge, the cup was brimmed, and the pale moon shone faintly in its depths, like the drowned pearl of the Egyptian queen.

. . . Our speed through this part of the country was terrible. Five hours away from Ogden, we were two hours and a half behind the time set for our arrival there. Some three-quarters of a million hung upon our arriving promptly[2] and getting the track clear for our-

31

selves beyond, not to mention many other important considerations that could scarcely be reckoned in figures; for a great government contract for mails would be either lost or won by morning.

A certain engineer, whose name was Foley—or words to that effect—was telegraphed to meet us at the next stop. He was a gentleman of Irish extraction who labored under an entire absence of physical timidity and who remarked with jovial determination, as he climbed into the cab, that he would "get us to Ogden—or hell, on time." Several times during that five hours' ride, the betting stood ten to one on the latter goal, and Hades was hot favorite. The grade at this part of the road has a descent of 93 feet in a mile, and the track corkscrewed through gorges and canyons with but small margin between us and destruction. To these considerations Mr. Foley was cheerfully indifferent, and pulling out the throttle, he let the engine have her head at the rate of sixty-five miles an hour. The train rocked like a ship at sea, and sleepers held to their berths in terror, the more nervous actually succumbing to mal de mer. The plunge of the engine, that now and again whimpered affrightedly in the darkness, could be felt through the whole train, as one feels beneath one the fierce play of the loins of a runaway horse. From the rear car the tracks were two lines of fire in the night. The telegraph pole reeled backwards from our course, and the land fled from under us with horrible nightmare weirdness. The officers of the train became alarmed and ordered *speed slackened; but Mr. Foley, consulting his watch, regretted with great firmness that he could not oblige them. One man rolled in an anguish of terror on the floor; and the general manager, engaged in a late game of whist, regarding the sufferer with sympathetic interest as he took the odd trick with the thirteenth trump, remarked that it was such episodes as this in American life that made us a nation of youthful gray-heads.*

We arrived in Ogden on time.

Mr. Foley dismounted with alacrity from his cab, remarked that these night rides were prone to give a man cold, and went in pursuit of an antidote behind a swinging Venetian door on the corner, and we saw him no more.

From here the vast, desolate uplands, eight thousand feet high in the keen dry air, showed no further sign of human habitation between the stations and were ornamented only with the frequent jack rabbit, the occasional coyote, and now and then an arrangement of tepees. Indians crowded about the train at every stop; those of the female sex who were blessed with offspring permitting us to view the living contents of the corded parcels they carried on their backs in exchange for small current coin. The girls and boys from six to sixteen I found very pretty, with smooth red skins, glittering teeth and eyes, and black Vandyked [zigzagged] locks. Those whom years had overtaken were indescribably wrinkled and parched.

All through this country the air had a delicious dry

33

perfume, like the smell of parching vegetation, that was stimulating and wholesome as the resinous incense of pines.

The night before reaching San Francisco, we found our first trees again, at a little wayside eating station, where a long row of poplars stood up stiffly in the dusk near our path, and a tiny fountain plashed with an enchanting, cool melodiousness. . . . The air was soft and spring-like and the moist darkness pleasant with a smell as of white clover.

Sacramento stopped us for a moment at daylight, and here we found rich, juicy verdure, watery marshes. Still there were no trees. Only grassy, rounded hills, with white sea mists trailing among them.

. . . At fifteen minutes past nine, the nose of the ferryboat from Oakland touches the San Francisco wharf. We have crossed the continent in four days and twenty hours, and the distance between New York and the western metropolis is reduced by a whole day. A great achievement! There are crowds of reporters waiting to interview everybody; general manager, engineer, conductor—even me. We splash cheerfully through the warm rain and oozing mud—the wet season began two days ago—with pleased faces that our tremendous journey is over, walking with free strides and swinging arms because of the long, cramping confinement.

To my eyes, accustomed to the soaring loftiness of New York architecture, this city seems astonishingly low. Three or four stories at the most the average is.

Because of earthquake they say; but latterly these have almost entirely ceased to occur, as if the land had grown to realize that civilization would not tolerate such impulsive ways and had gradually abandoned them shamefacedly, as being in extremely bad taste. Consequently a few of the more recent buildings have begun to climb, Babel-like, into the dripping skies.

One gets a remarkable impression of newness here such as a Londoner might on his first landing in New York. Everyone tells you, "I have been here a year—six months—three months—three years." One begins to believe that no one was ever born here. All the buildings look new and fresh, and the whole atmosphere of the place is charged with a vigorous, disrespectful sort of youth.

The city, or at least the Spanish part of it, was founded in the year of the Declaration of Independence, but the American town is only forty or fifty years old. The hotel at which I stop was erected in 1875. It is a huge caravansary, built around a square and enclosing a vast asphalted court adorned with palms and ferns. There is an arcade within this court where the typical American hotel frequenter tips back his chair, reads the papers, and smokes. On the outer side of the arcade are shops of every description, so that one may purchase all the ordinary needs of life without leaving one's lodging place.

I find here that my progress must be arrested for two days, as the arrangements for hurrying the departure of the ship have fallen through; and I do not altogether grieve, for this tremendous pace for thousands of miles across the country has told upon my nerves to an absurd degree, and I wonder, as I shiver with exhaustion and tremble with nameless, undefined apprehensions, how the coming generation that is to travel a hundred and a hundred and fifty miles an hour will bear the strain of it. Some process of adaption to a nerve-destroying environment will take place doubtless, humanity being so elastic in such matters.

Meantime, there is some space to investigate this first one of the many great cities I must pass through. The editors of the San Francisco Examiner, *who have shown me every courtesy from the moment of my arrival, invite me to luncheon at the Cliff House, which stands on the very western edge of the continent, upon one of the pillars of the Golden Gate.*[3]

There is still a soft, warm rain falling when we start. Roses climb around the porches of the residences and hang heavy-drenched blossoms amid their shining wet leaves, perfuming the damp city streets with delicious garden odors. Should I shut my eyes to the hills I mount and descend, the warmth, the humidity, and the rose odors would make me believe myself in New Orleans again. . . . It gives me a sense of nostalgia, not for the people and city I have but just left [New York], but for an earlier home [New Orleans], where I would have found just such carelessly happy geniality as among these witty, good-looking men who regard the delays of a train with amiable indifference and see their day slip from them with the carelessness of a spendthrift.

We lunch, jovially and sumptuously, upon the sea's edge. On a balcony that overhangs the water, we watch the sunset. Three great crags stand up sharply two hundred yards away—Seal Rocks—covered with grumbling, barking sea lions, the city's pets, whom the law protects. They look much like fat pigs from this distance. At the last moment the sun flames out gloriously, reddens all the heavens, and gilds a rippling road for me across the waterly world I must traverse. It is a sign of promise, they tell me.

The ride home in the cable car is a curious experience. The streets are of the most astonishing steepness still, though millions have been spent in grading the hills. On each of the cars is a small open space in front where one may sit if one likes and enjoy the sensation of plunging down the most startling inclines and yet see the car stop short at perilous points to allow a traveler to leisurely dismount. The road leads past the famous Nob Hill, where the bonanza kings[4] have their residences—huge wooden palaces of the most rococo designs. It is said that these half-dozen residences cost $9,000,000 to build. James C. Flood's house is of brown stone, the only dwelling of that material in the state, all of the stone having been imported from the East at prodigious expense. One of these palaces—the property of a bonanza relict—is of a curious lead color, which, with its overwhelmingly ornate decorations, gives it an odd resemblance to a gigantic hot-air stove.

There were beautiful public gardens, great public buildings, and many relics of the ancient Spanish domination to be seen in this charming city, but my flight was too rapid to pause for these. That night I saw the quarter known locally as Chinatown, peeped into some of the huge, splendid theaters and restaurants, and then, at three o'clock the next day, set sail for Japan.

NOTES

1. This is likely a reference to the book of Revelation, written by the apostle John on Patmos, an island in the Aegean Sea that had been used by the Romans as a penal colony.

2. The United States Postal Service had offered the Union Pacific Railroad a contract worth $750,000 if the railroad could reduce the time of the New York-to-San Francisco trip from 118 hours to 108.

3. Golden Gate: the Golden Gate Strait connects San Francisco Bay with the Pacific Ocean. The famous bridge was not completed until 1937.

4. Bonanza kings: nickname for those who became immensely wealthy, especially through mining. The most spectacular fortunes were those of J. C. Flood and W. S. O'Brien.

STAGE TWO

BLY: THROUGH EUROPE

M R. & MRS. JULES VERNE have sent a special letter asking that if possible you will stop to see them," the London correspondent said to me, as we were on our way to the wharf.

"Oh, how I should like to see them!" I exclaimed, adding in the same breath: "Isn't it hard to be forced to decline such a treat?"

"If you are willing to go without sleep and rest for two nights, I think it can be done," he said quietly.

"Safely? Without making me miss any connections? If so, don't think about sleep or rest."

The boat that was landing us left much to be desired in the way of comfort. The only cabin seemed to be the hull, but it was filled with mail and baggage and lighted by a lamp with a smoked globe. I did not see any place to sit down, so we all stood on deck, shivering in the damp, chilly air, and looking in the gray fog like uneasy spirits.

The dreary, dilapidated wharf was a fit landing place for the antique boat. I silently followed the correspondent into a large, empty shed, where a few men with sleep in their eyes, and uniforms that bore ample testimony to the fact that they had slept in their clothes, were stationed behind some long, low tables.

"Where are your keys?" the correspondent asked me as he sat my solitary bag down before one of these weary-looking inspectors.

"It is too full to lock," I answered simply.

"Will you swear that you have no tobacco or tea?" the inspector asked my escort lazily.

"Don't swear," I said to him; then turning to the inspector I added: "It's my bag." He smiled and putting a chalk mark upon the bag freed us.

Passing through the custom house, we were made happy by the information that it had been decided to attach a passenger coach to the special mail train to oblige the passengers who wished to go to London without delay.

A porter took my bag and another man in uniform drew forth an enormous key with which he unlocked the door in the side of the car instead of the end, as in America. I managed to compass the uncomfortable long step to the door and striking my toe against some projection in the floor, went most ungracefully and unceremoniously onto the seat.

My escort after giving some order to the porter went out to see about my ticket, so I took a survey of an English railway compartment. The little square in which I sat looked like a hotel omnibus and was about as comfortable. The two red leather seats in it run across the car, one backing the engine, the other backing the rear of the train. There was a door on either side, and one could hardly have told that there was a dingy lamp there to cast a light on the scene had not the odor from it been so loud. I carefully lifted the rug that covered the thing I had fallen over, curious to see what could be so necessary to an English railway carriage as to occupy such a prominent position. I found a harmless object that looked like a bar of iron and had just dropped the rug in place when the door opened and the porter, catching the iron at one end, pulled it out, replacing it with another like it in shape and size.

"Put your feet on the foot warmer and get warm, miss," he said, and I mechanically did as he advised.

My escort returned soon after, followed by a porter who carried a large basket which he put in our carriage. With a newspaper spread over our laps for a tablecloth, we brought out what the basket contained and put in our time eating and chatting about my journey until the train reached London.

As no train was expected at that hour, Waterloo Station was almost deserted. It was some little time after we stopped before the guard unlocked the door of our compartment and released us. Our few fellow passengers were just about starting off in shabby cabs when we alighted. Once again we called goodbye and good wishes to each other, and then I found myself in a four-wheeled cab, facing a young Englishman who had come to meet us and who was glibly telling us the latest news.

I don't know at what hour we arrived, but my companions told me that it was daylight. I should not have known it. A gray, misty fog hung like a ghostly pall over the city. I always liked fog; it lends such a soft, beautifying light to things that otherwise in the broad glare of day would be rude and commonplace.

"How are these streets compared with those of New York?" was the first question that broke the silence after our leaving the station.

"They are not bad," I said with a patronizing air, thinking shamefacedly of the dreadful streets of New York, although determined to hear no word against them.

Westminster Abbey and the Houses of Parliament were pointed out to me, and the Thames, across which we drove. I felt that I was taking what might be called a bird's-eye view of London. A great many foreigners have taken views in the same rapid way of America, and afterwards gone home and written books about America, Americans, and Americanisms.

We drove first to the London office of the New York *World*. After receiving the cables that were waiting for my arrival, I started for the American Legation to get a passport as I had been instructed by cable.

Mr. McCormick,[1] secretary of the legation, came into the room immediately after our arrival and, after welcoming and congratulating me on the successful termination of the first portion of my trip, sat down and wrote out a passport.

My escort was asked to go into another part of the room until the representative could ask me an important question. I had never required a passport before, and I felt a nervous curiosity to know what secrets were connected with such proceedings.

"There is one question all women dread to answer, and, as very few will give a truthful reply, I will ask you to swear to the rest first and fill in the other question afterwards, unless you have no hesitancy in telling me your age."

"Oh, certainly," I laughed. "I will tell you my age, swear to it, too, and I am not afraid; my companion may come out of the corner."

"What is the color of your eyes?" he asked.

"Green," I said indifferently.

He was inclined to doubt it at first, but after a little inspection, both the gentlemen accepted my verdict as correct.

It was only a few seconds until we were whirling through the streets of London again. This time we went to the office of the Peninsular and Oriental Steamship Company, where I bought tickets that would cover at least half of my journey. A few moments again and we were driving rapidly to the Charing Cross station.

I was faint for food, and while my companion

43

dismissed the cab and secured tickets, I ordered the only thing on the Charing Cross bill of fare that was prepared, so when he returned, his breakfast was ready for him. It was only ham and eggs, and coffee, but what we got of it was delicious. I know we did not get much, and when we were interrupted by the announcement that our train was starting, I stopped long enough to take another drink of coffee and then had to run down the platform to catch the train.

There is nothing like plenty of food to preserve health. I know that cup of coffee saved me from a headache that day. I had been shaking with the cold as we made our hurried drive through London, and my head was so dizzy at times that I hardly knew whether the earth had a chill or my brains were attending a ball. When I got comfortable seated in the train, I began to feel warmer and more stable. The train moved off at an easygoing speed, and the very jog of it lulled me into a state of languor.

"I want you to see the scenery along here; it is beautiful," my companion said, but I lazily thought, "What is scenery compared with sleep when one has not seen bed for over twenty-four hours?," so I said to him, very crossly: "Honestly, now, I care very little for scenery when I am so sleepy." I said apologetically. "Those English farmhouses are charming and the daisy-dotted meadows (I had not the faintest conception as to whether there were daisies in them or not) are only equaled by those I have seen in Kansas, but if you will excuse me?"—and I was in the land that joins the land of death.

I slept an easy, happy sleep, filled with dreams of home until I was waked by the train stopping. "We change for the boat here," my companion said, catching up our bags and rugs, which he hauled to a porter.

A little walk down to the pier brought us to the place where a boat was waiting. Some people were getting off the boat, but a larger number stood idly about waiting for it to move off.

There has been so much written and told about the English Channel that one is inclined to think of it as a stream of horrors. It is also affirmed that even hardy sailors bring up the past when crossing over it, so I naturally felt that my time would come.

I remained on deck and watched the seagulls, or what I thought were these useful birds—useful for millinery purposes—and froze my nose. It was bitterly cold, but I found the cold bracing until we anchored at Boulogne, France. Then I had a chill.

At the end of this desolate pier, where boats anchor and where trains start, is a small, dingy restaurant. While a little English sailor, who always dropped his *h*'s and never forgot his "sir," took charge of our bags and went to secure accommodations for us in the outgoing train, we followed the other passengers into the restaurant to get something warm to eat.

I was in France now, and I began to wonder now what would have been my fate if I had been alone as I had expected. I knew my companion spoke French, the language that all the people about us were speaking, so I felt perfectly easy on that score as long as he was with me.

We took our places at the table, and he began to order in French. The waiter looked blankly at him until, at last, more in a spirit of fun than anything else, I suggested that he give the order in English. The waiter glanced at me with a smile and answered in English.

We traveled from Boulogne to Amiens in a compartment with an English couple and a Frenchman. During this trip, I tried to solve the reason for the popularity of these ancient, incommodious railway carriages. I very shortly decided that while they may be suitable for countries where little traveling is done, they would be thoroughly useless in thinly populated countries where people think less of traveling three thousand miles than they do about their dinner. I also decided that the reason why we think nothing of starting out on long trips is because our comfort is so well looked after, that living on a first-class railway train is as comfortable as living at a first-class hotel. The English railway carriages are wretchedly heated. One's feet will be burning on the foot warmer while one's back will be freezing in the cold air above. If one should be taken suddenly ill in an English railway compartment, it would be a very serious matter.

But talk about privacy! If it is privacy the English desire so much, they should adopt our American trains, for there is no privacy like that to be found in a large car filled with strangers. Everybody has and keeps his own place. It would make any American woman shudder, with all her boasted self-reliance, to think of sending her daughter alone on a trip, even of a few hours' duration, where there was every possibility that during those hours she would be locked in a compartment with a stranger.

Small wonder the American girl is fearless. She has not been used to so-called private compartments in English railway carriages, but to large crowds, and every individual that helps to swell that crowd is to her a protector. When mothers teach their daughters that there is safety in numbers, and that numbers are the bodyguard that shield all womankind, then chaperones will be a thing of the past, and women will be nobler and better.

As I was pondering over this subject, the train pulled into a station and stopped. My escort, looking out, informed me that we were at Amiens. We were securely locked in, however, and began to think that we would be carried past, when my companion managed to get his head out of the window and shouted for the guard to come to our release. Freed at last, we stepped out on the platform at Amiens.

47

*　　*　　*

M. JULES VERNE and Mme. Verne,[2] accompanied by Mr. R. H. Sherard,[3] a Paris journalist, stood on the platform waiting our arrival.

When I saw them, I felt as any other woman would have done under the same circumstances. I wondered if my face was travel-stained and if my hair was tossed. I thought, regretfully, had I been traveling on an American train, I should have been able to make my toilet en route, so that when I stepped off at Amiens and faced the famous novelist and his charming wife, I would have been as trim and tidy as I would had I been receiving them in my own home.

There was little time for regret. They were advancing towards us, and in another second I had forgotten my untidiness in the cordial welcome they gave me. Jules Verne's bright eyes beamed on me with interest and kindliness, and Mme. Verne greeted me with the cordiality of a cherished friend. There were no stiff formalities to freeze the kindness in all our hearts, but a cordiality expressed with such charming grace that before I had been many minutes in their company, they had won my everlasting respect and devotion.

M. Verne led the way to the carriages which waited our coming. Mme. Verne walked closely by my side, glancing occasionally at me with a smile,

Jules Verne

which said in the language of the eye, the common language of the whole animal world, alike plain to man and beast: "I am glad to greet you, and I regret we cannot speak together." M. Verne gracefully helped Mme. Verne and myself into a coupé, while he entered a carriage with the two other gentlemen. I felt very awkward at being left alone with Mme. Verne, as I was altogether unable to speak to her.

Her knowledge of the English language consisted of "No," and my French vocabulary consisted of "Oui," so our conversation was limited to a few apologetic and friendly smiles interluded with an occasional pressure of the hand. Indeed, Mme. Verne is a most charming woman, and even in this awkward position, she made everything go most gracefully.

It was early evening. As we drove through the streets of Amiens, I got a flying glimpse of bright shops, a pretty park, and numerous nursemaids pushing baby carriages about.

When our carriage stopped, I got out and gave my hand to Mme. Verne to help her alight. We stood on a wide, smooth pavement, before a high stone wall, over the top of which I could see the peaked outlines of the house.

M. Verne was not long behind us. He hurried up to where we were standing and opened a door in the wall. Stepping in, I found myself in a small, smoothly paved courtyard, the wall making two sides, and the house forming the square.

A large black shaggy dog came bounding forward to greet me. He jumped up against me, his soft eyes overflowing with affection, and though I love dogs and especially appreciated this one's loving welcome, still I feared that his lavish display of it would undermine my dignity by bringing me to my knees at the very threshold of the home of the famous Frenchman. M. Verne evidently understood my plight, for he spoke shortly to the dog, who, with a pathetic droop of his tail, went off to think it out alone.

We went up a flight of marble steps across the tiled floor of a beautiful little conservatory that was not packed with flowers but was filled with a display just generous enough to allow one to see and appreciate the beauty of the different plants. Mme. Verne led the way into a large sitting room that was dusky with the early shade of a wintry evening. With her own hands she touched a match to the pile of dry wood that lay in the wide-open fireplace.

Meanwhile M. Verne urged us to remove our outer wrappings. Before this was done, a bright fire was crackling in the grate, throwing a soft, warm light over the dark room. Mme. Verne led me to a chair close by the mantel, and when I was seated, she took the chair opposite. Cheered by the warmth, I looked quietly on the scene before me.

The room was large, and the hangings and paintings and soft velvet rug, which left visible but a border of polished hard wood, were richly dark. On the mantel, which towered above Mme. Verne's head, were some fine pieces of statuary in bronze and, as the fire gave frequent bright flashes as the flames greedily caught fresh wood, I could see another bronze piece on a pedestal in a corner. All the chairs artistically upholstered in brocaded silks, were luxuriously easy. Beginning at either side of the mantel they were placed in a semicircle around the fire, which was only broken by a little table that held several tall silver candlesticks.

A fine white Angora cat came rubbing up against my knee, then seeing its charming mistress on the opposite side, went to her and boldly crawled up in her lap as if assured of a cordial welcome.

Next to me in this semicircle sat Mr. Sherard. M. Jules Verne was next to Mr. Sherard. He sat forward on the edge of his chair; his snow-white hair, rather long and heavy, was standing up in artistic disorder; his full beard, rivaling his hair, in snowiness, hid the lower part of his face; and the brilliancy of his bright eyes that were overshadowed with heavy white brows and the rapidity of his speech and the quick movements of his firm white hands all bespoke energy—life—with enthusiasm.

The London correspondent sat next to Jules Verne. With a smile on her soft, rosy lips, Mme. Verne sat nursing the cat, which she stroked methodically with a dainty white hand, while her luminous black eyes moved alternately between her husband and myself.

She was the most charming figure in that group around the wood fire. Imagine a youthful face with a spotless complexion, crowned with the whitest hair, dressed in smooth, soft folds on the top of a dainty head that is most beautifully poised on a pair of plump shoulders. Add to this face pretty red lips that, opened, disclose a row of lovely teeth, and large, bewitching black eyes, and you have but a faint picture of the beauty of Mme. Verne.

This day when she met me she wore a sealskin jacket and carried a muff, and on her white head was a small black velvet bonnet. On taking her wraps off in the house, I saw she wore a watered-silk skirt, laid in side plaits in the front with a full straight black drapery that was very becoming to her short, plump figure. The bodice was of black silk velvet.

Mme. Verne is, I should judge, not more than five feet two in height; M. Verne about five feet five. M. Verne spoke in a short, rapid way, and Mr. Sherard in an attractive, lazy voice translated what was said for my benefit.

"Has M. Verne ever been to America?" I asked.

"Yes, once," the answer came translated to me. "For a few days only, during which time I saw Niagara. I have always longed to return, but the state of my health prevents my taking any long journeys.

I try to keep a knowledge of everything that is going on in America and greatly appreciate the hundreds of letters I receive yearly from Americans who read my books."

"How did you get the idea for your novel, *Around the World in Eighty Days?*" I asked.

"I got it from a newspaper" was his reply. "I took up a copy of *Le Siécle* one morning and found in it a discussion and some calculations showing that the journey around the world might be done in eighty days. The idea pleased me, and while thinking it over, it struck me that in their calculations they had not called into account the difference in the meridians, and I thought what a denouement such a thing would make in a novel, so I went to work to write one. Had it not been for the denouement, I don't think that I should ever have written the book.

"I used to keep a yacht, and then I traveled all over the world studying localities; then I wrote from actual observation. Now, since my health confines me to my home, I am forced to read up descriptions and geographies."

M. Verne asked me what my line of travel was to be, and I was very happy to speak one thing that he could understand, so I told him.

"My line of travel is from New York to London, then Calais, Brindisi, Port Said, Ismailia, Suez, Aden, Colombo, Penang, Singapore, Hong Kong, Yokohama, San Francisco, New York."

"Why do you not go to Bombay as my hero Phileas Fogg did?" M. Verne asked.

"Because I am more anxious to save time than a young widow,"[4] I answered.

"You may save a young widower before you return," M. Verne said with a smile. I smiled with a superior knowledge, as women, fancy free, always will at such insinuations.

I looked at the watch on my wrist and saw that my time was getting short. There was only one train that I could take from here to Calais, and if I missed it, I might just as well return to New York by the way I came, for the loss of that train meant one week's delay.

"If M. Verne would not consider it impertinent, I should like to see his study before I go," I said at last.

He said he was only too happy to show it me, and even as my request was translated, Mme. Verne sprang to her feet and lighted one of the tall wax candles. She started with the quick, springy step of a girl to lead the way. M. Verne, who walks with a slight limp, the result of a wound, followed, and we brought up the rear. We went through the conservatory to a small room up through which was a winding stair, or, more properly speaking, a spiral staircase. Mme. Verne paused at every curve to light the gas.

Up at the top of the house and along a hall that

Verne's hero, Phileas Fogg, saving a young Indian widow

corresponded in shape to the conservatory below, M. Verne went, Mme. Verne stopping to light the gas in the hall. He opened a door that led off the hall, and I stepped inside after him.

I was astonished. I had expected, judging from the rest of the house, that M. Verne's study would be a room of ample proportions and richly furnished. I had read so many descriptions of the studies of famous authors and have dwelt with something akin to envy (our space is so limited and expensive in New York) on the ample room, the beautiful hand-carved desks filled with costly trinkets, the rare etchings and paintings that covered the walls, the rich hangings, and, I will confess it, I have thought it small wonder that amid such surroundings authors were able to dream fancies that brought them fame.

But when I stood in M. Verne's study, I was speechless with surprise. He opened a latticed window, the only window in the room, and Mme. Verne, hurrying in after us, lighted the gas jet that was fastened above a low mantel.

The room was very small; even my little den at home was almost as large. It was also very modest and bare. Before the window was a flat-topped desk. The usual litter that accompanies and fills the desks of most literary persons was conspicuously absent, and the wastebasket that is usually filled to overflowing with what one very often considers their

57

most brilliant productions, in this case, held but a few little scraps.

On the desk was a neat little pile of white paper, probably 8x10 in size. It was part of the manuscript of a novel that M. Verne is engaged on at present. I eagerly accepted the manuscript when he handed it to me, and when I looked at the neat penmanship, so neat in fact that had I not known it was prose, I should have thought it was the work of a poet, I was more impressed than ever with the extreme tidiness of this French author. In several places he had most effectually blotted out something that he had written, but there was no interlining, which gave me the idea that M. Verne always improved his work by taking out superfluous things and never by adding.

One bottle of ink and one penholder was all that shared the desk with the manuscript. There was but one chair in the room, and it stood before the desk. The only other piece of furniture was a broad, low couch in the corner, and here in this room with these meager surroundings, Jules Verne has written the books that have brought him everlasting fame.

I leaned over the desk and looked out of the little latticed window which he had thrown open. I could see through the dusk the spire of a cathedral in the distance, while stretching down beneath me was a park, beyond which I saw the entrance to a railway tunnel that goes under M. Verne's house and through which many Americans travel every year on their way to Paris.

Leading off from the study is an enormous library. The large room is completely lined with cases from ceiling to floor, and these glass-doored cases are packed with handsomely bound books which must be worth a fortune.

While we were examining the wealth of literature that was there before us, M. Verne got an idea. Taking up a candle and asking us to follow, he went out into the hall; stopping before a large map that hung there, holding up with one hand the candle, he pointed out to us several blue marks. Before his words were translated to me, I understood that on this map he had, with a blue pencil, traced out the course of his hero, Phileas Fogg, before he started him in fiction to travel around the world in eighty days. With a pencil he marked on the map, as we grouped about him, the places where my line of travel differed from that of Phileas Fogg.

Our steps lagged as we descended the winding stair again. It had come time to take farewell, and I felt as if I was separating from friends. Down in the room where we had been before, we found wine and biscuit on the little table, and M. Jules Verne explained that, contrary to his regular rules, he intended to take a glass of wine, that we might have the pleasure of drinking together to the success of my strange undertaking.

They clinked their glasses with mine and wished me "God speed."

"If you do it in seventy-nine days, I shall applaud with both hands," Jules Verne said, and then I knew he doubted the possibility of my doing it in seventy-five, as I had promised. In compliment to me, he endeavored to speak to me in English and did succeed in saying, as his glass tipped mine: "Good luck, Nellie Bly."

Mme. Verne was not going to be outdone by her gallant husband in showing kindness to me. She told Mr. Sherard that she would like to kiss me goodbye, and when he translated her kind request, he added that it was a great honor in France, for a woman to ask to kiss a stranger.

I was little used to such formalities, or familiarities, as one may deem them, but still I had not one thought of refusing such delicate attention, so I gave her my hand and inclined my head, for I am taller than she, and she kissed me gently and affectionately on either check. Then she put up her pretty face for me to kiss. I stifled a strong inclination to kiss her on the lips, they were so sweet and red, and show her how we do it in America. My mischievousness often plays havoc with my dignity, but for once I was able to restrain myself and kissed her softly after her own fashion.

With uncovered heads, and despite our protestations, they followed us out into the cold courtyard, and as far as I could see, I saw them standing at the gate waving farewell to me, the brisk winds tossing their white hair.

*   *   *

WHEN M. AND MME. VERNE were no longer visible, my thoughts turned to my trip. I feared that the enjoyment of my visit to their home had jeopardized the success of my tour.

The driver had been told to make the best speed back to the station, but the carriage seemed to be rolling along so quietly that I could not rest until it was urged again upon the coachman to reach the station in the shortest possible time.

Some few moments after we reached there, the train came in. Bidding a hearty goodbye to Mr. Sherard, I started again on my tour of the world, and the visit to Jules Verne was a thing of the past. I had gone without sleep and rest; I had traveled many miles out of my way for the privilege of meeting M. and Mme. Verne, and I felt that if I had gone around the world for that pleasure, I should not have considered the price too high.

The train which carried us to Calais is, I infer from what I have heard, the pride of France. It is called the Club train, and is built on the plan of the vestibule trains in America. The carriages are so narrow that, after having been accustomed to wide ones, the Club train seems like a toy.

Shortly after we left Amiens, a porter announced that dinner was served in a front car. Everybody at once filed out and into the dining car. I have thought since that probably the train carried two dining cars, because the dinner, and an excellent one it proved to be, was served *table d'hôte*, and there seemed to be accommodations for all.

After we had our cheese and salad, we returned to our drawing-room car, where we were served with coffee, the men having the privilege of smoking with it. I thought this manner of serving coffee a very pleasing one, quite an improvement on our own system, and quite worthy of adoption.

When I reached Calais, I found that I had two hours and more to spend in waiting. The train that I intended to take for Brindisi is a weekly mail train that runs to accommodate the mails and not passengers. It starts originally from London, at eight o'clock Friday evening of each week. The mail and passengers are carried across the channel, and the train leaves Calais at 1:30 in the morning.

There are pleasanter places in the world to waste time in than Calais. I walked down along the pier and looked at the lighthouse, which I am told is one of the most perfect in the world, throwing its light farther away than any other.

470. AMIENS – Train sortant du Tunnel sous le Champ de Foire

L. Caron, photo-édit, Amiens

A train leaving Amiens, France

My escort took me into the restaurant, where we found something to eat, which was served by a French waiter who could speak some English and understand more. When it was announced that the boat from England was in, we went out and saw the be-bundled and be-baggaged passengers come ashore and go to the train which was waiting alongside. One thousand bags of mail were quickly transferred to the train, and then I bade my escort goodbye, and was shortly speeding away from Calais.

There is but one passenger coach on this train. It is a Pullman Palace sleeping car with accommodations for twenty-two passengers, but it is the rule never to carry more than twenty-one, one berth being occupied by the guard.

The next morning, having nothing else to occupy my time, I thought that I would see what my traveling companions looked like. I had shared the stateroom at the extreme end of the car with a pretty English girl who had the rosiest cheeks and the greatest wealth of golden brown hair I ever saw. She was going with her father, an invalid, to Egypt, to spend the winter and spring months. She was an early riser, and before I was awake had gotten up and joined her father in the other part of the car.

When I went out so as to give the porter an opportunity to make up my stateroom, I was surprised at the strange appearance of the interior of the car. All the head- and footboards were left in place, giving the impression that the coach was divided into a series of small boxes. Some of the passengers were drinking, some were playing cards, and all were smoking until the air was stifling. I never object to cigar smoke when there is some little ventilation, but when it gets so thick that one feels as if it is molasses instead of air that one is inhaling, then I mildly protest. It was soon this occasion, and I wonder what would be the result in our land of boasted freedom if a Pullman car should be put to such purposes. I concluded it is due to this freedom that we do not suffer from such things. Women travelers in America command as much consideration as men.

For the first day, food was taken on the train at different stations, and the conductor, or guard, as they called him, served it to the passengers. A dining car was attached in the evening, but I was informed by the women that it was not exactly the thing for us to eat in a public car with men, so we continued to be served in our staterooms.

I might have seen more while traveling through France if the car windows had been clean. From their appearance I judged that they had never been washed. We did not make many stops. The only purpose of stopping was for coal or water, as passengers are not taken on or off this train between Calais and Brindisi.

In the course of the afternoon, we passed some high and picturesque mountains that were covered with a white frost. I found that even wearing my ulster and wrapped in a rug I was none too warm. About eight o'clock in the morning, we reached Modena. The baggage was examined there, and all the passengers were notified in advance to be prepared to get out and unlock the boxes that belonged to them. The conductor asked me several times if I was quite certain that I had no more than the handbag with me, telling me at the same time if any boxes were found locked, with no owner to open them, they would be detained by the custom inspectors.

Half an hour later we were in Italy. I was anxiously waiting to see that balmy, sunny land, but though I pressed my face close to the frosty window pane, bleak night denied me even one glimpse of sunny Italy and its dusky people. I went to bed early. It was so very cold that I could not keep warm out of bed, and I cannot say that I got much warmer in bed. The berths were provided with only one blanket each. I piled all my clothing on the berth and spent half the night lying awake thinking how fortunate the passengers were the week previous on this train. Just in the very same place that we were traveling through Italian bandits had attacked the train, and I thought, with regretful envy, if the passengers then felt the scarcity of blankets, they at least had some excitement to make their blood circulate.

When I got awake in the morning, I hastily

threw up the window shade and eagerly looked out. I fell back in surprise, wondering, if for once in my life I had made a mistake and waked up early. I could not see any more than I had the night before on account of a heavy gray fog that completely hid everything more than a yard away. Looking at the watch on my wrist, I found that it was ten o'clock, so I dressed with some haste, determined to find the guard and demand an explanation of him.

"It is a most extraordinary thing," he said to me; "I never saw such a fog in Italy before."

All day I traveled through Italy—sunny Italy, along the Adriatic Sea. The fog still hung in a heavy cloud over the earth, and only once did I get a glimpse of the land I had heard so much about. It was evening, just at the hour of sunset, when we stopped at some station. I went out on the platform, and the fog seemed to lift for an instant, and I saw on one side a beautiful beach and a smooth bay dotted with boats bearing oddly shaped and brightly colored sails, which somehow looked to me like mammoth butterflies, dipping, dipping about in search of honey. Most of the sails were red, and as the sun kissed them with renewed warmth, just before leaving us in darkness, the sails looked as if they were composed of brilliant fire.

A high, rugged mountain was on the other side of the train. It made me feel dizzy to look at the white buildings perched on the perpendicular side.

I noticed the road that went in a winding line up the hill had been built with a wall on the ocean side; still I thought I would not care to travel up it.

We arrived at Brindisi two hours late. When the train stopped, our car was surrounded with men wanting to carry us as well as our baggage to the boats. Their making no mention of hotels led me to wonder if people always passed through Brindisi without stopping. All these men spoke English very well, but the guard said he would get one omnibus and escort the English women, the invalid man and his daughter, and myself to our boats, and would see that we were not charged more than the right fare.

We drove first to the boat bound for Alexandria, where we took leave of my roommate and her father. Then we drove to the boat that we expected to sail on.

I alighted from the omnibus and followed my companions up the gangplank. I dreaded meeting English people with their much-talked-of prejudices, as I knew I would shortly have to do. I was earnestly hoping that everybody would be in bed. As it was after one in the morning, I hardly expected the trial of facing them at once. The crowds of men on the deck dispelled my fond hope. I think every man on board that boat was up waiting to see the new passengers. They must have felt but illy paid for their loss of sleep, for besides the men who came on board, there were only two large English women and my own plain, uninteresting self.

These women were more helpless than I. As they were among their own people, I waited for them to take the lead; but after we had stood at the foot of the stairs for some time, gazed at by the passengers, and no one came forward to attend to our wants, which were few and simple, I gently asked if that was the usual manner of receiving passengers on English boats.

"It is strange, very strange. A steward, or someone, should come to our assistance" was all they could say.

At last a man came down below, and as he looked as if he was in some way connected with the boat, I ventured to stop him and inquire if it was expecting too much to ask if we might have a steward to show us to our cabins. He said there should be some about and began lustily to call for one. Even this brought no one to us, and as he started to find one himself, I started in the opposite direction.

Among the crowd that stood about was but one man that dared to speak without waiting for an introduction before he could be commonly polite. "You will find the purser in his office the first door to the left there," he said; and I went that way, followed by the guard from the train.

Sitting in the office was the purser and a man I

supposed to be the doctor. I gave my ticket and a letter I had been given at the P&O office in London, to the purser. This letter requested that the commanders and pursers of all the P&O boats on which I traveled should give me all the care and attention it was in their power as such officers to bestow.

After leisurely reading the letter, the purser very carelessly turned around and told me the number of my cabin. I asked for a steward to show me the way, but he replied that there did not seem to be any about, that the cabin was on the port side, and with this meager information, he impolitely turned his back and busied himself with some papers on the desk before him.

The train guard, who still stood by my side, said he would help me find the cabin. After a little search, we did find it. I opened the door and stepped in, and the sight that met my eyes both amused me and dismayed me. At the opening of the door, two bushy heads were stuck out of the two lower berths, and two high-pitched voices exclaimed simultaneously with a vexed intonation, "Oh!" I looked at the bandboxes, boots, handbags, gowns, and the upper berth that was also filled with clothes, and I echoed their "Oh!" in a little different tone and retired.

I returned to the purser and told him I could not sleep in an upper berth and would not occupy a cabin with two other women. After looking again over the letter I had brought him, as if to see how much weight he should give it, he referred me to another cabin. This time a steward made his appearance, and he took the part of an escort.

I found a pretty girl in that cabin, who lifted her head anxiously, and then gave me a friendly smile when I entered. I put my bag down and returned to the guard, who was waiting to take me to the cable office. I stopped to ask the purser if I had time to make the trip, to which he replied in the affirmative, with the proviso, "If you hurry."

The guard took me down the gangplank and along several dark streets. At last, coming to a building where a door stood open, he stopped, and I followed him in. The room in which we stood was perfectly bare and lighted by a lamp whose chimney was badly smoked. The only things in the room were two stationary desks. On the one lay a piece of blank paper before an ancient inkwell and a much used pen.

I thought that everybody had retired for the night and the cable would have to wait until I reached the next port, until the guard explained to me that it was customary to ring for the operator, who would get up and attend to the message for me. Suiting the action to the words, the guard pulled at a knob near a small closed window, much like a postage stamp window. The bell made quite a clatter; still I had begun to think that hopeless, when the window opened with a clink, and a head appeared at the opening. The guard spoke in Italian, but hearing me speak English, the operator replied in the same language.

I told him I wanted to send a cable to New York. He asked me where New York was! I explained as best I could; then he brought out a lot of books, through which he searched first, to know by which line he could send the message— at least, so he explained—then what it would cost. The whole thing was so new and amusing to me that I forgot all about the departure of the boat until we had finished the business and stepped outside.

A whistle blew long and warningly. I looked at the guard; the guard looked at me. It was too dark to see each other, but I know our faces were the picture of dismay. My heart stopped beating, and I thought with emotions akin to horror, "My boat was gone—and with it my limited wardrobe!"

"Can you run?" the guard asked in a husky voice. I said I could, and he taking a close grasp of my hand, we started down the dark street with a speed that would have startled a deer. Down the dark streets, past astonished watchmen and late pedestrians, until a sudden bend brought us in full view of my ship still in port. The boat for Alexandria had gone, but I was saved.

Bisland: Westward across the Pacific

THE WHITE STAR STEAMSHIP *Oceanic, of the Occidental and Oriental Line[5]—Charles H. Kempson commander—sailed from San Francisco at three o'clock Thursday afternoon of November the 21st, and I found it a very exciting thing to leave one's country for the first time.*

Many of the pleasant acquaintances I had made in this short visit to San Francisco had come to bid me God speed, accompanied by a delegation who had got wind of my eccentric performance and came with no other credentials than a desire to gape. The whole army of martyrs to curiosity had afflicted me sorely in those two days on the Pacific coast, sending up their cards in the hotel with urgent messages and, on admission, confessing with placid impudence that their sole excuse for this intrusion was a desire to look at me—presumably as a sort of inexpensive freak show. Experience demonstrated, however, the high and delightful effectiveness of an elaborate and astonished civility that never failed to reduce their robust self-confidence to limp and writhing embarrassment in exactly three minutes, after which discovery I put the heathen to the edge of that manner and smote them hip and thigh. . . .

It must be admitted that my emotions on the occasion of this departure were much less tastefully mingled than I had planned they should be, low spirits and loneliness being such active ingredients that they disguised all other flavors, and it is to a little incident I shall forever remember with pleasure that I did not leave America quite unmixedly miserable. At the moment when the gong had warned all visitors ashore, there was handed up to me from the wharf a great nosegay of white chrysanthemums and roses, to which was attached a card inscribed "J. M. Prather," and bearing "good wishes" and "New Orleans" penciled in the corner. A hat was lifted from a handsome gray head, and two kind dark Southern eyes gave me a smile of such friendliness and goodwill that it warmed my heart like a greeting from my own people. This unknown gentleman taking the trouble to bid me a silent, fragrant farewell seems to me the most delicate and charming impulse of that much misinterpreted and scoffed-at Southern chivalry, and should he ever see this, I wish him to know how pleasant and lasting was the perfume of his flowers and kindly thought.

Perhaps this is the proper moment to speak of a feature that was to me one of the most interesting of this unusual voyage. I was a young woman, quite alone, and doing a somewhat conspicuous and eccentric thing, yet throughout the entire journey, I never met with other than the most exquisite and unfailing courtesy and consideration; and if I had been a princess with a suite of half a hundred people, I could have felt no safer or happier. It seems to me this speaks very highly for the civilization existing in all traveled parts of the globe, when a woman's strongest protection is the fact that she is unprotected. I owe a gratitude beyond all adequate expression for the goodwill shown me everywhere. In every port I touched, I found the kindest of welcomes, and I believe I have put a girdle round the earth of warm and generous friends whom I shall always remember with affection and gratitude.

. . . The last wooden link with the shore is withdrawn. There is a fluttering storm of handkerchiefs—a brief space of water in the beautiful bay—and then we pass away to the west through the Gates of Gold.

. . . America sinks out of sight, slowly—a vision of green hills in level sunshine. We are divided from it now by a long ridge of whirling foam—the bar, where we begin to rise and fall with the first pulse of the sea. Even that vanishes at last, and we plunge forward lonelily on the heaving, dusky plain. The wind of the coming night is cold, and the fluttering paper prayers the Chinese passengers cast overboard to ensure a safe voyage, it catches and whips sharply away, like autumn leaves falling in the November night.

Even up on the hurricane deck, the chill sea wind is tainted with that clinging, pervasive odor that one comes to recognize as "the Chinese smell." Pierre Loti[6] declares it can be smelt on the Chinese coast, while the ship is still miles at sea. On analyzation, it appears to be compounded of the bitter fumes of opium and the smoke of incense sticks.

China has 500,000,000 of population, each unit

trained by generations of bitter struggle for survival to an industry and economy almost superhuman. California has already nearly 100,000 of them; 30,000 living in San Francisco. Every westward-going steamer carries from three to four hundred home, men who have in a short time secured a competence and are returning to enjoy it; and yet their number in America apparently suffers no diminution. Fenced out by law from California,[7] the wave flows around this obstacle into British Columbia and trickles back, drop by drop, into the United States. We do not assimilate them as we do our other immigration. They hold to their own national dress, manners, and food. That part of San Francisco abandoned to them grows daily liker a Chinese city. They gut standing houses and reconstruct the interiors to suit their needs. Outside, lanterns hang in front of doors that have Chinese signs, and above these, frail balconies are strung about the windows where jars of chrysanthemums droop their ragged blossoms over the sill. The air is thick with Oriental odors. Street stalls expose for sale vegetables and fruits unknown to us, and the tiny shops with their Chinese furnishings and inscriptions sell wares which no American seeks.

. . . At eleven at night this transplanted city of Cathay [China] is still all alive, the streets crowded with a moving stream of black blouses and yellow faces— every one cheerful, chattering, and wide awake. The shops stand open, and workmen continue their labors as if it were still high noon.

For the next four days my only memory of the Pacific Ocean is of a foaming flood of emerald that roars past my porthole, making a dull green twilight within. I see only this and the slats of the upper berth. There are six of these slats. Of this I am unwaveringly sure—though I am not usually accurate about figures—because I counted them several thousand times. It was the only mental process of which I was capable during the long nights while I lay and listened to the loud combat of the thundering squadrons outside, whose white plumes flashed into sight again with the first gray gleam of day—the battle still raging. Every plank in the ship creaked and groaned and shrieked without once pausing to take breath, and I regarded with contemptuous indifference the frantic tobogganing of my most treasured possessions all over the stateroom. What were the fleeting things of this world to one to whose unexampled sufferings death must soon put a period? It was comforting to think that one's last will and testament was made, but hateful the contemplation of burial at sea. It was such an unnecessarily tragical end to this ridiculous wild-goose chase.

The fifth day the boiling pot of the sea subsided, and I began to take beef tea and resolution to live. Other women were also beginning to straggle back to life on deck—pale, wan, and with neglected hair tied up in lace scarfs. They lay in steamer chairs swathed in rugs and were indifferent about their appearance and to the charms of conversation. The week was nearly done be-

*fore the whole ship's company assembled at table, and
we began to take note of our fellow voyagers in this
water caravansary.*

*It was a cosmopolitan crew—Norwegians, Russians, English, French, Japanese, Americans, Germans,
Hungarians, and even one Manxman (from the Isle of
Man)—our chief engineer, with a pleasant "out-country" flavor to his speech, and full of tales of a profoundly esoteric humor—a kindly, mellow nature, like
one of William Black's old Highland lairds.*[8]

*There is the Englishman who has made his fortune
in China and retired, and is bringing a new-made
wife out, by way of America, to see the East, where he
had lived so long—an angular English girl, containing
the potential British matron, who knits gray stockings
and keeps herself carefully aloof from acquaintances
that might be detrimental in the future.*

*The typical American girl is with us, traveling
alone—greyhound-waisted, tiny of foot, clad with tailormade neatness, and armed with an amateur photographer's outfit. She is on her way to visit the
American minister to Japan.*

*And a couple from Georgia, who have lived twenty
years in Los Angeles but have lost nothing of their genial old-fashioned Georgia ways and looks, and still
speak with a soft southern drawl.*

*We have a full cargo of missionaries—fifteen in
all—mostly young women, and, on this occasion, all
Presbyterians. There is much missionary travel back*

and forth on this line, for the work of proselytization in China and Japan goes briskly on. Among them is a young doctor, who has just taken her degree and is going to the East to save both souls and bodies. She wears "reform" clothes[9] and has a strong, well-cut face, from which the heavy hair is brushed smoothly back. She regards the ten years' exile into which she is entering as merely the apprenticeship of her professional career and is likely to consider the physical welfare of her patients of more importance than the acceptance of her creed. She is the plain, wholesome product of northwestern life and a northwestern female college—speaking the speech of that region with a broad and blurring R. . . . Her future is simple and pleasant to guess at.

One is less sure of the handsome, slim girl of twenty with deep-set gray eyes and the delicate pointed fingers of what the palmists call "the psychic hand," indicating undue spiritual intensity of nature. In a spasm of the romantic exaltation to which young women of her age are subject, she has condemned herself to a decade of lonely exile in a remote Japanese town; but a pair of enchanting dimples in her fresh young cheeks war with the maiden severity of her earnest eyes, and she is not indifferent to a young girl's natural joys, though she mentions them loftily as things in the remote past appealing to her—now forever put away. It would be pretty and amusing, as a girl's exalté fancies are sometimes, were not the sacrifice of her best young years to

79

indifferent heathen not so real and so melancholy to think on.

. . . The sea is becoming very blue. The emerald fades as we pass into these vast liquid fields, and the blue deepens and deepens until one finds no words to express, no simile to convey, the intensity of its burning azure. Sapphires would be pale and cold beside this sea—palpitating with wave shadows deep as violets, yet not purple, and with no touch of any color to mar its perfect hue. It flames with unspeakable, many-faceted splendor, under a sky that is wan by contrast with its profundity of tint, and the very foam that curls away from our wake is blue as the blue shadows in snow. The cutter-like prow of our ship flings up two delicate plumes of pearl, and the sunlight shining through these has wrought upon the blue floor beneath us a rainbow arch that encircles our onward path, moves with our moving, and shimmers upon the waving flood as the iris shimmers upon a peacock's breast. . . .

It is here enormously deep. The longest plummet line ever let into the sea went down here, and only found bottom at the depth of four thousand fathoms.

The voyage is a lonely one. In all these many thousand miles, we never see a sail or any shore. There is no sea life about us, save of the sword-winged birds that follow us from San Francisco to Japan without sign of fatigue, wheeling easily after us as we plunge onward at the rate of 350 miles a day, and having quite the appearance of loafing along and waiting for us to catch

Bisland on the Pacific steamer, an illustration from her article in
Cosmopolitan

up. It fills one with a sort of despair to get up every morning and see the same sea, the same horizon, the same birds—nothing to mark our progress except the figures marked each day at noon on the map hanging over the companionway.

Our small, circumscribed world daily grows in importance in our estimation. We know intimately the characters, tastes, and histories of our companions. We take each other's photographs and exchange warm professions of friendship; we advise each other about the future and confide the incidents of the past. We play draughts and quoits [ring toss] and cards; we get together in corners and criticize the missionaries and are criticized by them—and all the while go steadily westward and westward, driven by wind and steam.

This lonely vessel swarms with life. Down in the steerage are over four hundred yellow people. . . . All sorts and conditions of Chinamen going home with their earnings. Many are merchants who have a merchant's pass, which enables them to return to America when their business across the water is finished. One old gentleman with an iron-gray pigtail is a "Forty-niner." He came to California during the gold fever and is now going home to die in China, having thriftily calculated that it costs less to cross the waters alive than it does in a coffin. He was rich in those early days, but, as he explains in fluent and profane American, fan-tan [Chinese betting game], poker, euchre, and horse races have reduced his store to an immodest com-

petence. However, as he nears the Chinese shore, he feels he can afford to wear a magnificent and lurid pair of brocaded trousers, of the sort popular in China when he left, and still—after forty years—of the very latest fashion.

Down in these Chinese quarters, placed where he can catch the best of the healing salt breezes, is a young fellow of six-and-twenty, who lies motionless all day, with crossed hands and half-closed eyes. These hands and the sunken face are the color of old wax, as impassive as if indeed they were cut from some such substance.

It is common among the emigrants to America to fall sick with a consumption and to struggle back in this way to die at home. He seems afraid to breathe or move, lest he should waste the failing oil or snuff out the dying flame ere he reaches his yearned-for home— the Flowery Kingdom—the Celestial Empire![10]

On the afterdeck, fan-tan rages all day long; also an intricate game of chess, or dominoes, when a less dangerous amusement is desired. Forward, there is a space for women, where five or six retroussé-eyed females find a temporary home. They are gentle, mild-faced little creatures, who are quick to give smile for smile and answer English amiabilities with what appears to be equally amiable Chinese. All the sailors are Chinamen and are popular with the commanders. They are obedient, not given to strikes at inconvenient moments, and are under the control of a boatswain, one of their countrymen with a keen, shrewd face and an air of unques-

tioned authority. He hires them and pays them their wages, and the owners reckon with him alone. He is a person of consequence and wealth, and owns much real estate in San Francisco, sufficient proof that the Chinese, as the white Jack-tar (sailor), is the victim of fraud and oppression.

These ships, like those of the merchant Antonio, voyage to the East for cargoes of tea, silk, and spices. There are three lines between China and America; two, the Pacific Mail and the Oriental and Occidental— controlled by the Central Pacific Railway magnates, Huntington, Crocker, and Stanford—have their termini in the United States, and the Canadian Mail sails from Vancouver. They carry out to China returning subjects of the yellow emperor, passengers for the East, flour, Connecticut clocks, hats, shoes, and such select assortments of Yankee notions as are required by the Barbarian.

Returning, they fetch hundreds of bales of raw silk, worth $700 apiece, which must be rushed across the continent immediately upon arrival, and have left the ship and are on their way across the country to the eastern mills before the passengers have landed. The usual cargo is from 1,200 to 1,300 bales, and in June, the tea trade begins, 1,700 to 2,700 tons in every ship— the whole of the Formosa crop, some 6,000,000 tons, comes to us. The English will not drink the light, perfumed Oolong. They demand something coarser and stronger. Spices, pepper, and tapioca come from Singa-

pore, and gambier [an astringent extract] in great quantities for coloring American beer, with thousands of bales of gunnysacks from Calcutta for American wheat, and, from Manila, hemp and jute.

At last there comes a day when one rises in the morning and the sailors, pointing to the horizon, say, "That is Japan," and one cries with cheerful excitement, "Yes! Yes!" though there is nothing but the same monotonous sea and sky visible to the unpracticed eye.

The missionaries all land here and are full of emotion at arriving at the scene of their labors to save immortal souls. The Chinese steerage clatter more noisily than ever, pleased to behold this outlying portal of their home. The Japanese poet Kachi, returning from travels in America, where he has been arranging for translations of his works into English, lifts his head again. He is a grave, mysterious-eyed person, who has not spoken to anyone during the voyage and has usually had his face—his dark, smooth, mask-like face—hidden behind a French novel.

This face is lit now with a fine patriotic glow as a delicate gray cloud grows up along the edge of the water and slowly a vast cone-like cumulus, a lofty rosy cloud, takes shape and form, gathers clearness of outline, deepens its hue of pink and pearl, melts softly into the gray beneath, soars sharply into the blue above, and reveals—Fujiyama . . . the divine mountain!

Having seen it, one no longer marvels that it dominates the Japanese imagination; that every fan, screen,

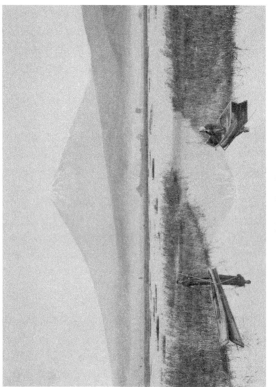

Mount Fuji, Japan

and jar, every piece of lacquer and porcelain, bears somewhere its majestic, its exquisite outline. Twelve thousand three hundred and sixty-five feet high, it rises up alone and unmarred by surrounding peaks; alone in fair calm beauty—the highest mountain in all the islands. In the old Ainu tongue[11]—the Ainus whom the warlike Japanese conquered and drove northward—"Fuji" signified "Mother of Fire," and the Japanese added the word "yama," their general term for all mountains. For more than two hundred years the Mother of Fire has been clad in snows and has made no sign. Traces of terrible ancient rages lie along her ravaged sides, but her passions are all stilled; peace and purity crown her; and he who hath seen Fujiyama's fair head lifted out of the blue sea and flushed with the dream of the coming day layeth his hand upon his mouth and is silent, but the memory of it passeth not away while he lives.

Notes

1. Robert Sanderson McCormick (1849–1919), American diplomat. Born in Virginia but at an early age moved to Chicago, where his relatives established the McCormick Reaper Company, later International Harvester. He married Katherine van Etta Medill, daughter of Joseph Medill, journalist and owner of the *Chicago Tribune*. His elder son, Joseph Medill McCormick was a U.S. senator; his younger son, Col. Robert R. McCormick, was publisher of the *Tribune*. (See Lakeside Classic 2014.)

2. Mme. Verne: Honorine Anne Hebe du Fraysse de Viane Morel (1829–1910), a widow who married Verne in 1857.

3. Robert Harborough Sherard (nee Kennedy) (1861–1943), English journalist and author.

4. One of Fogg's most dramatic adventures was saving an Indian widow from forced suttee (burning on a funeral pyre).

5. The Occidental and Oriental Line (O&O) was a United States steamship line (1874–1908) founded by the Central Pacific Railroad and the Union Pacific Railroad. It chartered ships from the White Star Line and operated between San Francisco and Asian ports.

6. Pierre Loti: pseudonym of Louis-Marie-Julien Viaud (1850–1923), French novelist.

7. In 1882, the U.S. Congress passed the Chinese Exclusion Act, which barred Chinese immigrants from entering the country for the next ten years; it was the first federal law ever to ban a group of immigrants on the basis of their race or nationality.

8. William Black (1841–98), Scottish novelist popular in the mid-nineteenth century.

9. The women's dress reform movement of the late nineteenth century advocated making women's clothing less cumbersome and more comfortable, practical, and healthful. It included fashions such as bloomers, trousers, and softly draped fabrics.

10. Flowery Kingdom and Celestial Empire: poetic terms for China derived from translations of native names. Its people were also called Celestials.

11. Ainu tongue: the language of the Ainus, aboriginal people of northern Japan.

STAGE THREE

Bly: The Middle East

I HAD NOT BEEN ASLEEP LONG, it seemed to me, until I waked to find myself standing upright beside my berth. It required but a second, a glance at my drenched self, and the sounds of vigorous scrubbing on the deck above to explain the cause of my being out of bed before I knew it. I had gone to sleep with the porthole open, and as my berth was just beneath it, I received the full force of the scrub water as it came pouring over the sides. I managed to let the heavy window down and went back to bed, wet, but confident that I would not again be caught napping under such circumstances.

I had not been asleep many moments until I heard a voice call: "Miss, will you have your tea now?" I opened my eyes and saw a steward standing at the door awaiting a reply. I refused the tea, as did the English girl on the other side of my cabin, managing to answer her bright smile with a very tired one, and then I was off to sleep again.

"Miss, will you have your bath now?" a voice broke in on my slumbers shortly afterwards. I looked up in disgust at a little white-capped woman who was bending over me, tempted to say I had just had my bath, a shower-bath, but thought better of it before speaking. I know I said something about "in a few minutes," and then I was asleep again.

"Well, you are a lazy girl! You'll miss your bath and breakfast if you don't get up the instant" was my third greeting.

The steward was the next one to put in an appearance. "Miss, this ship is inspected every day, and I must have this cabin made up before they come," he said complainingly. "The captain will be here presently."

There was nothing to do but to get up, which I did. After dressing, I wandered up on the next deck and was told breakfast was over long ago. I went out on deck, and the very first glimpse of the lazy-looking passengers in their summer garments, lounging about in comfortable positions or slowly promenading the deck, which was sheltered from the heat of the sun by a long stretch of awnings; and the smooth, velvety-looking water, the bluest I had ever seen, softly gurgling against the side of the ship as it almost imperceptibly steamed on its course; and the balmy air, soft as a rose leaf and just as sweet, air such as one dreams about but seldom finds; standing there alone among strange people, on strange waters, I thought, How sweet life is!

Before an hour had passed, I was acquainted with several persons. I had thought and expected that the English passengers would hold themselves aloof from a girl who was traveling alone, but my cabin companion saw me before I got away from the door and came forward to ask me to join herself and friends.

Shortly before noon, I became acquainted with an Englishman who belongs to the Civil Service in Calcutta. He had been in India for the last twenty years, during which time he had repeatedly visited England, which made this trip an old story to him. He had made the same trip from Calais on the India express as I had and said he noticed me on the train. Learning that I was traveling alone, he devoted most of his time looking out for my comfort and pleasure.

The bugle blew for luncheon, which is always called by the Indian title "tiffin" on ships traveling in Eastern seas. The Englishman asked if I would go with him to tiffin, and as I had gone without breakfast, I was only too anxious to go at the first opportunity. The dining hall is on the second deck. It is a small room nicely decorated with tropical foliage plants and looks quite cozy and pretty, but it was never intended to accommodate a ship carrying more than seventy-five first-class passengers.

The head waiter, who stood at the door, stared at us blankly as we went in. I hesitated, naturally thinking that he would show us to some table, but as he did not, I suggested to the gentleman with me that he ask before we take our places. "Sit anywhere" was the polite reply we received, so we sat down at the table nearest.

We had just been served, when four women ranging from twenty-four to thirty-five came in, and with indignant snorts of surprise, seated themselves at the same table. They were followed by a short, fat woman with a sweeping walk and air of satisfied assurance, who eyed us in a supercilious way and then turned to the others with an air of injured dignity that was intensely amusing. They were followed by two men, and as there were only places for seven at the table, the elderly man went out. Then we were made to suffer. All kinds of rude remarks were made about us. "They did hate people coming to their table"; "Too bad papa was robbed of his place"; "Shame people had to be crowded from their own table"; and similar pleasant speeches were hurled at us. The young woman who sat at my left was not content to confine her rudeness to her tongue, but repeatedly reached across my plate, brushing my food with her sleeves without one word of apology. I confess I never had a more disagreeable meal.

When dinner came, we found that we were debarred from the dining room. Passengers who got on at London were given the preference, and as there was not accommodations for all, the passengers who boarded the ship at Brindisi had to wait for second dinner.

One never realizes, until they face such contingencies, what an important part dinner plays in one's life. It was nine o'clock when the dining room was cleared that night and the Brindisi passengers were allowed to take their places at the table. I hardly believe they took much else. Everything was brought to us as it was left from the first dinner—cold soup, the remnants of fish, cut up bits of beef and fowl—all down the miserable course until at last came cold coffee! I had thought the food on the India express might have been better until after my experience on the P&O steamer *Victoria*, and then I decided it might have been worse.

Travelers who care to be treated with courtesy, and furnished with palatable food, will never by any chance travel on the *Victoria*. It is all rule and no practice on that ship. The impudence and rudeness of the servants in America is a standing joke, but if the servants on the *Victoria* are a sample of English servants, I am thankful to keep those we have, such as they are.

The commander of the ship set an example for rudeness. Although I had brought a letter to the captain, he never noticed me in any way. The captain had a tongue for gossip, too. Every time I heard a slighting story about any of the passengers and would ask where it came from, the answer would always be the captain had told it to somebody.

Notwithstanding all annoying trifles, it was a very happy life we spent in those pleasant waters. The decks were filled all the day, and when the lights were put out at night, the passengers reluctantly went to their cabins. The passengers formed two striking contrasts. There were some of the most refined and lovely people on board, and there were some of the most ill-bred and uncouth. Most of the women whose acquaintance I formed were very desirous of knowing all about American women, and frequently expressed their admiration for the free American woman, many going so far as to envy me, while admiring my unfettered happiness. Two clever Scotch women I met were traveling around the world but are taking two years at it. One Irishwoman, with a laugh that rivaled her face in sweetness, was traveling alone to Australia. My cabin-mate was bound for New Zealand, but she was accompanied by her brother, a pleasant young Englishman, who insisted on relinquishing his place at first dinner in my favor and who stayed away despite my protests and my determination not to deprive him of a warm dinner.

In the daytime the men played cricket and quoits. Sometimes, in the evenings, we had singing, and other times we went to the second-class deck and listened to better music given by second-class passengers. When there were no chairs, we would all sit down on the deck, and I remember nothing that was more enjoyable than these little visits.

Better than all to me, it was to sit in a dark corner on deck, above where the sailors had their food, and listen to the sounds of a tom-tom and a weird musical chanting that always accompanied their evening meal. The sailors were lascars [East Indian sailors]. They were not interesting to look at, and doubtless, if I could have seen as well as heard them at their evening meal, it would have lost its charm for me. They were the most untidy looking lot of sailors I ever saw. Over a pair of white muslin drawers they wore a long muslin slip very like in shape to the old-time nightshirt. This was tied about the waist with a colored handkerchief, and on their heads they wore gaily colored turbans, which are really nothing but a crown of straw with a scarf-shaped piece of bright cloth, often six feet in length, wound about the head. Their brown feet are always bare. They chant, as all sailors do, when hoisting sails, but otherwise are a grim, surly-looking set, climbing about over the ship like a pack of monkeys.

I had not been on the *Victoria* many days until someone who had become friendly with me told me it was rumored on board that I was an eccentric American heiress, traveling about with a hairbrush and a bankbook. I judged that some of the attention I was receiving was due to the story of my wealth. I found it convenient, later on, to correct the report when a young man came to me to say that I was the kind of a girl he liked, and as he was the second son and his brother would get both the money and the title, his sole ambition was to find a wife who would settle £1,000 a year on him.

There was another young man on board who was

A native crewman, or lascar

quite as unique a character and much more interesting to me. He told me that he had been traveling constantly since he was nine years old and that he had always killed the desire to love and marry because he never expected to find a woman who could travel without a number of trunks and bundles innumerable. I noticed that he dressed very exquisitely and changed his apparel at least three times a day, so my curiosity made me bold enough to ask how many trunks he carried with him.

"Nineteen" was the amazing reply. I no longer wondered at his fears of getting a wife who could not travel without trunks.

*   *   *

IT WAS IN THE AFTERNOON WHEN the *Victoria* anchored at Port Said. We were all on deck eagerly watching for the first sight of land, and though that sight showed us a wide, sandy beach and some uninteresting two-storied white houses with arcade fronts, still it did not lessen our desire to go ashore. I suppose that would have been the result under the circumstances had Port Said been the most desolate place on earth. I know everybody was experiencing a slight weariness, though we should all have stoutly denied such a reflection on our constant companions, and gladly welcomed the change of a few hours on shore, where at least we might see new faces. A more urgent reason still for our going to land was the fact that this was a coaling port for the *Victoria*, and I never knew of anything that would make one more quickly feel that there are things in life much worse than death, if I may use the expression, than to have to stay on board a ship during the coaling operation.

Before the boat anchored, the men armed themselves with canes, to keep off the beggars they said, and the women carried parasols for the same purpose. I had neither stick nor umbrella with me and refused all offers to accept one for this occasion, having an idea, probably a wrong one, that a stick beats more ugliness into a person than it ever beats out.

Hardly had the anchor dropped than the ship was surrounded with a fleet of small boats, steered by half-clad Arabs, fighting, grabbing, pulling, yelling in their mad haste to be first. I never in my life saw such an exhibition of hungry greed for the few pence they expected to earn by taking the passengers ashore. Some boatmen actually pulled others out of their boats into the water in their frantic endeavors to steal each other's places.

Our party were about the first to go down the ladder to the boats. It had been our desire and intention to go ashore together, but when we stepped into the first boat, some were caught by rival boatmen and literally dragged across to other boats.

Having our party divided, there was nothing to do under the circumstances but to land and reunite on shore, so we ordered the Arabs to pull away. Midway between the *Victoria* and the shore, the boatmen stopped and demanded their money in very plain and forcible English. We were completely at their mercy, as they would not land us either way until we paid what they asked. One of the Arabs told me that they had many years' experience in dealing with the English and their sticks and had learned by bitter lessons that if they landed an Englishman before he paid, they would receive a stinging blow for their labor.

Walking up the beach, sinking ankle deep in the sand at every step, we came to the main street. Almost instantly we were surrounded by Arab boys who besought us to take a ride on the burros that stood patiently beside them. There were burros of all colors, sizes, and shapes, and the boys would cry out, most beseechingly, "Here's Gladstone![1] Take a ride; see Gladstone with two beautiful black eyes."

If one happened to be of a different political belief and objected to riding the Gladstone hobby, as it were, a choice could be made of almost any well-known, if not popular name. There were Mrs. Maybricks, Mary Andersons, Lillie Langtrys,[2] and all the prominent men of the time.

I knew all about burros, having lived for some time in Mexico,[3] but they proved to be quite a novelty to many of the passengers, almost all of whom were anxious to take a ride before returning to the boat. So, as many as could find animals to ride, mounted and went flying through that quaint, sleeping town, yelling with laughter, bouncing like rubber balls on their saddles, while half-naked Arab boys goaded the burros on by short, urgent hisses and by prodding them from behind with a sharp stick.

After seeing about fifty of our passengers started off in this happy manner, a smaller number of us went to a gambling house, and in a short time were deep in the sport of placing our English gold on colors and numbers and waiting anxiously for the wheel to go 'round to see the money at last swept in by the man at the table. I do not think that any one of us knew anything about the game, but we recklessly put our money on the table and laughed to see it taken in by the man who gave the turn to the wheel.

There was another attraction in this place which helped to win a number of young men from that very expensive table. It was an orchestra composed of young women, some of whom were quite pleasing both in looks and manners.

The longer we remained at this gambling house, the less money we had to spend in the shops. I went ashore with the determination not to buy anything, as I was very anxious not to increase my baggage. I withstood the tempting laces which were offered at wonderfully low prices, the quaint Egyptian curios, and managed to content myself by buying a sun hat, as everybody else did, and a pugaree [scarf] to wind about it, as is customary in the East.

Having bought a hat and seen all I cared to of the shops, I went strolling about with some friends, feasting my eyes on what were to me peculiarities of a peculiar people. I saw old houses with carved-wood fronts that would have been worth a fortune in America occupied by tenants that were unmistakably poor. The natives were apparently so accustomed to strangers that we attracted very little, if any, attention, except from those who hoped to gain something from our visit. Unmolested, we went about, finding no occasion to use sticks on the natives. We saw a great number of beggars who, true to their trade, whined forth, with outstretched hands, their plaintive appeals.

While standing looking after a train of camels that had just come in loaded with firewood, I saw some Egyptian women. They were small in stature and shapelessly clad in black. Over their faces, beginning just below the eyes, they wore black veils that fell almost to their knees. As if fearing that the veil alone would not destroy all semblance of features, they wear a thing that spans the face between the hair and the veil down the line of their noses. In some cases this appears to be of gold, and in others it is composed of some black material. One Egyp-

A street scene in Port Said showing an elaborately carved shop front

tian woman carried a little naked baby with her. She held it on her hips, its little black legs clinging to her waist much after the fashion of a boy climbing a pole.

Down at the beach we came upon a group of naked men clustered about an alligator that they had caught. It was securely fastened in some knotted rope, the end of which was held by some half dozen black fellows. The public water carriers, with well-filled goatskins flung across their backs, we met making their way to the town for the last trip that day.

Darkness came on us very suddenly and sent us rushing off for our ship. This time we found the boatman would not permit us even to enter their boats until we paid them to take us across to the *Victoria*. Their price now was just double what they had charged to bring us to land. We protested, but they said it was the law to double the price after sunset.

They were just finishing the coaling when we reached the ship, but the sight we caught of the coal barges, lighted by some sputtering, dripping stuff, held in iron cages on the end of long poles that showed the hurrying naked people rushing with sacks of coal up a steep gangplank between the barges and the ship, was one long to be remembered. Nor were they working quietly. Judging from the noise, every one of them was yelling something that pleased his own fancy and humor.

The next morning I got up earlier than usual so anxious was I to see the famous Suez Canal. Rushing up on deck, I saw we were passing through what looked like an enormous ditch, enclosed on either side with high sandbanks. We seemed to be hardly moving, which made us feel the heat very intensely. They tell me that, according to law, a ship must not travel through the canal at a speed exceeding five knots an hour, because a rapid passage of the ship would make a strong current that would wash in the sandbanks. The trip through the canal can be made in from twenty to twenty-four hours.

About noon of our first day in the canal, we anchored in the bay fronting Ismailia. Here passengers were taken on, which gave us time to see the khedive's [viceroy or ruler] palace, which is built a little way back from the beach in the heart of a beautiful green forest. Continuing the journey through the canal we saw little of interest. The signal stations were the only green spots that met the eye, but they were proof of what could be done, even in this sandy desert, by the expenditure of time and energy.

We passed several ships in the canal. Generally the passengers would call to the passengers on the other ships, but the conversation was confined mainly to inquiries as to what kind of a voyage had been theirs.

In the night the boat hung an electric light from

the front, and by the aid of this light, moving it from side to side, were able to continue on their way. Before the introduction of electric headlights for this purpose, the vessels were always compelled to tie up in the canal overnight because of the great danger of running into the sandbanks.

We saw, when near the end of the canal, several Arab encampments. They were both picturesque and interesting. First we would notice a small dull-red fire, and between that fire and us we could see the outlines of people and resting camels. At one encampment we heard music, but at the others we saw the people either working over the fire, as if preparing their evening meal, or in sitting positions crouching about it in company with their camels.

Shortly after this, we dropped anchor in the Bay of Suez. Hardly had we done so, when the ship was surrounded by a number of small sailboats that, in the semi-darkness, with their white sails before the breeze, reminded me of moths flocking to a light, both from their white, winged-like appearance and the rapid way in which numbers of them floated down on us. These sailboats were filled with men with native fruits, photographs, and odd shells to sell.

Where we anchored at Suez, some claim is the historic place where the Israelites crossed the Red Sea. Some people who bother themselves greatly about facts, figures, and ancient history, bought views, which showed that at certain stages of the tide, people, in even this day, can wade around there without any risk of life or comfort. The next morning when we arose, we were out of sight of land and well out on the Red Sea.

The *Victoria* is said to be the finest boat on the P&O Line; still it could not be more unsuited for the trip. It is very badly planned, being built so that a great number of cabins inside are absolutely cut off from light and air. It is a compliment to call them cabins, as they are really nothing more than small, dark, disagreeable, and unventilated boxes. The prices to ports that are touched at by rival steamship lines are rather reasonable, while to ports where they have the monopoly, they charge exorbitant rates. I have stated that the conduct of the officers and servants and the quality of the food left much to be desired by travelers.

The nights were so warm while on the Red Sea that the men left their cabins and spent their nights on deck. It is usually customary for the women to sleep on deck, one side of which, at such times, is reserved exclusively for them. During this trip, none of the women had the courage to set the example, so the men had the decks to themselves.

Sleeping down below was all the more reason why women arising early would go on the decks before the sun began to boil, in search of a refreshing spot where they could get a breath of cool air. At this hour the men were usually to be seen promenading about in their pajamas, but I heard no objections raised until, much to the dismay of the women, the captain announced that the decks belonged to the men until after eight o'clock in the morning and that the women were expected to remain below until after that hour.

Just before we came to Aden, we passed in the sea a number of high brown mountains. They are known as the Twelve Apostles. Shortly after this, we came in sight of Aden. It looked to us like a large, bare mountain of wonderful height, but even by the aid of glasses, we were unable to tell that it was inhabited. Shortly after eleven o'clock in the morning, we anchored in the bay. Our boat was soon surrounded by a number of small boats, which brought to us men who had things to sell and the wonderful divers of the East.

The passengers had been warned by the officers on board not to go ashore at Aden because of the intense heat. So the women spent their time bargaining with the Jews who came to the ship to sell ostrich feathers and feather boas. The men helped them to close with the sellers always to the sellers' advantage, much as they might congratulate themselves to the contrary.

I, in company with a few of the more reckless ones, decided to brave the heat and go ashore and see what Aden had to offer.

* * *

HIRING A LARGE BOAT, I went ashore with a half dozen acquaintances who felt they could risk the sun. The four oarsmen were black fellows, thin of limb but possessed of much strength and tireless good humor. They have, as have all the inhabitants of Aden, the finest white teeth of any mortals. This may be due to the care they take of them and the manner of that care. From some place, I am unable to state where, as I failed to see one living thing growing at Aden, they get tree branches of a soft, fibrous wood which they cut into pieces three and four inches in length. With one end of this stick, scraped free of the bark, they rub and polish their teeth until they are perfect in their whiteness. The wood wears into a soft pulp, but as one can buy a dozen sticks for a penny, one can well afford to throw the stick away after once using; although, if necessary, a stick can be used many times. I bought several sticks and found them the most efficient as well as pleasant toothbrush I had ever tried. I felt a regret that some enterprising firm had not thought of importing this useful bit of timber to replace the tooth-destroying brush used in America.

The man in charge of the boat that carried us to land was a small black fellow with the thinnest legs I ever saw. Around his neck and over his bare breast were twined strings of beads, black and gold and silver. Around his waist was a highly colored sash, and on his arms and ankles were heavy bracelets, while his fingers and toes seemed to be trying to outdo one another in the way of rings. He spoke English quite well, and to my rather impertinent question as to what number constituted his family, told me that he had three wives and eleven children, which number, he added piously, by the grace of the power of his faith, he hoped to increase.

His hair was yellow, which, added to his very light dress of jewelry and sash, gave him rather a strange look: the bright yellow hair and the black skin forming a contrast which was more startling than the black eyes and yellow hair that flashed upon the astonished vision of the American public some years ago but has become since an old and tiresome sight.[4] Some of the boatmen had their black wool pasted down and hidden under a coating of lime. I was very curious about it until the first man explained that they were merely bleaching their hair; that it was always done by covering the head with lime, which, being allowed to remain on for several days, exposed to the hot sun and the water, bleached the hair yellow or red at the expiration of that time. This bleaching craze, he also informed me, was confined to the men of Aden. So far, none of the women had tried to enhance their black beauty in that way, but it was considered very smart among the men.

We landed at a well-built pier and walked up the finely cut white-stone steps from the boat to the land. Instantly we were surrounded by half-clad black people, all of whom, after the manner of hack drivers at railway stations, were clamoring for our favor. They were not all drivers, however. Mingling with the drivers were merchants with jewelry, ostrich plumes, and boas to sell, runners for hotels, beggars, cripples, and guides. This conglomeration besought us to listen to every individual one of them until a native policeman, in the queen's uniform, came forward and pushed the black fellows back with his hands, sometimes hastening their retreat with his boot.

A large board occupied a prominent position on the pier. On it was marked the prices that should be paid drivers, boatmen, and like people. It was, indeed, a praiseworthy thoughtfulness that caused the erection of that board, for it prevented tourists being robbed. I looked at it and thought that even in that land there was more precaution taken to protect helpless and ignorant strangers than in New York City, where the usual custom of night hack men is to demand exorbitant prices, and if they are not forthcoming, to pull off their coats and fight for it.

Perched on the side of this bleak, bare mountain is a majestic white building, reached by a fine road cut in the stone that forms the mountain. It is a clubhouse, erected for the benefit of the English soldiers who are stationed on this barren spot. In the harbor lay an English man-of-war, and near a point where the land was most level, numbers of white tents were pitched for soldiers.

From the highest peak of the black, rocky mountain, probably 1,700 feet above sea level, floated the English flag. As I traveled on and realized more than ever before how the English have stolen almost all, if not all, desirable seaports, I felt an increased respect for the level-headedness of the English government, and I cease to marvel at the pride with which Englishmen view their flag floating in so many different climes and over so many different nationalities.

Near the pier were shops run by Parsees.[5] A hotel, post office, and telegraph office are located in the same place. The town of Aden is five miles distant. We hired a carriage and started at a good pace, on a wide, smooth road that took us along the beach for a way.

The roads at Aden are a marvel of beauty. They are wide and as smooth as hardwood, and as they twist and wind in pleasing curves up the mountain, they are made secure by a high, smooth wall against mishap. Otherwise their steepness might result in giving tourists a serious roll down a rough mountainside.

On the road we saw black people of many different tribes. A number of women I noticed, who walked proudly along, their brown, bare feet stepping lightly on the smooth road. They had long purple-black hair, which was always adorned with a long, stiff feather, dyed of brilliant red, green, purple, and like striking shades. They wore no other ornament than the colored feather, which lent them an air of pride when seen beside the much bejeweled people of that quaint town. Many of the women, who seemed very poor indeed, were lavishly dressed in jewelry. They did not wear much else, it is true, but in a place as hot as Aden, jewelry must be as much as anyone would care to wear.

To me the sight of these perfect, bronze-like women, with a graceful drapery of thin silk wound about the waist, falling to the knees, and a corner taken up the back and brought across the bust, was most bewitching. On their bare, perfectly modeled arms were heavy bracelets, around the wrist and muscle, most times joined by chains. Bracelets were also worn about the ankles, and their fingers and toes were laden with rings. Sometimes large rings were suspended from the nose, and the ears were almost always outlined with hoop rings that reached from the inmost edge of the lobe to the top of the ear joining the head. So closely were these rings placed that, at a distance, the ear had the appearance of being rimmed in gold. A more pleasing style of nose ornament was a large gold ornament set in the nostril and fastened there as screw rings fasten in the ear. Still, if that nose ornamentation was more pleasing than the other, the ear adornment that accompanied it was disgusting. The lobe of the ear was split from the ear, and pulled down to such length that it usually rested on the shoulder. The enormous loop of flesh was partially filled with large gold knobs.

At the top of the hill we came to a beautiful, majestic stone double gate, the entrance to the English fort and also spanning the road that leads to the town. Sentinels were pacing to and fro, but we drove past them without stopping or being stopped, through a strange, narrow cut in the mountain that towered at the sides a hundred feet above the road-bed. Both these narrow, perpendicular sides are strongly fortified. It needs but one glance at Aden, which is in itself a natural fort, to strengthen the assertion that Aden is the strongest gate to India.

The moment we emerged from the cut, which, besides being so narrow that two carriages pass with great difficulty, is made on a dangerous steep grade, we got a view of the white town of Aden, nestling in the very heart of what seems to be an extinct volcano. We were driven rapidly down the road, catching glimpses of gaudily attired mounted po-

A street scene in Aden

licemen, water carriers from the bay, with their well-filled goatskins flung across their backs, camels loaded with cut stone, and black people of every description.

When we drove into the town, which is composed of low adobe houses, our carriage was surrounded with beggars. We got out and walked through an unpaved street, looking at the dirty, uninviting shops and the dirty, uninviting people in and about them. Very often we were urged to buy, but more frequently the natives stared at us with quiet curiosity. In the heart of the town we found the camel market, but beyond a number of camels standing, lying, and kneeling about, the sight was nothing extraordinary. Nearby was a goat market, but business seemed dull in both places.

Without buying anything, we started to return to the ship. Little naked children ran after us for miles, touching their foreheads humbly and crying for money. They all knew enough English to be able to ask us for charity.

When we reached the pier, we found our driver had forgotten all the English he knew when we started out. He wanted one price for the carriage, and we wanted to pay another. It resulted in our appealing to a native policeman, who took the right change from us, handed it to the driver, and gave him, in addition, a lusty kick for his dishonesty.

Our limited time prevented our going to see the

water tanks, which are some miles distant from Aden. When we returned to the ship, we found Jews there, selling ostrich eggs and plumes, shells, fruit, spears of swordfish, and such things. In the water, on one side of the boat, were numbers of men, Somali boys, they called them, who were giving an exhibition of wonderful diving and swimming.

They would actually sit in the water looking like bronze statues, as the sun rested on their wet, black skins. They sat in a row, and turning their faces up towards the deck, would yell methodically, one after the other, down the entire line: "Have a dive! Have a dive! Have a dive!"

The other half, meanwhile, would put their hands before their widely opened mouths, yelling through their rapidly moving fingers with such energy that we gladly threw over silver to see them dive and stop the din.

The moment the silver flashed over the water, all the bronze figures would disappear like flying fish, and looking down, we would see a few ripples on the surface of the blue water—nothing more. After a time that seemed dangerously long to us, they would bob up through the water again. We could see them coming before they finally appeared on the surface, and one among the number would have the silver between his teeth, which would be most liberally displayed in a broad smile of satisfaction. Some of these divers were children not more than eight years old, and they ranged from that up to any age. Many of them had their hair bleached. As they were completely naked, excepting a small cloth twisted about the loins, they found it necessary to make a purse out of their cheeks, which they did with as much ease as a cow stows away grass to chew at her leisure.

No animal water-born and -bred could frisk more gracefully in the water than do these Somali boys. They swim about, using the legs alone or the arms alone, on their backs or sides, and, in most cases, with their faces under water. They never get out of the way of a boat. They merely sink and come up in the same spot when the boat passes.

After a seven hours' stay at Aden, we left for Colombo, being followed a long ways out from land by the divers. One little boy went out with us on the ship, and when he left us, he merely took a plunge from the upper deck into the sea and went happily back towards Aden, on his side, waving a farewell to us with his free hand.

The passengers endeavored to make the time pass pleasantly between Aden and Colombo. The young women had some tableaux vivants[6] one evening, and they were really very fine. In one they wished to represent the different countries. They asked me to represent America, but I refused, and then they asked me to tell them what the American flag looked like! They wanted to represent one as nearly as possible and to raise it to drape the young woman who was to represent America. Another evening we had a lantern-slide exhibition that was very enjoyable.

The loyalty of the English to their queen on all occasions, and at all times, had won my admiration. Though born and bred a staunch American, with the belief that a man is what he makes of himself, not what he was born, still I could not help admiring the undying respect the English have for their royal family. During the lantern-slide exhibition, the queen's picture was thrown on the white sheet and evoked warmer applause than anything else that evening. We never had an evening's amusement that did not end by everybody rising to their feet and singing "God Save the Queen." I could not help but think how devoted that woman, for she is only a woman after all, should be to the interests of such faithful subjects.

With that thought came to me a shamed feeling that there I was, a freeborn American girl, the native of the grandest country on earth, forced to be silent because I could not in honesty speak proudly of the rulers of my land, unless I went back to those two kings of manhood, George Washington and Abraham Lincoln.

AND IT CAME TO PASS *that on the morning of the 8th day of December we rose up and perceived that we had come unto Fan-land . . . to the Islands of Porcelain . . . to Shikishima—the Country of Chrysanthemums. The place across whose sky the storks always fly by day, and the ravens by night—where cherry branches with pink-and-white blossoms grow out of nothing at all to decorate the foreground, and where ladies wear their eyes looped up in the corners, and gowns in which it is so impossible that any two-legged female should walk that they pass their lives smiling and motionless upon screens and jars. . . .*

Sailing so long due west, we had at last reached the East. The real East, not east of anywhere, but the East . . . the birthplace of Man, and of his Religions . . . of Poetry and Porcelains, of Tradition, and of Architecture. And I who had come to it from the country of common sense, of steam-ploughs and newspaper enterprise, bowed my head reverently in the portal of this great Temple of the World, and fell upon my knees, awed by its mysterious age and vastness. . . . My heart within me was stirred, and I was led to great recklessness in the use of capital letters.

There lies here, by the gates of the East, a land, as we discovered, stranger and more wonderful even than we had dreamed. Captain Kempson had steered us in sixteen days from the coast of America to where a mountain of pink pearl rose out of the sea; and when the gray clouds about its base resolved themselves into land, we found they were the green hills of fairyland. All who have ever set foot on these shores bear the same testimony to the elfin witchery of Nippon—the land of the rising sun. I spent, alas! less than two days in these fairy islands.

We double a headland, pass a slim white pharos [lighthouse], and we make our way up the long bay to Yokohama. The town has been in existence only since 1859, when Japan opened a few ports to foreign trade, but already it is a place of size and importance, for what the Japanese did, they did thoroughly. They jettied the harbor, built ample wharves and godowns [warehouses], and bade their own people confine themselves to the inner town across the canal and not encroach upon the Europeans.

The queerest craft come to meet us in the bay—light-winged junks [flatbottomed ships] with gray and russet sails, so carelessly and crazily built, that were the sea to but give them a playful slap, she would crush them in an instant to kindling wood. Their feebleness ensures her gentleness, it would seem, for they spread their great butterfly wings and skim along without fear, going far afield for the fishing. Many large ships lie at anchor in the harbor—American men-of-war, English, French, and German merchant vessels, and a few neat Japanese coasters.

A cloud of sampans descend upon us as we an-

chor—craft as crazy as the junks—made of three un-painted boards lightly fastened together, with a sharp prow and wide, high stern, across which the standing boatman lays a long oar and waggles it carelessly in the water, attaining thereby an astonishing speed. Like a certain famous epitaph, it is "simple but sufficient."[7]

. . . These boatmen are the vanguard of elves from Elfland—small, lithe creatures with good-looking yellow countenances, bearing no resemblance to the flat-faced Chinese, and with thick, shining black locks, through which is twisted a blue fillet. Their dress is of dark blue cotton, sometimes the gown shape called a kimono and worn by both sexes, but for the most part a costume much like that worn in England in the time of Henry II—cloth hose to the waist, a short jerkin, and loose sleeveless coat reaching to the hips. These blue coats have on the back a great white circle surrounding decorative Japanese characters which set forth the owner's occupation so that he who runs may read. The intention is business-like, but utilitarianism in Japan is inseparable from the picturesque, and these portable advertisements only add a new charm to the wearer's delightful queerness. There are boys of ten or twelve in some of the boats with the men—quaint little brats with varying patterns shaved on the tops of their heads, entering into the contest to secure part of the carrying trade with the stern and enthusiastic vigor known only to the small boy of all countries.

I attach myself for the time being to a party of agree-

able Americans. One of them, a pretty brown-eyed girl named Madge, finds everything as dear and astonishing a delight as do I. The Gentleman from Germany—always pleased in the pleasure of others—is indulgently sympathetic. We—Madge and I—secretly desire to be ferried over to the pier by one of these elfish ferrymen; but the others are so lofty that we meekly submit to allow a commonplace steam launch to set us on shore, making the journey with the missionaries, who have much exaltation and baggage.

More medieval folk in blue stand about on the stone pier and welcome us with friendly smiles, and we charter their jinrikishas to take us to the hotel. Now, the jinrikisha is exactly the vehicle in which one would expect to ride in this land of fairy children—large perambulators that hold one person comfortably; but instead of being trundled from behind by a white-capped nursemaid, one of the Henry II gentlemen, who wears also straw sandals and an enormous blue mushroom hat on his head, ensconces himself between the little shafts in front and prances noiselessly away with it. He has legs as light and muscular as a thoroughbred horse and can spin along with the 'rikisha at the rate of five miles an hour. He can, with few intervals for rest, keep this up all day; he will charge you seventy-five cents for the whole; he will not be winded at all; and will be in a gay and charming temper when the day is done. . . .

Our way lies along the Bund, a broad, handsome street on the waterfront, with a fringe of slim pine trees

A Japanese woman riding in a jinricksha

strange of outline as are those one is familiar with upon fans. Other jinrikishas are scampering about. Tonsured doll babies in flowered gowns, such as one buys at home in the Oriental shops, are walking about here alive and flying queer-shaped kites, with a sort of calm unconscious elfishness befitting dwellers in fairyland. Two little Japanese ladies with pink cheeks and black hair clasped with jade pins toddle by on wooden pattens [wooden-soled sandals or clogs] that clack pleasantly on the pavement. Their kimonos are of gay crape, and their sashes tied behind like bright-tinted wings. Every one—even the funny little gendarme who stands outside of his sentry box like a toy soldier—gives us back smile for smile.

The Grand Hotel is at the upper end of the Bund, and here another specimen of the Moyen-âge [Middle Ages] in his stocking feet shows us into beautiful rooms facing the water—rooms with steam heat and electric bells! . . . The darkness closes down swiftly, but charming things are still to be seen from our veranda. The air is crisp and keen; gay cries and clinking pattens tinkle in melodious confusion from the street below. The 'rikishas have swinging from their shafts now crimped pink and white paper lanterns, and flit by in the dark like fireflies.

After dinner we are lucky enough to fall into the hands of Lieutenant McDonald. He is a paymaster in the American Navy and has been here two years. He knows the place well and offers to be our guide tonight through the native town. In the flowery hotel court we find our 'rikishas standing in a row in the moonlight, each with one of the pretty lanterns swinging; and we too flit away behind our sandaled steeds. Only the whir of our wheels and our calls and laughter sound through the city's quiet, moon-washed ways. Here in the European town, the houses of two stories of stone stand flush with the narrow asphalt-paved street. A tiny footpath runs under the shadow of their tiled caves; but as these are paved with little cobblestones, and the roadway is smooth and clean as a table, no one by any chance ever walks in the footpaths.

We skim around corners with a shrill ki-yi! of warning; debouch into a great square upon which churches and public buildings face; cross a broad canal where acres of sampans are huddled for the night; and find on the other side Shichiu, the native town. Hanchodori lies before us, the wide main thoroughfare from which spring hundreds of narrow branches, all swarming with a frolicsome, chattering crowd tinkling about in pattens, their multitudinous tapping making a vibrant musical undertone to the sound of the many voices. . . .

The houses, delicate little matchboxes of thin, unpainted wood, fifteen or twenty feet high, and divided into two stories, crowd close together and give upon the street. The fronts of these houses—indeed, the greater part of the walls all around—are sashes of many tiny panes glazed with white, semitransparent paper,

*through which the inner light shines as from a lantern;
and the shop fronts are mere curtains of bamboo, rolled
up during business hours and let down when the shop
is closed for the night.*

*. . . Business is not nearly over yet. The Japanese are
as little inclined to early bed as the Chinese, it seems,
and the tide of trade runs strong. . . . From all the eaves
swing soft bubbles of tinted light—lanterns of many
shapes and sizes. The shops are lit and busy, and contain every need, from crabs to curios, that Japanese
flesh is heir to. Here and there cluster flocks of light,
portable booths, each also with a swaying lantern,
where steaming tea is sold in thimble-cups; where saki
may be drunk hot and hot, poured from long-necked
porcelain bottles; or trays of queer, toothsome-looking
sweetmeats are to be had for coins of infinitesimal
value. Along the street lie heaps of fresh vegetables—
making pretty bouquets of color, all clean and ready for
the pot—or fruits of many sorts massed with skill and
beauty . . . little red oranges in bamboo nets, set about
with their own green leaves; plums, pomelos, and fruits
whose names we do not know. Everything, everywhere,
is radiantly clean, dainty, and inviting.*

*We are on our way to the theater—one of the hum-
bler sort, where acrobats do their feats for a few cents,
where stage and auditorium are on a level, and both
merely platforms. A little gallery to one side is reserved
for the moon-eyed babies with whimsically shaved
heads; but they come down occasionally and rollick*

A Japanese food market

about as they wish, quite unreproved. They are never harsh with children in this fair country, and in return, the children display a courteous tolerance of the foibles of their elders that is extremely soothing. A group of tumblers on the stage are going through some supple contortions to the sound of a shrill little pipe and a blattering wooden drum, playing out of time with one another. The whole front of the theater, a curtain of matting, is rolled up at intervals and, when the feat in progress is at its most thrilling climax, is let fall. This artful proceeding stimulates the interest of the passers-by to such poignancy that they succumb in platoons to the pangs of curiosity, and so crowd the little platform that we depart hastily. . . .

More moon and lanterns, more laughter and flutter, more clacking of sandals, and then a Japanese Madame Tussauds, with pleasing little horrors in wax at the entrance as earnest of more of the same cheerful entertainment within. Farther up the street is a large and fashionable playhouse, where we may see the best talent of Nippon. At the box office are piles of flat sticks, six inches long and two wide, painted with numbers in the native character, which, inquiry reveals, are shoe checks for the many sandals hanging on rows of pegs by the door; for here, as in every other house in Japan, one enters in stocking feet. In consideration of our being benighted foreigners, we are allowed to retain our shoes. . . .

The interior is large and lofty. The common folk

Actors performing in a Japanese theater

occupy the level floor of the pit, marked into squares, where family parties sit on small wadded rugs and are quite at home, bringing their little charcoal braziers to warm their fingers, furnish lights for their tiny pipes, and keep the teapot steaming. The galleries on two sides are divided into matting-lined boxes, one of which they furnish with chairs, seeing that we display small skill in sitting on our heels. We enter during an entr'acte; and before the stage, which is not deep, but lofty, sways lightly in the draft a gay crape curtain. The men in the pit are smoking or curled up in their rugs snatching a nap, while the women drink tea and gossip, and the children romp all over the house. High up on either side of the stage comes from a latticed box the sound of the samisen [three-stringed guitar] and other stringed instruments that make a soft, plaintive, and pleasing music. The play has been going on for three weeks and is to end tonight. I should like to see how it all turns out; but the smile of the Gentleman from Germany is growing wan, so we go home.

A nipping and an eager air blows among the rose trees in the court next morning when Madge and I start out for early shopping. Lieutenant McDonald, magnificent in brown cords and laced Russia-leather riding boots, offers us his pony carriage, but we scoff at anything less foreign than a jinrikisha and set off together for Benton-dori, the fashionable shopping street of Shichiu. In spite of the fall in the thermometer, the spirits of the public in general appear in no way chilled.

The bare feet in straw sandals look red and uncomfortable, but the owners of them merely acquire great plumpness of appearance by adding three or four more cotton-wadded kimonos to their costume, tuck their chilly fingers away in their ample sleeves, and laugh at the passing discomfort. Everything looks ridiculously tiny by day, and deliciously absurd. One has a feeling that it is all a game that one is playing to amuse the children. We sit on the edge of the little platform that forms the floor of the shop, and, in the baby talk that is called pidgin English, bargain with the amiable shopkeeper seated on his own heels and within easy reach of all his goods. We have been instructed not to pay more than half that is asked, but the prices are so delightfully low that we give them joyfully and without haggling. We wander from shop to shop, received with an air of affectionate friendliness everywhere; we warm our fingers at many different braziers, and might drink little thimble-cups of tea at every hospitable place of business were we so minded. The really valuable bric-à-brac is costly here as elsewhere; but many charming things in common use among the people, pretty proofs of their universal love of beauty, are to be picked up for a mere trifle.

In the silk shops we find the very poetry of fabrics . . . crapes like milky opals, with the pale iris hues of rainbows; crapes with the faint purple and rose of clear sunset skies, embroidered with wheeling flights of white storks. Out of a sweet-smelling box comes a mass of shining stuff that the low-voiced fourteenth-century-looking shopkeeper calls by three musical syllables, which, translated, signify the Garments of the Dawn. Its threads shimmer like the crystals of dry snow, and amid its folds, the whiteness blushes to rose, deepens to gold, or pales to blue, while through it here and there runs a sort of impalpable cloudiness like a morning mist. He shows us moon-cloths, duskily azure with silver gleams . . . crapes, pearl-white and rich with needlework in patterns of delicate bamboo fronds or loose-petaled chrysanthemum blossoms . . . fairy garments all, woven of rainbows and moonbeams!

. . . We are in the train going to Tokyo. It is a funny train, as absurdly toy-like and doll-housey as is everything else in this country; and our destinies are committed today into the hands of a sweet-mannered gentleman in a gray kimono and an American hat, who is to guide us amid the beauties of his country's capital. . . . Delicious little pictures run past our car windows, astonishing us with the sudden revelation of what nonsense the Occident has talked about the conventionality of Japanese art, when, in truth, it is the most exquisite fidelity to the nature the artist has seen about him. The world the Japanese artist has painted has been the world just as it exists in his own country, and, moreover, he has in his art caught and expressed with perfect and subtle veracity its atmosphere of gay grotesquerie—of delicate fantasticality—its crisp and fragile fairy likeness—the soul of things about him that

has so far escaped the brush of every foreign artist en-deavoring to portray the outward forms of things Japanese. . . .

The charm of all we see from our car—the Tokaido (the great imperial highway that intersects the whole empire), the queer little farmhouses and railway sta-tions, and even the water-soaked paddy fields, reaped of their rice—lies in the exquisite, faultless cleanliness and propriety of it all.

Arrived at Tokyo, we go to the residence of the American minister, who is very agreeably housed, and where we find—as in all private dwellings throughout the East—a most astonishing profusion of flowery plants blooming and bourgeoning in every corner of the mansion.

We take our tiffin in a little latticed glove box of a teahouse, the polished daintiness of whose interior will not permit of our wearing our shoes; and a grotesque spectacle they make—those American shoes, standing in a row just inside the entrance while we tiptoe awk-wardly and shamefacedly in our stocking feet up the stairs. A mild diffused light through the paper panes illuminates our tiny upper chamber, whose only fur-nishings are sweet-smelling mattings, a kakemono[8] hanging on the wall, and a tall jar full of red-berried branches in the corner. We are served by a moon-faced little maid in a flowered gown, who bows at each entry and draws in her breath to signify what a privilege it is to breathe the same air with us . . . one of the customs of a national courtesy so thorough and far-reaching that even the domestic animals are civilly addressed as Mr. Cat and Mr. Dog. . . . She brings us braziers to warm our fingers and wadded rugs to sit upon, tailorwise, and serves us delicious tea, sugarless and straw-colored, in tiny cups without handles, and bowls of rice across which are laid crisp, freshly broiled eels—a delightful dish that we eat with polished black chopsticks.

. . . The 'rikishas race away with us quite to the other side of town—past great forts and fosses [moats], past the mikado's [emperor's] palaces and gardens, to the famous temples at Shiba. The road is smooth and broad and overshadowed by pines. A superb gilded and lacquered gateway admits us to the temple grounds, and here the guide goes in search of a shaven-headed priest who will show us his treasures. Immediately before us stands a lovely red temple, rich with gold and carvings and lacquered figures, and with a marble-paved veranda polished as onyx; but we cannot wait to examine it. We go to the left and climb the hill by stone steps strewn with crimson petals of the camellia blossoms. . . . At the end of an avenue of tall gray stone lanterns—where lights shine during the great religious festivals—stands the tomb of Iemitsu, the son of Ieyasu, the great shogun who usurped supreme authority and reduced the mikado to the position of a primate.[9] *But the little finger of Iemitsu was thicker than his father's loins. He consolidated the feudal system, and chivalry under his rule achieved its noblest development; Japa-*

nese arms were feared and respected abroad and at home; and under the sun of his kingly favor, Japanese art blossomed into its supreme, consummate flower. Today the curios of his period are worth their weight in gold, and all the knightly traditions of the land cluster about his name and reign.

Laying down a life of power, he yearned for an immortality of beauty—to be magnificent and impressive even in death; and, choosing this spot, he spent millions in glorifying his last resting place. Never monarch slept among sweeter verdure, space, and calm.

We race across the city again in our 'rikishas to the great park of Uyeno, to see the sun go down behind Fujiyama . . . to look out across the city's vast hive with its million or more of folk whose myriad lights begin to twinkle in the violet dusk. . . . We worship a moment before a gigantic, calm-lidded stone Buddha set on a little hill, amid a thicket of roses.

Then the railroad again . . . a broad, yellow moon shining on the ever-present Fujiyama . . . regretful farewells to the charming Americans and Lieutenant Mc-Donald, and then the visit to fairyland is over. . . . I must pass on in my swift course and be ready for new sights and friends.

NOTES

1. William Ewart Gladstone (1809–99) was the current prime minister of Britain.

2. Well-known, if not popular name: American-born Florence Maybrick had just been convicted of murdering her English husband; Mary Anderson and Lillie Langtry were actresses.

3. In 1885, as a reporter for the *Pittsburg Dispatch*, Bly spent five months living in Mexico, where she covered local politics and culture. She returned to the U.S. after government officials threatened to arrest her for violating a law that barred foreigners from participating "in any way" in Mexican politics. See *Six Months in Mexico* by Nellie Bly (New York, American Publishers Corporation, 1888).

4. American women began bleaching their hair with hydrogen peroxide in the 1860s.

5. Parsees: followers of Zoroastrianism, a pre-Islamic religion that originated in Iran but spread to other places, especially India. Adherents have also been called "fire-worshipers" because they face a light or flame when praying.

6. Tableaux vivants: performances in which people form posed, motionless scenes to depict characters or events

7. In his *Memoir of Thomas Moore*, the English poet and biographer Charles Kent referred to Moore's epitaph—"THOMAS MOORE, THE POET AND PATRIOT OF IRELAND"—as "simple but sufficient."

8. Kakemono: a vertical scroll that can be rolled up.

9. Tokugawa Iemitsu (1604–51) was the third shogun of the Tokugawa dynasty of Japan. His edict of 1639 forbade Japanese ships from sailing to, or returning from, foreign countries, thus isolating Japan from the outside world. Iemitsu was actually the grandson—not son—of Ieyasu, the founder of the Tokugawa shogunate.

STAGE FOUR

BLY: CEYLON AND MALAYA

ABOUT NINE O'CLOCK in the morning we anchored in the bay at Colombo, Ceylon.[1] The island, with its abundance of green trees, was very restful and pleasing to our eyes after the spell of heat we had passed through on the ocean coming from Aden.

Preparations had been made by the passengers before we anchored, to go ashore, and as we came slowly into the small harbor, where a number of vessels were lying, we all stood impatiently on deck waiting for the first opportunity to desert the ship.

With all our impatience we could not fail to be impressed with the beauties of Colombo and the view from the deck of our incoming steamer. As we moved in among the beautiful ships lying at anchor, we could see the green island dotted with low arcaded buildings which looked, in the glare of the sun, like marble palaces. In the rear of us was the blue, blue sea, jumping up into little hills that formed into snow drifts which softly sank into the blue again. Forming the background to the town was a high mountain, which they told us was known as Adam's Peak. The beach, with a forest of tropical trees, looked as if it started in a point away out in the sea, curving around until near the harbor it formed into a blunt point, the line of which was carried out to sea by a magnificent breakwater surmounted by a lighthouse. Then the land curved back again to a point where stood a signal station, and on beyond a wide road ran along the water's edge until it was lost at the base of a high green eminence that stood well out over the sea, crowned with a castle-like building glistening in the sunlight.

Accompanied by a friend, I was the first to step ashore. Some passengers who started in advance of us took a steam launch. My escort said that he would give me a novel experience and also show me a small boat that traveled faster than a steam launch. The gentleman, who had offered to be my escort during our jaunt on land, was a traveler of vast experience. He has averaged a yearly tour of the world for several years and knows the Eastern countries as he knows his home. Still, when I saw the boat in which he intended to take me ashore, I rather doubted his judgment, but I said nothing.

The boat was a rudely constructed thing. The boat proper was probably five feet in length and two feet in width across the top, narrowing down to the keel, so that it was not wide enough to allow one's feet to rest side by side in the bottom. There were two seats in the middle of the boat facing one another. They are shaded by a bit of coffee sack that must be removed to give room for passengers to get in. The two men sit at either end of this peculiar boat, and with one paddle each. The paddle is a straight pole, with a board the shape and size of a cheese-box head tied to the end of it, and with both those paddles on the same side, they row us ashore. The boat is balanced by a log the length of the boat and fastened out by two curved poles, probably three feet from the boat. These boats are called by tourists, outriggers, but are called by the people of Ceylon, catamarans.

With but slight exertion, the men sent the boat cutting through the water, and in a few moments we had distanced the steam launch and had accommodations engaged at the hotel before the launch had landed its passengers.

A nearer view of the hotel, the Grand Oriental, did not tend to lessen its attractiveness—in fact it increased it. It was a fine, large hotel, with tiled arcades, corridors airy and comfortable, furnished with easy chairs and small marble-topped tables which stood close enough to the broad armrests for one to sip the cooling lime squashes or the exquisite native tea, or eat of the delicious fruit while resting in an attitude of ease and laziness. I found no place away from America where smoking was prohibited, and in this lovely promenade the men smoked, consumed gallons of whiskey and soda, and perused the newspapers, while the women read their novels or bargained with the pretty little copper-colored women who came to sell dainty handmade lace, or with the clever, high-turbaned merchants who would snap open little velvet boxes and expose, to the admiring gaze of the charmed tourists, the most bewildering gems. There were deeply dark emeralds, fire-lit diamonds, exquisite pearls, rubies like pure drops of blood, the lucky cat's-eye with its moving line, and all set in such beautiful shapes that even the men, who would begin by saying, "I have been sold before by some of your kind," would end by laying down their cigars and papers and examining the glittering ornaments that tempt all alike. No woman who lands at Colombo ever leaves until she adds several rings to her jewel box.

For the first time since leaving America I saw American money. It is very popular in Colombo and commands a high price—as jewelry! It goes for nothing as money. When I offered it in payment for my bills, I was told it would be taken at sixty percent discount. The Colombo diamond merchants are very glad to get American twenty-dollar gold pieces and pay a high premium on them. The only use they make of the money is to put a ring through it and hang it on their watch chains for ornaments.

Leading off from this corridor, pleasant in its coolness, interesting in its peculiarities, is the dining hall, matching the other parts of the hotel with its picturesque stateliness. The small tables are daintily set and are richly decorated daily with the native flowers of Colombo, rich in color, exquisite in form, but void of perfume. From the ceiling were suspended embroidered punkahs, that invention of the East which brings comfort during the hottest part of the day. The punkahs are long strips of cloth, fastened to bamboo poles that are suspended within a short distance of the tables. They are kept in motion by a rope pulley, worked by a man or boy. They send a lazy, cooling air through the building, contributing much to the ease and comfort of the guest. Punkahs are also used on all the ships that travel in the East.

Very good food was served at the hotel—which was all the more palatable to the passengers from the *Victoria* after the trials they had had for the past fortnight in eating the same kind of food under daily different names. Sinhalese [native] waiters were employed, and they were not only an improvement on the English stewards, to whose carelessness and impudence we had been forced to submit, but they were interesting to the Westerner.

They managed to speak English very well and understood everything that was said to them. They are not unpleasing people, being small of stature and fine of feature, some of them having very attractive, clean-cut faces, light bronze in color. They wore white linen apron-like skirts and white jackets. Noiselessly they move over the smooth tile floor, in their bare brown feet. Their straight black hair is worn long, twisted in a Psyche knot[2] at the back of the head. On the crown of the head, instead of circling it from ear to ear, is always set a tortoiseshell comb, like those worn by American school children. It was some time before I could tell a Sinhalese man from a Sinhalese woman. It is not difficult to distinguish the different sexes after one knows that the Sinhalese men wear the comb, which is as distinct a feature of their dress as men's trousers in America. Sinhalese women would not think of donning this little comb any more than a sensitive American woman would think of wearing men's apparel.

At tiffin I had some real curry, the famous native dish of India. I had been unable to eat it on the *Victoria,* but those who knew said it was a most delicious dish when prepared rightly, and so I tested it on shore. First, a divided dish containing shrimps and boiled rice was placed before me. I put two spoonfuls of rice on my plate, and on it put one spoonful of shrimps; there was also chicken and beef for the meat part of the curry, but I took shrimps only. Then was handed me a much divided plate containing different preserved fruits, chuddah [sic][chutney], and other things hot with pepper. As instructed, I partook of three of this variety and put it on top of what had been placed first on my plate. Last came little dried pieces of stuff that we heard before we saw, its odor was so loud and unmistakable. They called it Bombay duck. It is nothing more or less than a small fish, which is split open, and after being thoroughly dried, is used with the curry. One can learn to eat it.

After all this is on the plate, it is thoroughly mixed, making a mess very unsightly, but very palatable, as I found. I became so given to curry that I only stopped eating it when I found, after a hearty meal, curry threatened to give me palpitation of the heart.

After tiffin we drove to Mount Lavinia. We went along the smoothest, most perfectly made roads I ever saw. They seemed to be made of red asphalt, and I was afterwards told that they are constructed by convicts. Many of these roads were picturesque bowers, the overreaching branches of the trees that lined the waysides forming an arch of foliage above our heads, giving us charming telescopic views of people and conveyances along the road. Thatched huts of the natives and glimpses of the dwellers divided our attention with the people we passed on the road.

Mount Lavinia we found to be the place we had noticed on entering the harbor. It is a fine hotel situated on an eminence overlooking the sea and is a favorite resort during the hot seasons. It is surrounded by a smooth green lawn and faces the blue sea, whence it gets a refreshing breeze all the year through.

After dinner, everybody at the Grand Oriental

Hotel went out for a drive, the women, and many of the men going bareheaded, driving through the town, down the wide streets, past beautiful homes set well back in tropical gardens, to the Galle Face drive that runs along the beach just out of reach of the waves that break on the sandy banks with a more musical roar than I ever heard water produce before. The road lies very close to the water's edge, and by the soft rays of the moon, its red surface was turned to silver, the deep blue of the sea was black, and the foamy breakers were snowdrifts. In the soft, pure light we would see silent couples strolling along arm and arm, apparently so near the breakers that I felt apprehensive, lest one, stronger than the others, should catch them unawares and wash them out to that unknown land where we all travel to rest. One night I saw a native standing waist-deep, fishing in the roaring breakers. They tell me that many of the fish bite more freely after night, but I thought how easily the fisherman might be washed away, and no one would be the wiser until his absence was noticed by his friends.

Early next morning I was awakened by a Sinhalese waiter placing coffee and toast on a small table which he drew up close to my curtained bed, after which he went out. I arose earlier than was my habit because I had a desire to see what there might be to see while I had the opportunity. After a cool, refreshing bath, I dressed hastily and went down below. I found almost all of my friends up, some having already started out to enjoy the early morning.

In a light wagon we again drove down Galle Face road, and out past a lake in which men, women, children, oxen, horses, buffalo, and dogs were sporting. It was a strange sight. Off on a little green island, we saw the laundry folk at work, beating, sousing [soaking], and wringing the clothes, which they afterwards spread upon the grass to dry. Almost all of the roads through which we drove were perfect with their picturesque curves and often bordered and arched with magnificent trees, many of which were burdened with beautiful brilliant blossoms.

Everybody seemed to be out. The white people were driving, riding, riding bicycles, or walking. The breakwater, which is a good half mile in length, is a favorite promenade for the citizens of Colombo. Morning and evening, gaily dressed people can be seen walking back and forth between the lighthouse and the shore. When the stormy season comes, the sea dashes full forty feet above this promenade, which must be cleansed of a green slime, after the storms are over, before it can be traveled with safety. The Prince of Wales laid the first stone of this beautiful breakwater in 1875, and ten years later it was finished.

Colombo reminded me of Newport, R.I. Possibly—in my eyes, at least—Colombo is more beautiful. The homes may not be as expensive, but

28. - The Lake, Colombo.

Ceylonese men washing laundry in a lake

they are more artistic and picturesque. The roads are wide and perfect; the view of the sea is grand; and while unlike in its tropical aspect, still there is something about Colombo that recalls Newport.

I went one night to a Parsee theater. At the entrance were groups of people, some of whom were selling fruits, and some were jinricksha men waiting to haul the people home after the performance. There was no floor in the building. The chairs were placed in rows on the ground. The house was quite well filled with native men, women, and children who were deeply interested in the performance which had begun before we reached there.

The actors were all men; my escort had told me women never think of going on the stage in that country. The stage was not unlike any other stage, and the scenery, painted by native artists, was quite as good as is usually seen. On the left of the stage, close to the wing, was a man, sitting cross-legged on a raised platform, beating a tom-tom. A tom-tom was undoubtedly the mother to the drum. It is made on the same principle, but instead of being round, is inclined to be long in shape. The player uses his hands instead of drumsticks, and when one becomes accustomed to it, I do not think the sound of a tom-tom can be called unmusical.

On the right, directly opposite to the tom-tom player, was a man whose duty it was to play a strange-looking organ. He only used one hand, the left, for playing, and with the right he held a book, which he steadily perused throughout the entire performance, reading and playing mechanically without once looking at the actors.

The story of the opera was not unlike those in other countries. The basis or plot of the play was a tale of love and tragedy. A tall young man, with his face painted a death-like white, sang shrilly through his very high-arched nose to another young man, dressed in the costume of a native woman. The latter was the lady, and the heroine of the play, and he sang sharply through his nose like his, or her, lover. All the actors sang through their noses, and the thinner their voices and the more nasal sound they employed, the more the audience applauded.

I rode home from the theater in a bullock hackery. It was a very small springless cart on two wheels with a front seat for the driver, and on the back seat, with our backs to the driver and our feet hanging over, we drove to the hotel. The bullock is a strange, modest-looking little animal with a hump on its back and crooked horns on its head. I feared that it could not carry us all, but it traveled at a very good pace. There was a sound of grunt, grunt, grunting that concerned me very much until l found it was the driver and not the bullock that was responsible for the noise. With grunts he urged the bullock to greater speed.

Among the natives that haunt the hotel are the

snake charmers. They are almost naked fellows, sometimes with ragged jackets on and sometimes turbans on their heads, but more often the head is bare. They execute a number of tricks in a very skillful manner. The most wonderful of these tricks, to me, was that of growing a tree. They would show a seed; then they would place the seed on the ground, cover it with a handful of earth, and cover this little mound with a handkerchief, which they first passed around to be examined, that we might be positive there was nothing wrong with it. Over this they would chant, and after a time, the handkerchief is taken off and then up through the ground is a green sprout. We look at it incredulously, while the man says: "Tree no good; tree too small," and covering it up again, he renews his chanting. Once more he lifts the handkerchief, and we see the sprout is larger, but still it does not please the trickster, for he repeats: "Tree no good; tree too small," and covers it up again. This is repeated until he has a tree from three to five feet in height. Then he pulls it up, shows us the seed and roots.

Although these men always asked us to "See the snake dance?," we always saw every other trick but the one that had caught us. One morning, when a man urged me to "See the snake dance?," I said that I would, but that I would pay to see the snake dance and for nothing else. Quite unwillingly the men lifted the lid of the basket, and the cobra crawled slowly out, curling itself up on the ground. The "charmer" began to play on a little fife, meanwhile waving a red cloth which attracted the cobra's attention. It rose up steadily, darting angrily at the red cloth, and rose higher at every motion until it seemed to stand on the tip end of its tail. Then it saw the charmer and it darted for him, but he cunningly caught it by the head and with such a grip that I saw the blood gush from the snake's mouth. He worked for some time, still firmly holding the snake by the head before he could get it into the basket, the reptile meanwhile lashing the ground furiously with its tail. When at last it was covered from sight, I drew a long breath, and the charmer said to me sadly: "Cobra no dance, cobra too young, cobra too fresh!" I thought quite right; the cobra was too fresh!

At Colombo I saw the jinricksha for the first time. The jinricksha is a small two-wheel wagon, much in shape like a sulky, except that it has a top which can be raised in rainy weather. It has long shafts joined at the end with a crossbar. The jinricksha men are black and wear little else than a sash. When the sun is hot, they wear large hats that look like enormous mushrooms, but most of the time these hats are hanging to the back of the 'ricksha. There are stands at different places for these men, as well as carriage stands. While waiting for patrons, they let their 'rickshas rest on the shafts and they sit in the bottom, their feet on the ground. Besides dressing in a sash, these men dress in an oil or grease, and when the day is hot and they run, one wishes they wore more clothing and less oil! The grease has an original odor that is entirely its own.

I had a shamed feeling about going around the town drawn by a man, but after I had gone a short way, I decided it was a great improvement on modern means of travel; it was so comforting to have a horse that was able to take care of itself! When we went into the shops, it was so agreeable not to have the worry of fearing the horses were not blanketed, and when we made them run, we did not have to fear we might urge them into a damaging speed. It is a great relief to have a horse whose tongue can protest.

I visited at the temples in Colombo, finding little of interest, and always having to pay liberally for the privilege of looking about. One day I went to the Buddhist college, and, while there, I met the famous high priest of Ceylon. He was sitting on a verandah that surrounded his low bungalow, writing on a table placed before him. His gown consisted of a straight piece of old gold silk wrapped deftly around the body and over the waist. The silk had fallen to his waist, but after he greeted us, he pulled it up around his shoulders. He was a copper-colored old fellow, with gray hair that was shaved very close to the head. He spoke English quite well, and among other things told me he received hundreds of letters from the United States every year and that they found more converts to the Buddhist religion in America than in any other land.

The two newspapers in Colombo are in the charge of two young Englishmen who are very clever. They are very kind to strangers, and I am indebted to them for a great deal of pleasure during my stay in Ceylon. The hotel manager is a German of high birth. He is untiring in his efforts to make his guests comfortable. His wife is a very pretty little woman, with a beautiful voice. Through her kindness I learned of a tailor in Ceylon who makes gowns that for style and fit are not excelled. I have seen gowns from Worth that could not equal them, and this man charges for making a gown, five rupees! Five rupees are about two dollars and a half. He will make a gown in two days.

The praises of Kandy had been sung to me, so one morning at seven o'clock I started for Kandy with the Spanish representative, who was going to Peking [Beijing] and a jolly Irish lad who was bound for Hong Kong, both of whom had traveled with me from Brindisi. We drove to the station and were passed with the people, through the gate to the train. English cars, and ones that leave everything to be desired, are used on this line. We got into a compartment where there was but one seat, which, luckily for us, happened to be facing the way we traveled. Our tickets were taken at the station, and then the doors were locked and the train started. Before the start, we had entered our names in a book which a guard brought to us with the information that we could have breakfast on the train if so desired. As it was too early for breakfast at the hotel, we were only too glad to get an opportunity to eat. At eight o'clock the train stopped and the guard unlocked our door, telling us to go front to the dining car. It seemed strange to be compelled to get out of a train, instead of walking through it, in order to get to the other end of it.

The dining car was fitted up with stationary tables which almost spanned the car, leaving a small space for people to walk along. There were more people than could be accommodated, but as the train had started, they were obliged to stand. Several persons had told me that the breakfast served on this train was considered remarkably good. I thought, on seeing the bill of fare, they had prepared a feast for a chicken hawk. First, there was fish dressed in vinegar and onions, followed by chicken soup, chicken aspic, grilled chicken, boned chicken, fried chicken, boiled chicken, cold chicken, and chicken pie!

The road to Kandy is spoken of as being very beautiful. It winds up the mountainside and is rather pretty, but nothing wonderful in that respect. It is a tropical land, but the foliage and flowers are

The road to Kandy, Ceylon

very ordinary. About the prettiest things to be seen are the rice beds. They are built in terraces, and when one looks down into the deep valley, seeing terrace after terrace of the softest, lightest green, one is forced to cry: "How beautiful!"

Arriving at Kandy at last, we hired a carriage and went to see the lake, the public library, and the temples. In one old temple, surrounded by a moat, we saw several altars, of little consequence, and a bit of ivory which they told us was the tooth of Buddha. Kandy is pretty, but far from what it is claimed to be. They said it was cool, but we found it so hot that we thought with regret of Colombo. Disgusted with all we found worth seeing, we drove to Peradeniya to see the great botanical garden. It well repaid us for the visit. That evening we returned to Colombo. I was tired and hungry, and the extreme heat had given me a sick headache.

I went to bed that night too ill to eat my dinner. The next morning I had intended to go to the pearl market but felt unequal to it, and when my acquaintances returned and told me that at the very end of the sale a man bought some leftover oysters for one rupee and found in them five hundred dollars' worth of pearls, I felt sorry that I had not gone, although there was great danger of getting cholera.

*   *   *

ONE NIGHT, after I had been five days in Colombo, the blackboard in the hotel corridor bore the information that the *Oriental* would sail for China the following morning, at eight o'clock. I was called at five o'clock and some time afterwards left for the ship.

When farewells had been said, and I was on the *Oriental,* I found my patience had given way under the long delay. The ship seemed to be deserted when I went on deck, with the exception of a handsome elderly man, accompanied by a young blond man in a natty white linen suit, who slowly promenaded the deck, watching out to sea while they talked. I was trying to untie my steamer chair so as to have some place to sit, when the elderly man came up and politely offered to assist me.

"When will we sail?" I asked shortly.

"As soon as the *Nepaul* comes in," the man replied. "She was to have been here at daybreak, but she hasn't been sighted yet. Waiting for the *Nepaul* has given us this five days' delay. She's a slow old boat."

"There is the *Nepaul*," I said, pointing out a line of smoke just visible above the horizon. They doubted it, but a few moments proved that I was correct. "I am very ill-natured," I said, glancing from the kindly blue eyes of the elderly man to the

156

laughing blue eyes of the younger man; "but I could not help it. After being delayed for five days I was called at five o'clock because they said the ship was to sail at eight, and here it is nine o'clock and there's no sign of the ship sailing and—I am simply famished."

As they laughed at my woes, the gong sounded for breakfast, and they took me down. I was the only woman that morning, and a right jolly breakfast we had.

The captain, a most handsome man, and as polite and courteous as he was good looking, sat at the head of the table. Officers that any ship might boast of were gathered about him. Handsome, good-natured, intelligent, polite, they were, every single one of them. I found the elderly man I had been talking to was the chief engineer, and the young man was the ship's doctor.

The dining hall was very artistic and pleasant, and the food was good. The ship, although much smaller than the *Victoria*, was very much better in every way. The cabins were more comfortable, the ship was better ventilated, the food was vastly superior, the officers were polite and good-natured, the captain was a gentleman in looks and manners, and everything was just as agreeable as it could be.

It was well on to one o'clock before the passengers were transferred from the *Nepaul* to the *Oriental*. In the meantime the ship was amply peopled with merchants from the shore who were selling jewels and lace. How they did cheat the passengers! They would ask, and sometimes get, fabulous prices for things, and when the ship was ready to sail, they offered to sell at any price.

At one o'clock we sailed. The first day and the two days following were passed lazily on deck. I found it a great relief to be again on the sweet, blue sea, out of sight of land and free from the tussle and worry and bustle for life which we are daily, hourly even, forced to gaze upon on land. Although the East is, in a very great measure, free from the dreadful crowding for life, still one is bound to see signs of it even among the most indolent of people. Only on the bounding blue, the grand, great sea, is one rocked into a peaceful rest at noon of day, at dusk of night, feeling that one is drifting, drifting, not seeing, or knowing, or caring, about fool mortals striving for life. True, the sailors do this and that, but it has an air far from that of elbowing each other for a living. To the lazy passengers it seems that they merely hoist a sail or pull it down, that they may drift—dream—sleep—talk—live for happiness and not for gain.

The fourth day out was Sunday. The afternoon was spent on deck looking at the most beautiful green islands which we slowly passed. Sometimes we would lazily conjecture as to whether they were inhabited or not.

The next day we anchored at Penang, or Prince of Wales Island, one of the Straits Settlements. As the ship had such a long delay at Colombo, it was said that we would have but six hours to spend on shore. With an acquaintance as escort, I made my preparations and was ready to go to land the moment we anchored. We went ashore in a sampan, an oddly shaped flat boat with the oars, or rather paddles, fastened near the stern. The Malay oarsman rowed hand over hand, standing upright in the stern, his back turned towards us as well as the way we were going. Frequently he turned his head to see if the way was clear, plying his oars industriously all the while. Once landed, he chased us to the end of the pier demanding more money, although we had paid him thirty cents, just twenty cents over and above the legal fare.

Hiring a carriage, we drove to where a waterfall comes bounding down the side of a naturally verdant mountain which has been transformed, halfway up, into a pleasing tropical garden.

On the way to the town we visited a Hindu temple. Scarcely had we entered, when a number of half-clad, barefooted priests rushed frantically upon us, demanding that we remove our shoes. The temple being built open, its curved roof and rafters had long been utilized by birds and pigeons as a bedroom. Doubtless ages had passed over the stone floor, but I could swear nothing else had, so I refused emphatically and unconditionally to un-boot myself. I saw enough of their idols to satisfy me. One was a black god in a gay dress; the other was a shapeless black stone hung with garlands of flowers, the filthy stone at its base being buried 'neath a profusion of rich blossoms.

English is spoken less in Penang than in any port I visited. A native photographer, when I questioned him about it, said: "The Malays are proud, miss. They have a language of their own, and they are too proud to speak any other."

A Chinese joss house [temple or shrine containing images], the first I had seen, was very interesting. The pink and white roof, curved like a canoe, was ornamented with animals of the dragon tribe, with their mouths open and their tails in the air. The straggling worshippers could be plainly seen from the streets through the arcade sides of the temple. Chinese lanterns and gilt ornaments made gay the dark interior. Little josses, with usual rations of rice, roast pig, and smoldering joss sticks [incense sticks] disbursing a strangely sweet perfume, were no more interesting than a dark corner in which the superstitious were trying their luck, a larger crowd of dusky people than were about the altars. In fact, the only devotee was a waxed-haired Chinese woman, with a slit-eyed brown babe tied on her back, bowing meekly and lowly before a painted, be-bangled joss.

Some priests with shaven heads and old-gold silk garments, who were in a summer house in the garden, saw us when we were looking at the goldfish ponds. One came forth, and, taking me by the hand, gracefully led me to where they were gathered. They indicated their wish that we should sit with them and drink tea with them, milkless and sugarless, from child-like china cups, which they refilled so often that I had reasons for feeling thankful the cups were so like unto play dishes. We were unable to exchange words, but we smiled liberal smiles at one another.

Mexican silver is used almost exclusively in Penang. American silver will be accepted at the same value, but American gold is refused, and paper money is looked on with contempt. The Chinese jinricksha men in Penang, compared with those in Colombo, are like overfed pet horses beside racers in trim. They were the plumpest Chinamen I ever saw; such round, fat legs and arms!

When we started back to the ship, the bay was very rough. Huge waves angrily tossed our small boat about in a way that blotted the red from my escort's cheeks and caused him to hang his head in a care-for-nothing way over the boat's side. I could not help liking the sea to a coquette, so indifferent and heedless is it to the strange emotions it raises in the breast of man. It was a reckless spring that landed us on the ship's ladder, the rolling of the coal barge helping to increase the swell which had threatened to engulf us. Hardly had we reached deck, when the barge was ordered to cut loose; even as this was being done, the ship hoisted anchor and started on its way. Almost immediately, there was a great commotion on board. About fifty ragged black men rushed frantically on deck to find that while depositing their last sacks of coal in the regions below, their barge and companions had cast off and were rapidly nearing the shore. Then followed dire chattering, wringing of hands, pulling of locks, and crying after the receding barge, all to no avail. The tide was coming in, a very strong tide it was, too, and despite the efforts of those on it, the barge was steadily swept inland.

The captain appeased the coolies'[3] fears by stating that they should go off in the pilot's boat. We all gathered to see the sight, and a funny one it was! The tug being lashed to the ship, they first tried to take the men off without slowing down, but after one man got a dangerous plunge bath and the sea threatened to bury the tug, then the ship was forced to slow down. Some coolies slid down a cable, their comrades grabbing and pulling them, wet and frightened white, onto the tug. Others went down the ladder, which lacked five feet of touching the pilot boat. Those already on board would clutch the hanging man's bare legs, he meanwhile clinging despairingly to the ladder, fearing to loosen his grasp and only doing so when the ship officers would threaten to knock him off.

The pilot, a native, was the last to go down. Then the cable was cast off, and we sailed away seeing the tug, so overloaded that the men were afraid to move even to bail it out, swept back by the tide towards the place where we had last seen the land.

It was so damply warm in the Strait of Malacca that for the first time during my trip I confessed myself uncomfortably hot. It was sultry and foggy and so damp that everything rusted, even the keys in one's pockets, and the mirrors were so sweaty that they ceased to reflect. The second day out from Penang, we passed beautiful green islands. There were many stories told about the straits being once infested with pirates, and I regretted to hear that they had ceased to exist, I so longed for some new experience.

We expected to reach Singapore that night. I was anxious that we should, for the sooner we got in, the sooner we should leave, and every hour lost meant so much to me. The pilot came on at six o'clock. I waited tremblingly for his verdict. A wave of despair swept over me when I heard that we should anchor outside until morning because it was too dangerous to try to make the port after dark. And this was the result of slowing down to leave off the coolies at Penang. The mail contract made it compulsory for the ship to stay in port twenty-four hours, and while we might have been consuming our stay and so helping me on in my race against time, I was wasting precious hours lying outside the gates of hope, as it were, merely because some black men had been too slow. Those few hours might mean the loss of my ship at Hong Kong; they might mean days to my record. What agony of suspense and impatience I suffered that night!

When I came on deck the next morning, the ship lay alongside the wharf, and naked Chinese coolies carrying, two by two, baskets of coal suspended between them on a pole, were constantly traversing the gangplank between the ship and shore, while in little boats about were peddlers with silks, photographs, fruits, laces, and monkeys to sell.

The doctor, a young Welshman, and I hired a gharry, a light wagon with latticed windows and comfortable seating room for four, with the driver's seat on the same level outside. They are drawn by a pretty spotted Malay pony, whose speed is marvelous compared with its diminutive size and whose endurance is of such quality that the law confines their working hours to a certain limit.

Driving along a road as smooth as a ballroom floor, shaded by large trees, made picturesque by native houses built on pins in marshy land on either side, which tended to dampen our surprise at the great number of graveyards and the generous way in which they were filled, we drove to the town. The graves were odd, being round mounds with walls shaped like horseshoes. A flat stone where the mound ends and the wall begins bears the inscriptions done in colored letters.

There are no sidewalks in Singapore, and blue and white in the painting of the houses largely predominate over other colors. Families seem to occupy the second story, the lower being generally devoted to business purposes. Through latticed windows, we got occasional glimpses of peeping Chinese women in gay gowns, Chinese babies bundled in shapeless, wadded garments, while down below through widely opened fronts we could see people pursuing their trades. Barbering is the principal trade. A chair, a comb, a basin, and a knife are all the tools a man needs to open shop, and he finds as many patrons if he sets up shop in the open street as he would under shelter. Sitting doubled over, Chinamen have their heads shaven back almost to the crown, when a spot about the size of a tiny saucer is left to bear the crop of hair which forms the pigtail. When braided and finished with a silk tassel, the Chinaman's hair is "done" for the next fortnight.

The people here, as at other ports where I stopped, constantly chew betel nut, and when they laugh, one would suppose they had been drinking blood. The betel nut stains their teeth and mouthfuls blood-red. Many of the natives also fancy tinting their fingernails with it.

Nothing is patronized more than the 'rickshas in Singapore, and while they are to be had for ten cents an hour, it is no unusual sight to see four persons piled in one jinricksha and drawn by one man. We visited a most interesting museum, and saw along the suburban roads the beautiful bungalows of the European citizens. People in dogcarts[4] and wheelmen on bicycles crowded the splendid drives.

We found the monkey cage, of course. There was, besides a number of small monkeys, one enormous orangoutang. It was as large as a man and was covered with long red hair. While seeming to be very clever, he had a way of gazing off in the distance with wide, unseeing eyes, meanwhile pulling his long red hair up over his head in an aimless, insane way that was very fetching. The doctor wanted to give him a nut but feared to put his hand through the bars. The grating was too small for the old fellow to get his hand through, but he did not intend to be cheated of his rights, so he merely stuck his lips through the gratings until they extended fully four inches. I burst into laughter at the comical sight. I had heard of mouths, but that beat anything I ever saw, and I laughed until the old fellow actually smiled in sympathy. He got the nut!

The doctor offered him a cigar. He did not take it but touched it with the back of his hand, afterwards smelling his hand, and then subsided into that dreamy state, aimlessly pulling his hair up over the back of his head.

At the cable office, in the second story of a building, I found the agents conversant with the English language. They would accept American silver at par, but they did not care to handle our other money.

We had dinner at the Hotel de l'Europe, a long, low, white building set back in a wide, green lawn, with a beautiful esplanade, faced by the sea, fronting it. Upon the verandah were long white tables where a fine dinner was served by Chinamen.

On our return, I heard a strange, weird din as of many instruments in dire confusion and discord, very like in sound to a political procession the night after the presidential election. "That's a funeral," my Malay driver announced.

"Indeed! If that is the way you have funerals here, I'll see one," I said. So he pulled the gharry [horse-drawn carriage] to one side, where we waited eagerly for a funeral that was heralded by a blast of trumpets. First came a number of Chinamen with black and white satin flags, which, being flourished energetically, resulted in clearing the road of vehicles and pedestrians. They were followed by musicians on Malay ponies, blowing fifes, striking cymbals, beating tom-toms, hammering gongs, and pounding long pieces of iron, with all their might and main. Men followed carrying on long poles roast pigs and Chinese lanterns, great and small, while in their rear came banner bearers. The men on foot wore white trousers and sandals, with blue top dress, while the pallbearers wore black garments bound with blue braid. There were probably forty pallbearers. The casket, which rested on long poles suspended on the shoulders of the men, was hidden beneath a white-spotted scarlet cloth with decorations of Chinese lanterns or inflated bladders on arches above it. The mourners followed in a long string of gharries. They were dressed in white satin from head to toe and were the happiest-looking people at the funeral. We watched until the din died away in the distance, when we returned to town as delighted as if we had seen a circus parade.

Laughing and jesting about what had to us no suggestion of death, we drove back to see the temples. None of us were permitted to pass beneath the gate of the Mohammedan temple, so we went on to a Hindu temple. It was a low stone building, enclosed by a high wall. At the gateway leading to it were a superfluity of beggars, large and small, lame and blind, who asked for alms, touching their foreheads respectfully. The temple was closed, but some priests rushed forth to warn us not step on the sacred old dirty stone passage leading to it with our shoes on. Its filth would have made it sacred to me with my shoes off! My comrades were told that removing their shoes would give them admission, but I should be denied that privilege because I was a woman.

A Chinese funeral in Singapore

"Why?" I demanded, curious to know why my sex in heathen lands should exclude me from a temple, as in America it confines me to the side entrances of hotels and other strange and incommodious things.

"No, señora, no mudder," the priest said with a positive shake of the head.

"I'm not a mother!" I cried so indignantly that my companions burst into laughter, which I joined after a while, but my denials had no effect on the priest. He would not allow me to enter.

In some sheds which lined the inner part of the high wall we saw a number of fantastically shaped carts of heavy build. Probably they were juggernauts.[5] Nearby, we saw through the bars, a wooden image of a woman. Her shape was neither fairy-like nor girlish; her features were fiendish in expression and from her mouth fell a long string of beads. As the mother of a poor man's family, she would have been a great success. Instead of one pair of arms, she had four. One pair was employed in holding a stiff wooden baby before her, and the other three pairs were taking care of themselves much like the legs of a crab.[6] They showed us a white wooden horse mounted on wheels, images of most horrible devils; in short, we saw so many images of such horrible shapes that it would be impossible to recall them all.

On the lawn, fastened to a slight pin, was a white cow, the only presentable cow I saw during my trip.

Hindoo Temple   SINGAPORE

A Hindu temple in Singapore

The people in Singapore have ranks as have people in other lands. There they do not wait for one neighbor to tell another or for the newspapers to inform the public as to their standing, but every man, woman, and child carries his mark in gray powder on the forehead so that all the world may look and read and know his caste.[7]

We stopped at the driver's humble home on our way to the ship, and I saw there on the ground floor, his pretty little Malay wife dressed in one wrapping of linen, and several little brown naked babies. The wife had a large gold ring in her nose, rings on her toes and several around the rim of her ears, and gold ornaments on her ankles. At the door of their home was a monkey. I did resist the temptation to buy a boy at Port Said and also smothered the desire to buy a Sinhalese girl at Colombo, but when I saw the monkey, my willpower melted, and I began straightway to bargain for it. I got it.

"Will the monkey bite?" I asked the driver, and he took it by the throat, holding it up for me to admire as he replied:

"Monkey no bite." But he could not under the circumstances.

Hong kong! . . . *I like the name of my next port. It has a fine clangorous significance, like two slow, loud notes of some great brazen-lunged bell. . . . Hong—Kong!*

We have one more glimpse of Fujiyama the next morning as Japan sinks out of sight. . . . During the day, the young Chinaman with the pallid waxen hands dies. He has struggled hard to keep the flame burning until he sees his own land, but the crisp breath of the Japanese coast puffs it suddenly out. A canvas screen is hung across one corner of the steerage deck, and the doctor goes back and forth from behind it. . . . They will carry him back to his country, though he will not be glad or aware. But the sea knows she is being defrauded of her rights, and wakes and rages. For two days, we steam in the face of the northwest gale she has raised, and for three, the ship plunges like a spurred horse.

On Sunday, the 15th [of December], we reach Hong Kong. The sea turns to a cool profound emerald, and we descry again on the horizon the bamboo wings of the fishing and coasting junks. These sails are somewhat larger and deeper of hue than those of Japan, and still more resemble the fans of giant yellow and russet butterflies.

. . . More treeless mountains rise out of the green waters. They are broken and rugged, of volcanic origin,

and where the scant herbage fails, their naked sides show tawny as a lion's hide. It is one of the three beautiful harbors of the world, the water winding deeply inland between the hills and flowing around island mountains ringed with girdles of foam. At one o'clock we are in the broad antechamber of the port, known as the Lyee-Moon, and are signaled from the lofty peak to the inhabitants of the town lying at its foot. At two o'clock we drop anchor in the roadstead amid a great host of shipping of all character and nations—twenty-three days out from San Francisco. The White Star people had instructed Captain Kempson to make all due haste for my sake, and it is one of the swiftest voyages ever known at this season of the year, when the winds are contrary, coming to the west. We were sixteen days to Japan, where we remained thirty-six hours, and five days from Yokohama to Hong Kong.

The island of Hong Kong is a cluster of lofty abrupt hills with scanty vegetation, seized by England in 1842 after a struggle with China. At that time the town was an insignificant fishing village, but the value of the site was great commercially and strategically. It is a convenient and safe harbor for the squadron detailed to watch and menace the Russian navy in the Pacific; and the English have elevated the village into a flourishing city and made it the fourth shipping port of the world. The harbor is navigable for the largest merchant vessels and men-of-war in existence, and is perfectly sheltered and easy of access.

As in Japan, sampans swarm about us as soon as we are made fast to the buoy, but they are far less picturesque than were those. Each sampan wears a bamboo hood in the stern, and here the owner houses his wife and rears his family. A brood of babies is in each one of these little hutches, and while the pigtailed subject of the Celestial Emperor stands and rows in the bow, his helpmeet sculls in the stern with a long oar that serves as a tiller. The Chinese woman of the working class, I find, decided centuries ago the question still in its stormy infancy with us—of the divided skirt. She clothes herself in a pair of wide black trousers, a loose tunic, jade earrings, and cork-soled shoes, and is ready for all the emergencies of life. Should they take the form of marriage with a sampan owner, she will but rarely set her foot on shore again, but will, in common with something like twenty thousand of the "water population" of Hong Kong, work, sleep, eat, bear her children, rear them, and die in this crazy little boat.

I am very regretful at leaving the *Oceanic,* where I have received so much kindness; but "hateful is the dark blue ocean" after more than three weeks of it, and delightful the thought of even three precious days on land. I am to stay with personal friends in Hong Kong in order that I may see something of domestic life in the East, and I am taken ashore in their private steam launch. Chairs and bearers are waiting for us on the dock—comfortable fauteuils of bamboo, trimmed with silver and supported by long bamboo poles. This is even

A Common Scene along the Wharves in Hong Kong

more amusing than the 'rikishas. There are four China-
men for each chair, dressed in my friend's livery—loose
trousers and tunic of white cotton bordered with rose
color. Their feet are bare, and their queues [pigtails]
are gathered into Psyche knots, on the back of their
heads, like the hair of the shop girls in America.

They lift the poles to their shoulders and start off in
a swift swinging trot. We pass across the narrow strip
of level land that lies on the water's edge—the business
quarter of the city built handsomely and solidly of na-
tive stone—and begin to mount the broad steep ways
that lead to the residence quarter. These are cool and
shadowy with great trees, with the clattering feathered
spears of the tall bamboos, with gigantic ferns, and
prodigious satiny leaves of tropical lilies. The streets are
paved with asphalt and have no sidewalks; here and
there they resolve themselves into broad flights of shal-
low steps up which the bearers carry us with perfect
ease. . . . The verdure is magnificent; the town is sub-
merged in it, and flowers are everywhere. Every nook
and corner that will hold a jar is filled with bloom,
and the rarest orchids are strewn carelessly about, in-
dustriously producing flowers, in delicious provincial
ignorance of their own value and of what they might
exact in the way of expensive attention.

. . . We meet the most astonishing varieties of the
human race. All sorts and conditions of Chinamen—
elegant dandies in exquisitely pale-tinted brocades;
grave merchants and compradors [senior servants/stew-

ards], richly but soberly clad; neat amahs[8] *with the tiny deformed Chinese feet, sitting at the street corners, taking in sewing by the day; street sellers of tea, shrimp, fruit, sweetmeats, and rice; women working side by side with the men, mending the streets . . . horrible old women, wizened and wrinkled beyond all imagining, all the femininity shriveled out of them, their only head covering a bit of black cloth across their seamed and humble foreheads, and the last pathetic spark of the female instinct for adornment displaying itself in the big jade and silver rings in their ears.*

. . . From windows shaded by light bamboo blinds look out coarse olive faces—heavy and dull of eye, repulsively sensual. These are Portuguese, descendants of the hardy sailors who explored and ruled these southern seas before the English supplanted them. They have bred in with the natives everywhere and have grown an indolent mongrel race. . . . Plump and prosperous-looking gentlemen go by in European dress and with tight-fitting purple satin coal hods [scuttle-shaped hats] on their heads. Their complexions are dark and their features—dug out of a mat of astonishingly thick beards—are aggravatedly Hebraic in their cast. They are Parsees, and look uncommonly like the lost tribes— exhibiting also, I am told, the same eminent abilities in business probably possessed by those much-sought-for Hebrew truants.

. . . At the corner stands a haughty jewel-eyed prince of immense stature—straight and lithe as a palm—in

178

whose high-featured bronze countenance are unfath-
omable potentialities of pride and passion. . . . He
wears a soldier's dress and sword, and a huge scarlet
turban of the most intricate convolutions. I cry out
with astonishment at the sight of this superb creature.

"Is it an emperor?" I demand, in breathless admiration.

"An emperor! Poof! It's only a Sikh policeman. There
are hundreds about the place quite as splendid as he."

It gives me my first real impression of the power of
England, who tames these mountain lions and sets
them to do her police duty. It would seem incredible
that this rosy commonplace Tommy Atkins[9] who comes
swaggering down the street in his scarlet coat can be the
weapon that tamed the fine creature in the turban. . . .

Here comes one of the conquerors of India, a kilted
Highlander, swinging down the road in his plaided
petticoats, with six inches of bare stalwart pink legs
showing, and a fine hearty self-confidence in his mien
that signifies his utter disbelief in the power of anything human to conquer him.

We leave this olla-podrida [Spanish stew] of nations
behind and mount into a broad street curved around
the flank of the hill. On the upper side of it is the heavy
wall of the Portuguese convent, once painted a lovely
light blue and now freaked [streaked] and stained a
thousand charming tints by time and weather. A beautiful work is done inside in teaching Chinese girls the
sweet decencies of life and pretty feminine arts. Opposite is my friend's house—two stories of stone sur-

No. 29.   Travelling in Sedan Chair, Hongkong.

A Western woman rides in a sedan chair in Hong Kong

rounded by great verandas. The coolies run down a curving flight of steps and deposit us at the door.

These Hong Kong houses have admirable interiors. A lofty hall divides this one, terminating on a rear veranda, with a wide view of the precipitous white city, buried in verdure, sloping down to the flashing emerald of the bay that is ringed with tawny hills. The hall is filled with more potted plants and massive furniture of Indian ebony and marble. To the left is a great drawing room, fifty feet long and eighteen high, with a dozen windows. Here are more palms and ferns, rich European fittings, and Eastern bric-à-brac.

My bedchamber is another huge shadowy place, with a dressing room and bath as large as the ordinary drawing room at home, furnished with old mahogany and silver fittings brought from Germany two generations ago. Its airy, unencumbered spaces remind me of the fine old bedchambers in the plantation houses at home in the South. . . . Here I am awakened in the morning by another pigtailed gentleman, who brings me my tea, prepares my bath, and arranges all things ready for my toilet. Female servants in Hong Kong are rare; and after the first surprise is over, these clean, grave male-maids seem perfectly efficient and convenable servitors. Our meals are stately functions—adorned, of course, with profuse greenery and flowers—with fine wines and delicate food exquisitely prepared. . . . A sumptuous Eastern life that flows on with cool and unhasting repose and gravity.

. . . In all our expeditions about the place, we are luxuriously carried by our coolies, who apparently put forth no special effort or haste, but with whom a rapid walker with no burden is unable to keep pace. The streets are a panorama of unending interest. 'Rikishas are employed occasionally in the level part of the town, but the general mode of traveling in the steeper streets is by chairs, the distinctive livery of private bearers consisting of the color of the border of their white garments. Stout, haughty, red-faced Englishmen go by in these chairs, and occasionally a covered one is met, with bamboo blinds, in which sits an equally fat and haughty mandarin. Coolies run about at a dog-trot, bearing immense burdens swung at the two ends of a pole carried on their naked muscular yellow shoulders. Pretty round-faced children, dressed exactly like their elders, play in the doorways and exchange smiles with the passerby. There is a general public amiability—without the gay and gracious vivacity of Japan—in all save the lowest class of laborers. These toil terribly and incessantly for infinitesimal sums, and by the most minute economies manage to exist— to continue these labors and privations. They are old in youth, parched, callous, and dully indifferent. Incapable of further disappointment, they exist with the stolid patience of those who expect only stones and serpents, having abandoned all hopes of bread and fish. . . .

The town is growing and prosperous. The shops, ho-

tels, clubs, and counting houses are handsome stone buildings with deep arcade-like verandas surrounded by pointed arches. The banks and public buildings are imposing and massive, and the place is noisy with the sound of mason's tools. The harbor for two hundred yards in front of the Praya (the broad water street) is shallow, and preparations are being made to fill it up and give Hong Kong the benefit of this extra width of level land. The same was done some years ago at Kowloon, on the opposite side of the harbor, where England owns a strip of the mainland. On this reclaimed land, fine wharves lined with godowns (warehouses) have been built, and huge dry docks and shipyards established where shipbuilding goes industriously on and the largest vessels afloat can put in for repairs. The export trade in cotton, tea, silk, spices, and rice is enormous, and the place develops year by year considerable manufacturing industries.

Though three great lines of trans-Pacific steamers ply between Hong Kong and America, there is only one resident of that nationality in the city besides the consul. The English, Germans, Parsees, and Chinamen conduct its business. The strategic importance of Hong Kong is so great that four or five war ships are always in its harbor or cruise in the neighborhood, and two full regiments are kept in garrison.

The climate of Hong Kong at this season is of Eden. The sun is pleasantly hot at midday, and the mornings and evenings are dewily cool. My friends are loath that

I should lose a single pleasure, and we are out all day long in this adorable weather. One of our paths lies through the green twilight of the Botanical Gardens, filled with such vegetation as I have always regarded with a doubting eye in the picture of the Asiatic half of the geographies. We pass under the tremulous lacey shadows of ferns twenty feet high, through trellises weighted with ponderous vines that blow a myriad perfumed purple trumpets up to the golden noon, and emerge upon sunny spaces where fountains are sprinkling silver rain upon banks of crimson and orange flowers. The flaxen-haired, muslin-clad English children play here, cared for by prim trousered Chinese amahs; and we meet pretty blue-eyed German ladies in their chairs, taking this road home.

Another expedition leads to the top of the peak, whose head is two thousand feet above the water and up whose side the town climbs year by year. Our way— at an angle of forty-five degrees—is by a tram dragged up the mountain by means of an endless chain. This peak is the city's summer resort and pleasuring ground. Handsome bungalows cling to its steep sides—built in the Italian style, of warm cream-white stone. There is ten degrees difference in temperature between the summit and the town, and a summer hotel is in process of construction at the top. . . . We can see from here how the water flows between the hills and how the harbor broadens to bays and narrows to straits between the

island mountains. Only at Rio [de] Janeiro and Syd-
ney, they tell me, is there a harbor whose beauty com-
pares to this.

Our chairs have come up another way, and we are
to be carried down the long winding road that sinks by
slow stages to the town. During the first stage, we are
in full sunlight, passing under the walls of the white
palace-like bungalows with smooth-shaven tennis
courts, where ruddy-cheeked, spare-loined young Eng-
lishmen toss the ball to fair-haired, light-footed English
girls. Then the road—the earth here is a thousand
beautiful shades of buff and rose—winds about to the
east, and we pass into the shadows. A tiny Greek
church with a sparsely populated graveyard clings to
the declivity above us, and from far below comes the
faint cool sound of waters foaming round the foot of
the hills.

. . . The sun has set; only the utmost heights are
gilded now, and the twilight deepens on our path. We
swing around the hills—in and out, and down, down,
with smooth, easy motion—to the regular pad, pad,
pad of the bearers' feet. Here and there in the dusk we
discern the scarlet turbans of Sikh warders, standing
motionless as bronze statues. Below in the harbor, the
lights of the town, the ships, and the flitting sampans
sparkle through the faint evening mist like multitudi-
nous fireflies. The town climbs the hill to meet us, and
we pass into the still heavier gloom of trees.

> *"In Xanadu did Kubla Khan*
> *A stately pleasure-dome decree —"*[10]

Kubla Khan did come to tiffin one day—a handsome dark gentleman of forty years or so, with very white teeth and eyes like black velvet. He wore extremely well-fitting London clothes, and in his soft, slow voice he signified that on the morrow he would take us to see the pleasure dome—not yet entirely complete. . . . Kubla Khan was his name in Xanadu of course, but in Hong Kong, for the sake of convenience and brevity, he was called Catchik Chater. Also for convenience and brevity, he gave it out that he was a British subject, resident in China, born in India, and with a certain mixture of Greek and Armenian blood in his veins. It had been his fancy to come to Hong Kong twenty years before, neglecting to bring with him any drafts on his treasury, and in the interim, he had collected something like a million pounds it was said. It was he who had made the long waterfront at Kowloon, rescuing it from the sea, and had covered it with great godowns filled with merchandise of the East, and it was he who was proposing the same feat on the opposite side of the harbor. He had interested himself more or less in the banks, the shipyards, and manufactures of various sorts, and he now felt prepared to erect in China a repetition of the Xanadu pleasure dome. He took us first to see his docks and godowns, resounding with the loud clangors of trade, and then through the grassy

A street in Hong Kong

Kowloon plains, by a wide red road shadowed with banana trees, to this lordly pavilion set on the crest of many flowering terraces

It is like the sumptuous fancy of some splendid Roman noble, proconsul of an Eastern province. The pavilion for the moment is in the hands of workmen, so we may not dine there; but we do dine with the Khan in his townhouse, eating through many courses, drinking many costly wines, and served by a phalanx of Celestials in rustling blue gowns.

Another day we go to the shops and turn over costly examples of Chinese art—coming home through the many-colored ways of the native town—steep streets that climb laboriously up and down stairs, and so narrow that there is hardly room for our chairs to pass through the multitudes who swarm there. Sixteen hundred residents to the acre they average in this part of the town, buzzing and humming like the unreckonable myriads insects bred from the fecund slime of a marsh. Two-thirds of their life is passed out of doors in the streets, and all seem to be patiently and continuously busy. Children are as the flies in number and activity. The place smells violently; smells of opium, of the dried ducks and fish hanging exposed for sale in the sun, of frying pork and sausages, and of the many strange repulsive-looking meals being cooked on hissing braziers in the streets and in doorways. There is no lack of color. The shops are faced with a broad fretwork

*richly gilded, and the long perpendicular signs are or-
namentally lettered with large black characters. Every
house is lime-washed some strong tint, and the whole
leaves upon the eye the color-impression one gets from
Chinese porcelains—of sharp green, gold, crimson, and
blue, all vigorous, definite, and mingled with grotesque
tastefulness.*

*My plan had been to sail from Hong Kong on the
Norddeutscher Lloyd ship* Preussen, *but a Peninsular
and Oriental steamer sails three days earlier; I am advised to go in her as far as Ceylon, and I do. So on the
morning of the 18th of December, I find myself on the
deck of the* Thames, *surrounded by the charming
friends and acquaintances of this Hong Kong episode,
who have come to give me a final proof of their goodness and wish me speed on my journey.*

*This boat is as polyglot as the land I have just left,
and swarms with queer people. The sailors are lascars,
clad in close trousers and tunic of blue cotton check and
red turbans. Many of the Parsees in their purple coal
hods come aboard to bid farewell to a parting friend.
One of the Highlanders is going home, and his comrades
have brought the pipes to give him a last tune. Grief and
Scotch whiskey move them finally to "play a spring and
dance it round" in spite of the heat, which brings the
sweat pouring down their faces. Sampans cluster about
with pretty little Chinese dogs, bamboo steamer chairs,
and canary birds for sale, driving a few final bargains.*

. . . The bell warns them all away. I wave goodbye to my friends and to the beautiful city with the keenest regret.

. . . The fifth stage of my journey has begun under the shadow of the Union Jack.

NOTES

1. Ceylon is now known as Sri Lanka. As a strategically located island in the Indian Ocean, it attracted Europeans' interest in the early sixteenth century. It passed from Portuguese to Dutch to British control, becoming a crown colony in 1805, a Commonwealth dominion in 1948, and the Democratic Socialist Republic of Sri Lanka in 1972.

2. Psyche knot: a popular Victorian hairstyle in which hair is twisted into a coil and knotted at the top of the nape of the neck.

3. Coolies: Unskilled Asian laborers. (The term is now considered offensive.)

4. Dogcarts: light two-wheeled carriages with two seats set back to back.

5. Juggernaut: a large, heavy cart that was used to convey a statue of Krishna. Sometimes devotees threw themselves under its wheels. Now used for a heavy vehicle like a truck or lorry.

6. The Hindu goddess Periyachi, most often seen in Singaporean temples, is the protector of children; she is usually depicted in a fearsome manner, with four pairs of arms that hold weapons and a baby.

7. Caste: the hereditary class into which Indian society is traditionally divided.

8. Amahs: Usually baby nurses or nannies, but here it seems to mean working women.

9. Tommy Atkins: slang for a British private soldier.

10. "In Xanadu . . .": the opening lines from the poem "Kubla Khan" by the English poet Samuel Taylor Coleridge (1772–1834).

STAGE FIVE
Bly: China

THAT EVENING WE SAILED for Hong Kong. The next day the sea was rough, and headwinds made the run slower than we had hoped for. Towards noon almost all the passengers disappeared. The roughness increased, and the cook enjoyed a holiday.

The terrible swell of the sea during the monsoon was the most beautiful thing I ever saw. I would sit breathless on deck watching the bow of the ship standing upright on a wave, then dash headlong down as if intending to carry us to the bottom. Although there was a dreadful swell, still the atmosphere was heavy and close. Sometimes I felt as if I would smother.

The monkey proved a good seaman. One day when I visited it, I found the young men had been toasting its health. It was holding its aching head when I went in, and evidently thinking I was the cause of the swelling, it sprang at me, making me seek safety in flight.

One night during the monsoon, the sea washed over the ship in a frightful manner. I found my cabin filled with water, which, however, did not touch my berth. Escape to the lower deck was impossible, as I could not tell the deck from the angry, pitching sea. As I crawled back into my bunk a feeling of awe crept over me and with it a conscious feeling of satisfaction. I thought it very possible that I had spoken my last word to any mortal, that the ship would doubtless sink, and with it all I thought, if the ship did go down, no one would be able to tell whether I could have gone around the world in seventy-five days or not. The thought was very comforting at that time, for I felt then I might not get around in one hundred days.

I could have worried myself over my impending fate had I not been a great believer in letting unchangeable affairs go their way. "If the ship does go down," I thought, "there is time enough to worry when it's going. All the worry in the world cannot change it one way or the other, and if the ship does not go down, I only waste so much time." So I went to sleep and slumbered soundly until the breakfast hour.

The ship was making its way laboriously through a very frisky sea when I looked out, but the deck was drained, even if it was not dry.

Later in the day the rolling was frightful. I was sitting on deck when all at once the ship went down at one side like a wagon in a deep rut. I was thrown in my chair clear across the deck. A young man endeavored to come to my assistance just as the ship went the other way in a still deeper sea rut. It flung me back again, and only by catching hold of an iron bar did I save my neck at least, for in another moment I would have been dashed through the skylight into the dining hall on the deck below.

As I caught the bar, I saw the man who had rushed to my assistance turned upside down and land on his face. I began to laugh, his position was so ludicrous. When I saw he made no move to get up, I ran to his side, still convulsed with laughter. I found his nose was bleeding profusely, but I was such an idiot that the sight of the blood only served to make the scene to me the more ridiculous. Helping him to a chair, I ran for the doctor and from laughing could hardly tell him what I wanted. The man's nose was broken, and the doctor said he would be scarred for life. Even the others laughed when I described the accident, and, although I felt a great pity for the poor fellow, hurt as he was in my behalf, still an irresistible impulse to laugh would sweep over me every time I endeavored to express my appreciation of his attempt to assist me.

Our passengers were rather queer. I always enjoy the queerness of people. One day, when speaking about the boat, I said: "Everything is such an improvement on the *Victoria*. The food is good, the passengers are refined, the officers are polite, and the ship is comfortable and pleasant."

When I finished my complimentary remarks about the ship, a little bride who had been a source of interest to us looked up and said: "Yes, everything is very nice; but the life preservers are not quite comfortable to sleep in."

Shocked amazement spread over the countenances of all the passengers, and then in one grand shout that dining room resounded with laughter. The bride said that ever since they left home on their bridal tour they had been sleeping in the life preservers. They thought it was the thing to do on board a ship.

But I never knew how queer our passengers were until we reached Hong Kong, which we did two days ahead of time, although we had the monsoon against us. When we landed, a man sued the company for getting him in ahead of time. He said he bought his tickets to cover a certain length of time, and if the company got him in before it expired, they were responsible for his expenses, and they had to pay his hotel bill.

The captain asked a minister who was on board to read the service one Sunday. He did so, and when he reached Hong Kong, he put in a bill for two pounds! He said he was enjoying a vacation and did not propose to work during that time unless he was paid for it! The company paid but warned the officers not to let ministers read the service thereafter until they knew their price.

The evening of December 22 we all sat on deck in a dark corner. The men were singing and telling stories. The only other woman who was able to be up and I were the interested and appreciative audience. We all felt an eagerness for morning, and yet the eagerness was mingled with much that was sad.

Knowing that early in the day we would reach Hong Kong, and while it would bring us new scenes and new acquaintances, it would take us from old friends.

*   *   *

WE FIRST SAW THE CITY of Hong Kong in the early morning. Gleaming white were the castle-like homes on the tall mountainside. We fired a cannon as we entered the bay, the captain saying that this was the custom of mail ships. A beautiful bay was this magnificent basin, walled on every side by high mountains. Mirror-like was the bay in the bright sun, dotted with strange craft from many countries. Heavy ironclads, torpedo boats, mail steamers, Portuguese lorchas [local sailing vessels], Chinese junks and sampans. Even as we looked, a Chinese ship wended its way slowly out to sea. Its queer, broad stern hoisted high out of the water and the enormous eye gracing its bow were to us most interesting. A graceful thing I thought it, but I heard an officer call it most ungraceful and un-shapely.

Hong Kong is strangely picturesque. It is a ter-raced city, the terraces being formed by the castle-like arcaded buildings perched tier after tier up the mountain's verdant side. The regularity with which the houses are built in rows made me wildly fancy them a gigantic staircase, each stair made in imitation of castles.

The doctor, another gentleman, and I left the boat, and walking to the pier's end, selected sedan chairs, in which we were carried to the town. The carriers were as urgent as our hackmen around railway stations in America. There is a knack of getting into a chair properly. It is placed upon the ground, the carrier tilts the shafts down, and the patron steps inside, back towards the chair, and goes into it backward. Once seated, the carriers hoist the chair to their shoulders and start off with a monotonous trot, which gives the chair a motion not unlike that of a pacing saddlehorse.

We followed the road along the shore, passing warehouses of many kinds and tall balconied buildings filled with hundreds of Chinese families, on the flat-house plan. The balconies would have lent a pleasing appearance to the houses had the inhabitants not seemed to be enjoying a washing jubilee, using the balconies for clotheslines. Garments were stretched on poles, after the manner of hanging coats so they will not wrinkle, and those poles were fastened to the balconies until it looked as if every family in the street had placed their old clothing on exhibition.

The town seemed in a state of untidiness, the road was dirty, the mobs of natives we met were filthy, the houses were dirty, the numberless boats lying along the wharf, which invariably were crowded with dirty people, were dirty, our carriers were dirty fellows, their untidy pigtails twisted around their half-shaven heads. They trotted steadily ahead, snorting at the crowds of natives we met to clear the way. A series of snorts or grunts would cause a scattering of natives more frightened than a tie walker would be at the tooting of an engine's whistle.

My only wish and desire was to get as speedily as possible to the office of the Oriental and Occidental Steamship Company to learn the earliest possible time I could leave for Japan, to continue my race against time around the world. I had just marked off my thirty-ninth day. Only thirty-nine days since leaving New York, and I was in China. I was leaving particularly elated, because the good ship *Oriental* not only made up the five days I had lost in Colombo, but reached Hong Kong two days before I was due, according to my schedule. It was the *Oriental*'s maiden trip to China, and from Colombo to Hong Kong, she had broken all previous records.

I went to the O&O office feeling very much elated over my good fortune, with never a doubt but that it would continue. "Will you tell me the date of the first sailing for Japan?" I asked a man in the office.

"In one moment," he said, and going into an inner office, he brought out a man who looked at me inquiringly, and when I repeated my question, said: "What is your name?"

"Nellie Bly," I replied in some surprise.

"Come in, come in," he said nervously.

We followed him in, and after we were seated, he said: "You are going to be beaten."

"What? I think not. I have made up my delay," I said, still surprised, wondering if the Pacific had sunk since my departure from New York, or if all the ships on that line had been destroyed.

"You are going to lose it," he said with an air of conviction.

"Lose it? I don't understand. What do you mean?" I demanded, beginning to think he was mad.

"Aren't you having a race around the world?" he asked, as if he thought I was not Nellie Bly.

"Yes; quite right. I am running a race with Time," I replied.

"Time? I don't think that's her name."

"Her! Her!!" I repeated, thinking, "Poor fellow, he is quite unbalanced," and wondering if I dared wink at the doctor to suggest to him the advisability of our making good our escape.

"Yes, the other woman; she is going to win. She left here three days ago."

I stared at him; I turned to the doctor; I wondered if I was awake; I concluded the man was quite mad, so I forced myself to laugh in an unconcerned manner, but I was only able to say stupidly:

"The other woman?"

"Yes," he continued briskly; "did you not know? The day you left New York another woman started out to beat your time, and she's going to do it. She left here three days ago. You probably met somewhere near the Strait of Malacca. She says she has authority to pay any amount to get ships to leave in advance of their time. Her editor offered one or two thousand dollars to the O&O if they would have the *Oceanic* leave San Francisco two days ahead of time. They would not do it, but they did do their best to get her here in time to catch the English mail for Ceylon. If they had not arrived long before they were due, she would have missed that boat and so have been delayed ten days. But she caught the boat and left three days ago, and you will be delayed here five days."

"That is rather hard, isn't it?" I said quietly, forcing a smile that was on the lips but came from nowhere near the heart.

"I'm astonished you did not know anything about it," he said. "She led us to suppose that it was an arranged race."

"I do not believe my editor would arrange a race without advising me," I said stoutly. "Have you no cables or messages for me from New York?"

"Nothing" was his reply.

"Probably they do not know about her," I said more cheerfully.

"Yes they do. She worked for the same newspaper you do until the day she started."

"I do not understand it," I said quietly, too proud to show my ignorance on a subject of vital importance to my well-doing. "You say I cannot leave here for five days?"

"No, and I don't think you can get to New York in eighty days. She intends to do it in seventy. She has letters to steamship officials at every point requesting them to do all they can to get her on. Have you any letters?"

"Only one, from the agent of the P&O, requesting the captains of their boats to be good to me because I am traveling alone. That is all," I said with a little smile.

"Well, it's too bad; but I think you have lost it. There is no chance for you. You will lose five days here and five in Yokohama, and you are sure to have a slow trip across at this season.

Just then a young man, with the softest black eyes and a clear pale complexion, came into the office. The agent, Mr. Harmon, introduced him to me as Mr. [Fred W.] Fuhrmann, the purser of the *Oceanic*, the ship on which I would eventually travel to Japan and America. The young man took my hand in a firm, strong clasp, and his soft black eyes gave me such a look of sympathy that it only needed his kind tone to cheer me into a happier state.

"I went down to the *Oriental* to meet you; Mr.

Harmon thought it was better. We want to take good care of you now that you are in our charge, but, unfortunately, I missed you. I returned to the hotel, and as they knew nothing about you there, I came here, fearing that you were lost."

"I have found kind friends everywhere," I said, with a slight motion towards the doctor, who was speechless over the ill-luck that had befallen me. "I am sorry to have been so much trouble to you."

"Trouble! You are with your own people now, and we are only too happy if we can be of service," he said kindly. "You must not mind about the possibility of someone getting around the world in less time than you may do it. You have had the worst connections it is possible to make, and everybody knows the idea originated with you and that others are merely trying to steal the work of your brain, so, whether you get in before or later, people will give you the credit of having originated the idea."

"I promised my editor that I would go around the world in seventy-five days, and if I accomplish that, I shall be satisfied," I stiffly explained. "I am not racing with anyone. I would not race. If someone else wants to do the trip in less time, that is their concern. If they take it upon themselves to race *against* me, it is their lookout that they succeed. I am not racing. I promised to do the trip in seventy-five days, and I will do it; although had I been permitted to make the trip when I first proposed it over a year ago, I should then have done it in sixty days."

We returned to the hotel, where a room had been secured for me, after arranging the transfer of my luggage and the monkey from the *Oriental* to the *Oceanic*.

Having but the one dress, I refused to attend any dinners or receptions that were proposed in my honor. During the afternoon, the wife of a prominent Hong Kong gentleman waited upon me to place herself and her home at my disposal. She was anxious that I should make her home mine during my stay, but I told her I could not think of accepting her kindness because I would wish to be out most of the time and could not make my hours conform to the hours of the house and still feel free to go, come, and stay as I pleased. Despite her pleadings, I assured her I was not on pleasure bent, but business, and I considered it my duty to refrain from social pleasures, devoting myself to things that lay more in the line of work.

I had dinner on the *Oriental*. As I bade the captain and his officers farewell, remembering their kindness to me, I had a wild desire to cling to them, knowing that with the morning light, the *Oriental* would sail and I would be once again alone in strange lands with strange people.

It is said people do not grow old in Hong Kong. Their youthful looks bear ample testimony to the statement. I asked the reason why, and they said it is because they are compelled to invent amusements for themselves, and, by inventing, they find, not time to grow blasé, but youth and happiness.

The theater in Hong Kong knows few professional troupes, but the amateur actors in the English colony leave little to be desired in the way of splendid entertainments. I went one night to see *Ali Baba and the Forty Thieves* as given by the Amateur Dramatic Club of Hong Kong. It was a new version of the old story filled with local hits arranged for the club by a military captain; the music was by the bandmaster of the Argyll and Sutherland Highlanders. The beautiful and artistic scenery was designed and executed by two army men, as were the limelight effects.

Inside, the scene was bewitching. A rustling of soft gowns, the odor of flowers, the fluttering of fans, the sounds of soft, happy whispering, a maze of lovely women in evening gowns mingling with handsome men in the regulation evening dress—what could be prettier? If American women would only ape the English in going bonnetless to the theaters, we would forgive their little aping in other respects, and call it even. Upon the arrival of the governor the band played "God Save the Queen," during which the audience stood.

Afterwards, the sight of handsomely dressed women stepping into their chairs, the daintily colored Chinese lanterns, hanging fore and aft, marking the course the carriers took in the darkness, was very oriental and affective. It is a luxury to have a carriage, of course, but there is something even more luxurious in the thought of owning a chair and carriers. Every member of a well-established household in Hong Kong has his or her own private chair. Many men prefer a coverless willow chair with swinging step, while many women have chairs that close entirely so they can be carried along the streets secure against the gaze of the public. Convenient pockets, umbrella stands, and places for parcels are found in all well-appointed chairs.

At every port I touched, I found so many bachelors, men of position, means, and good appearance that I naturally began to wonder why women do not flock that way. It was all very well some years ago to say, "Go West, young man," but I would say, "Girls, go East!" There are bachelors enough and to spare! And a most happy time do these bachelors have in the East. They are handsome, jolly, and good-natured. They have their own fine homes with no one but the servants to look after them. Think of it, and let me whisper, "Girls, go East!"

The second day after my arrival, Captain Smith, of the *Oceanic,* called upon me. I expected to see a hard-faced old man; so, when I went into the drawing room and a youthful, good-looking man, with the softest blue eyes that seemed to have caught a tinge of the ocean's blue on a bright day, smiled down at me, I imagine I must have looked very stupid indeed. "You were so different to what I imagined you would be," I said afterwards, when we talked over our first meeting.

"And I could not believe you were the right girl, you were so unlike what I had been led to believe," he said, with a laugh, in a burst of confidence. "I was told that you were an old maid with a dreadful temper. Such horrible things were said about you that I was hoping you would miss our ship. I said if you did come, I supposed you would expect to sit at my table, but I would arrange so you should be placed elsewhere."

The captain took me out to see "Happy Valley" that day before we separated. In jinrickshas we rode by the parade and cricket grounds where some lively games are played, the city hall, and the solid, unornamented barracks; along smooth, tree-lined roads, out to where the mountains make a nest of one level, green space. This level has been converted into a racecourse. The judges' stand was an ordinary, commonplace racecourse stand, but the stands erected by and for private families were built of palms and were more pleasing because they were out of the usual.

During the month of February, races are held here annually. They last three days, and during that period, everybody stops work, rich and poor alike

Happy Valley Race Course and Cemetery in Hong Kong

flocking to the racecourse. They race with native-bred Mongolian ponies, having no horses, and the racing is pronounced most exciting and interesting.

"Happy Valley" lines the hillside. There are congregated the graveyards of all the different sects and nationalities in Hong Kong. The Fire Worshipers lie in ground joining the Presbyterians, the Episcopalians, the Methodists, and the Catholics, and Mohammedans are just as close by. That those of different faiths should consent to place their dead together in this lovely tropical valley is enough to give it the name of Happy Valley, if its beauty did not do as much. In my estimation it rivals in beauty the public gardens, and visitors use it as a park. One wanders along the walks looking at the beautiful shrubs and flowers, never heeding that they are in the valley of death, so thoroughly is it robbed of all that is horrible about graveyards.

We rode back to town through the crowded districts, where the natives huddle together in all their filth. It is said that over one hundred thousand people live within a certain district in Hong Kong not exceeding one-half square mile, and they furthermore positively affirm that sixteen hundred people live in the space of an acre. This is a sample of the manner in which the Chinese huddle together. They remind me of a crowd of ants on a lump of sugar. An effort is being made in Hong Kong to compel owners to build differently so as to make the huddling and packing impossible, for the filth that goes with it invariably breeds disease.

Queen's Road is interesting to all visitors. In it is the Hong Kong Club, where the bachelors are to be found, the post office, and greater than all, the Chinese shops. The shops are not large, but the walls are lined with black-wood cabinets, and one feels a little thrill of pleasure at the sight of the gold, the silver, ivory carvings, exquisite fans, painted scrolls; and the odor of the lovely sandalwood boxes coming faintly to the visitor creates a feeling of greed. One wants them all—everything.

The Chinese merchants cordially show their goods or follow as one strolls around, never urging one to buy, but cunningly bringing to the front the most beautiful and expensive part of their stock.

"*Chin chin*," which means "Good day," Goodbye," "Good night," "How are you?," or anything one may take from it, is the greeting of Chinamen. They all speak mongrel English, called "pidgin" or "pigeon" English. It is impossible to make them understand pure English, consequently Europeans, even housekeepers, use pidgin English when addressing the servants. The servants are men, with the exception of the nurses, and possibly the cooks.

While strolling about the Chinese localities, seeing shops more worthy a visit, being more truly Chinese, I came upon an eating house, from which a conglomeration of strange odors strolled out and down the road. Built around a table in the middle of the room was a circular bench. The diners perched on this bench like chickens on a fence, not letting their feet touch the floor, or hang over, nor "hunkering" down, nor squatting crossed-legged like a Turk or tailor, but sitting down with their knees drawn up until knees and chin met; they held large bowls against their chins, pushing the rice energetically with their chopsticks into their mouths. Cup after cup of tea is consumed, not only at meals, but at all hours during the day. The cup is quite small and saucerless, and the tea is always drank minus sugar and cream.

Professional writers, found in nooks and recesses of prominent thoroughfares, are interesting personalities. Besides writing letters for people, they tell fortunes, and their patrons never go away without having their fates foretold. I noticed when paying for articles, merchants invariably weigh the money. It is also customary for merchants to put their private stamp upon silver dollars as an assurance of its legality and worth. Much silver is beaten into such strange shapes by this queer practice that at first I was afraid to accept it in change.

I saw a marriage procession in Hong Kong. A large band of musicians, who succeeded in making themselves heard, were followed by coolies carrying curious-looking objects in blue and gilt, which, I was told, represent mythical and historical scenes. A

Peak Tramway, Hongkong.　　　　H. 16

The tramway to the Hong Kong European neighborhood on Victoria Peak

number of very elegant Chinese lanterns and gorgeous-looking banners were also carried along. I was told that in such processions, they carry roast pig to the temples of the josses, but it is afterwards very sensibly carried off by the participants.

It would be a hopeless thing for a man to go to Hong Kong in search of employment. The banking and shipping houses, controlled by Europeans, certainly employ numbers of men, but they are brought from England under three- and five-years' contracts. When a vacancy occurs from a death or a transfer, the business house immediately consults its representatives in London, where another man signs an agreement and comes out to Hong Kong to work.

One day I went up to Victoria Peak, named in honor of the queen. It is said to be 1,800 feet high, the highest point on the island. An elevated tramway is built from the town to Victoria Gap, 1,100 feet above the sea. It was opened in 1887. Before that time, people were carried up in sedans.

The first year after its completion 148,344 passengers were carried up the mountainside. The fare is thirty cents up and fifteen cents down. During the summer months, Hong Kong is so hot that those who are in a position to do so seek the mountain top, where a breeze lives all the year round. Level places for buildings are obtained by blasting, and every brick, stone, and bit of household furniture is carried by coolies from the town up to the height of 1,600 feet.

At the gap we secured sedan chairs and were carried to the Hotel Craigieburn, which is managed by a colored man. The hotel—Oriental in style—is very liberally patronized by the citizens of Hong Kong, as well as visitors. After the proprietor had shown us over the hotel and given us a dinner that could not be surpassed, we were carried to Victoria Peak. It required three men to a chair ascending the peak. At the Umbrella Seat, merely a bench with a peaked roof, everybody stops long enough to allow the coolies to rest; then we continue on our way, passing sightseers and nurses with children. After a while, they stop again, and we travel on foot to the signal station.

The view is superb. The bay, in a breastwork of mountains, lies calm and serene, dotted with hundreds of ships that seem like tiny toys. The palatial white houses come halfway up the mountainside, beginning at the edge of the glassy bay. Every house we notice has a tennis court blasted out of the mountainside. They say that after night, the view from the peak is unsurpassed.

Early one morning a gentleman, who was the proud possessor of a team of ponies, the finest in Hong Kong, called at the hotel to take me for a drive. In a low, easy phaeton [open carriage] behind the spirited ponies that seem like playthings in their smallness but giants in their strength, we whirled along through the town and were soon on the road edging the bay. We had a good view of the beautiful dry dock on the other side, which is constructed entirely of granite and is said to be of such size that it can take in the largest vessels afloat. I thought there were other things more interesting, so I refused to go over to it.

During our drive, we visited two quaint and dirty temples. One was a plain little affair with a gaudy altar. The stone steps leading to it were filled with beggars of all sizes, shapes, diseases, and conditions of filth. They were so repulsive that instead of appealing to one's sympathy, they only succeed in arousing one's disgust.

At another temple, nearby a public laundry where the washers stood in a shallow stream slapping the clothes on flat stones, was a quaint temple hewed, cave-like, in the side of an enormous rock. A selvage of rock formed the altar, and to that humble but picturesque temple, Chinese women flock to pray for sons to be born unto them that they may have someone to support them in their old age.

After seeing everything of interest in Hong Kong, I decided to go to a real simon-pure [authentic] Chinese city. I knew we were trying to keep the Chinamen out of America, so I decided to see all of them I could while in their land. Pay them a farewell visit, as it were! So, on Christmas Eve, I started for the city of Canton [Guangzhou].

*   *   *

THE O&O AGENT escorted me to the ship *Powan*, on which I was to travel to Canton. He gave me in charge of Captain Grogan, the *Powan*'s commander, an American, who has lived for years in China. A very bashful man he was, but a most kindly, pleasant one.

Soon after we left, night descended. I went on deck, where everything was buried in darkness. Softly and steadily the boat swam on, the only sound—and the most refreshing and restful sound in the world—was the lapping of the water.

To sit on a quiet deck, to have a starlit sky the only light above or about, to hear the water kissing the prow of the ship, is, to me, paradise. They can talk of the companionship of men, the splendor of the sun, the softness of moonlight, the beauty of music, but give me a willow chair on a quiet deck, the world with its worries and noise and prejudices lost in distance, the glare of the sun, the cold light of the moon blotted out by the dense blackness of night. Let me rest rocked gently by the rolling sea, in a nest of velvety darkness, my only light the soft twinkling of the myriads of stars in the quiet sky above; my music, the round of the kissing waters, cooling the brain and easing the pulse; my companionship, dreaming my own dreams. Give me that, and I have happiness in its perfection.

But away with dreams. This is a workaday world, and I am racing Time around it. After dinner, when the boat anchored, waiting for the tide which was to carry us safely over the bar, I went below to see the Chinese passengers. They were gambling, smoking opium, sleeping, cooking, eating, reading, and talking, all huddled together on one deck, which was in one large room, not divided into cabins. They carry their own beds, a bit of matting, and their own food, little else than rice and tea.

Before daybreak we anchored at Canton. The Chinamen went ashore the moment we landed, but the other passengers remained for breakfast.

While we were having breakfast, the guide whom the captain had secured for us came on board and quietly supervised the luncheon we were to take with us. A very clever fellow was that guide, Ah Cum. The first thing he said to us was "A Merry Christmas!" and as it had even slipped our minds, I know we all appreciated the polite thoughtfulness of our Chinese guide. Ah Cum told me later that he had been educated in an American mission located in Canton, but he assured me, with great earnestness, that English was all he learned. He would have none of the Christian religion. Ah Cum's son was

Shameen   European Settlement in Canton with part of the Church.

The Western settlement of Shamian (Shameen) in Canton

also educated in an American mission, and, like his father, has put his learning to good account. Besides being paid as guide, Ah Cum collects a percentage from merchants for all the goods bought by tourists. Of course the tourists pay higher prices than they would otherwise, and Ah Cum sees they visit no shops where he is not paid his little fee.

Ah Cum is more comely in features than most Mongolians, his nose being more shapely and his eyes less slit-like than those of most of his race. He had on his feet beaded black shoes with white soles. His navy blue trousers, or tights, more properly speaking, were tied around the ankle and fitted very tight over most of the leg. Over this he wore a blue, stiffly starched shirt-shaped garment, which reached his heels, while over this he wore a short padded and quilted silk jacket, somewhat similar to a smoking jacket. His long, coal-black queue, finished with a tassel of black silk, touched his heels, and on the spot where the queue began rested a round black turban.

Ah Cum had chairs ready for us. His chair was a neat arrangement in black, black silk hangings, tassels, fringe, and black wood poles finished with brass knobs. Once in it, he closed it and was hidden from the gaze of the public. Our plain willow chairs had ordinary covers, which, to my mind, rather interfered with sightseeing. We had three coolies to each chair. Those with us were barefooted, with tousled pigtail and navy-blue shirts and trousers, much the worse for wear both in cleanliness and quality. Ah Cum's coolies wore white linen garments, gaily trimmed with broad bands of red cloth, looking very much like a circus clown's costume.

Ah Cum led the way, our coolies following. For a time I was only conscious of a confused mass of black faces and long pigtails, though shortly I became accustomed to it and was able to distinguish different objects along the crowded thoroughfare, could note the different stands and the curious looks of the people. We were carried along dark and dirty narrow ways, in and about fish stands, whence odors drifted, filling me with disgust, until we crossed a bridge which spanned a dark and sluggish stream.

This little island, guarded at every entrance, is Shamian, or Sandy Face, the land set aside for the habitation of Europeans. An unchangeable law prohibits Celestials from crossing into this sacred precinct because of the hatred they cherish for Europeans. Shamian is green and picturesque, with handsome houses of Oriental design, and grand shade trees, and wide, velvety green roads, broken only by a single path, made by the bare feet of the chair carriers.

Here, for the first time since leaving New York, I saw the stars and stripes. It was floating over the gateway to the American Consulate. It is a strange fact that the farther one goes from home, the more

218

loyal one becomes. I felt I was a long ways off from my own dear land; it was Christmas Day, and I had seen many different flags since last I gazed upon our own. The moment I saw it floating there in the soft, lazy breeze, I took off my cap and said: "That is the most beautiful flag in the world, and I am ready to whip anyone who says it isn't."

No one said a word. Everybody was afraid! I saw an Englishman in the party glance furtively towards the Union Jack, which was floating over the English Consulate, but in a hesitating manner, as if he feared to let me see.

Consul [Charles] Seymour received our little party with a cheery welcome. He was anxious that we should partake of his hospitality, but we assured him our limited time only gave us a moment to pay our respects, and then we must be off again.

Mr. Seymour was an editor before he went to China with his wife and only daughter, to be consul. Since then, he has conceived a hobby for embroideries and carved ivories, which he is able to ride to the top of his bent in Canton. When tourists go there, he always knows someplace where he can guide them to bargains. Mr. Seymour is a most pleasant, agreeable man, and a general favorite. It is to be hoped that he will long have a residence in Shamian, where he reflects credit upon the American Consulate.

What a different picture Canton presents to

Shamian. They say there are millions of people in Canton. The streets, many of which are roughly paved with stone, seem little over a yard in width. The shops, with their gaily colored and handsomely carved signs, are all open, as if the whole end facing the street had been blown out. In the rear of every shop is an altar, gay in color and often expensive in adornment. As we were carried along the roads, we could see not only the usually rich and enticing wares, but the sellers and buyers. Every shop has a bookkeeper's desk near the entrance. The bookkeepers all wear tortoise-shell-rimmed glasses of an enormous size, which lend them a look of tremendous wisdom. I was inclined to think the glasses were a mark of office, for I never saw a man employed in clerical work without them.

I was warned not to be surprised if the Chinamen should stone me while I was in Canton. I was told that Chinese women usually spat in the faces of female tourists when the opportunity offered. However, I had no trouble. The Chinese are not pleasant-appearing people; they usually look as if life had given them nothing but trouble; but as we were carried along, the men in the stores would rush out to look at me. They did not take any interest in the men with me but gazed at me as if I was something new. They showed no sign of animosity, but the few women I met looked as curiously at me, and less kindly.

A street in Canton

The thing that seemed to interest the people most about me were my gloves. Sometimes they would make bold enough to touch them, and they would always gaze upon them with looks of wonder.

The streets are so narrow that I thought at first I was being carried through the aisles of some great market. It is impossible to see the sky, owing to the signs and other decorations, and the compactness of the buildings; and with the open shops, just like stands in a market, except that they are not even cut off from the passing crowd by a counter, the delusion is a very natural one. When Ah Cum told me that I was not in a market house, but in the streets of the city of Canton, my astonishment knew no limit.

I was very anxious to see the execution ground, so we were carried there. We went in through a gate where a stand erected for gambling was surrounded by a crowd of filthy people. Some few idle ones left it to saunter lazily after us. The place is very unlike what one would naturally suppose it to be. At first sight it looked like a crooked back alley in a country town. There were several rows of half-dried pottery. A woman, who was molding in a shed at one side, stopped her work to gossip about us with another female who had been arranging the pottery in rows. The place is probably seventy-five feet long by twenty-five wide at the front, and narrowing down at the other end. I noticed the ground in one place was very red, and when I asked Ah Cum about it, he said indifferently, as he kicked the red-colored earth with his white-soled shoe: "It's blood. Eleven men were beheaded here yesterday."

He added that it was an ordinary thing for ten to twenty criminals to be executed at one time. The average number per annum is something like four hundred. The guide also told us that in one year, 1855, over fifty thousand rebels were beheaded in this narrow alley.

While he was talking, I noticed some roughly fashioned wooden crosses leaned up against the high stone wall, and supposing they were used in some manner for religious purposes before and during the executions, I asked Ah Cum about them. A shiver waggled down my spinal cord when he answered: "When women are condemned to death in China, they are bound to wooden crosses and cut to pieces. Men are beheaded with one stroke unless they are the worst kind of criminals," the guide added; "then they are given the death of a woman to make it the more discreditable."

I went to the jail and was surprised to see all the doors open. The doors were rather narrow, and when I got inside and saw all the prisoners with thick, heavy boards fastened about their necks, I no longer felt surprised at the doors being unbarred. There was no need of locking them.

I went to the court, a large, square, stone-paved

building. In a small room off one side, I was presented to some judges who were lounging about smoking opium! In still another room, I met others playing fan-tan! While I was there, they brought in two men who had been caught stealing. The thieves were chained with their knees meeting their chins, and in that distressing position were carried in baskets suspended on a pole between two coolies. The judges explained to me that as these offenders had been caught in the very act of taking what belonged not to them, their hands would be spread upon flat stones, and with smaller stones every bone in their hands would be broken. Afterwards they would be sent to the hospital to be cured.

Canton is noted for its many curious and interesting temples. There are over eight hundred temples in the city. The most interesting one I saw during my flying trip was the Temple of the Five Hundred Gods. While there, the guide asked me if I was superstitious, and upon my answering in the affirmative, he said he would show me how to try my luck. Placing some joss sticks in a copper jar before the luck-god, he took from the table two pieces of wood, worn smooth and dirty from frequent use, which, placed together, were not unlike a pear in shape. With this wood—he called it the "luck pigeon"—held with the flat sides together, he made circling motions over the smoldering joss sticks, once, twice, thrice, and dropped the luck pigeon to the floor. He explained if one side of the luck pigeon turned up and the other turned down, it meant good luck, while if they both fell in the same position, it meant bad luck. When he dropped it, they both turned the one way, and he knew he would have bad luck.

I took the luck pigeon then, and I was so superstitious that my arm trembled and my heart beat in little palpitating jumps as I made the motions over the burning joss sticks. I dropped the wood to the floor, and one piece turned one way and one the other, and I was perfectly happy. I knew I was going to have good luck.

I saw the Examination Hall, where there are accommodations for the simultaneous examination of 11,616 Celestial students, all male. We went to the entrance gate through a dirty park-like space where a few stunted trees grew feebly and a number of thin, black pigs rooted energetically. The open space is the principal entrance, then we go through a small gate called the gate of Equity, and later still another called the Dragon gate, which leads into the great avenue. A most strange and curious sight this avenue gives. An open space with a tower on the end, known as the watch tower, has a god of literature in the second story. On each side of the open green space are rows of whitewashed buildings, not unlike railway cattle yards in appearance. In these ranges of cells, cells that measure 5½ by 3 feet, 11,616 pigtailed students undergo their written examination. On the sides facing the avenue are Chinese inscriptions showing what study is examined in that range. In each cell is a board to sit on, and one a little higher for a desk. This roughly improvised desk must be slid out to allow the student to enter or depart unless he crawls under or jumps over. The same tests are given to all at daylight, and very often when essays are not finished at night, the students are kept overnight in their cells. The Hall is about 1,380 feet long by 650 feet wide, and is really a strangely interesting place well worth a visit. It is said the examinations are very severe, and from the large number of candidates examined, sometimes only 150 will be passed. The place in which the essays are examined is called the Hall of Auspicious Stars, and the Chinese inscription over the avenue, translated, reads, "The opening heavens circulate literature."

I had a great curiosity to see the leper village, which is commonly supposed to contain hundreds of Chinese lepers. The village consists of numbers of bamboo huts, and the lepers present a sight appalling in its squalor and filth. Ah Cum told us to smoke cigarettes while in the village so that the frightful odors would be less perceptible. He set the example by lighting one, and we all followed his lead. The lepers were simply ghastly in their misery. There are men, women, and children of all ages and conditions. The few filthy rags with which they endeavored to hide their nakedness presented no shape of any garment or any color, so dirty and ragged were they.

As we left the leper city, I was conscious of an inward feeling of emptiness. It was Christmas Day, and I thought with regret of dinner at home, although one of the men in the party said it was about midnight in New York. The guide said there was a building nearby which he wanted to show us, and then we would eat our luncheon. Once within a high wall, we came upon a pretty scene. There was a mournful sheet of water undisturbed by a breath of wind. In the background the branches of low, overhanging trees kissed the still water just where stood some long-legged storks, made so familiar to us by pictures on Chinese fans.

Ah Cum led us to a room which was shut off from the court by a large carved gate. Inside were hardwood chairs and tables. While eating, I heard chanting to the weird, plaintive sound of a tom-tom and a shrill pipe. When I had less appetite and more curiosity, I asked Ah Cum where we were, and he replied: "In the Temple of the Dead." And in the Temple of the Dead I was eating my Christmas luncheon.

It is customary at the death of a person to build a bonfire after night and cast into the fire household articles, such as money boxes, ladies' dressing cases, etc., composed of gilt paper, the priests meanwhile playing upon shrill pipes. They claim the devil which inhabits all bodies leaves the body to save the property of the dead, and once they play him out, he can never re-enter, so souls are saved.

I climbed high and dirty stone steps to the water clock, which, they say, is over five hundred years old and has never run down or been repaired. In little niches in the stone walls were small gods, before them the smoldering joss sticks. The water clock consists of four copper jars, about the size of wooden pails, placed on steps, one above the other. Each one has a spout from which comes a steady drop-drop. In the last and bottom jar is an indicator, very much like a foot rule, which rises with the water, showing the hour. On a blackboard hanging outside, they mark the time for the benefit of the town people. The upper jar is filled once every twenty-four hours, and that is all the attention the clock requires.

On our return to the *Powan*, I found some beautiful presents from Consul Seymour and the cards of a number of Europeans who had called to see me. Suffering from a sick headache, I went to my cabin, and shortly we were on our way to Hong Kong, my visit to Canton on Christmas Day being of the past.

I T IS A BEAUTIFUL SHIP, *like a fine yacht in its spacious commodiousness. Here and there hang canary cages thrilling with song. Narcissus bulbs in bowls are ablow with fluttering white flowers and everywhere are deep-colored jars full of palms and ferns. The space assigned to me is a large, pleasant, white room, from which a great square lifts up outward on the water side, leaving me on intimate terms with the milky, jade-tinted sea. Beneath this window is a broad divan, and here, laved in tepid sea winds and soothed by rippling whispers against the ship's side, I sleep—the languorous, voluptuous sleep of the tropics.*

Yea, verily, life is good in this magnificent equatorial world! Every day brings new marvels and new joys. I go to bed exhaustedly happy and wake up expectantly smiling. Everything pleases, everything amuses me; most of all perhaps the strong British atmosphere in which one finds one's self on board a P&O steamer. I am—with the exception of a charming little old lady from Boston, who after two years of travel in the East has suffered no diminution of her respect for the [Boston] Common and Phillips Brooks[i]—the only woman on the passenger list, so the British atmosphere has a pronounced masculine flavor; but despite even this limitation it is interesting.

The men, from captain to cook, are fine creatures. Their physical vigor is superb—such muscles! Such crisply curled hair! Such clear ruddy skins, white teeth, and turquoise eyes. They are flat-backed and lean-loined; they carry their huge shoulders with a lordly swagger; they possess a divine faith in themselves and in England; and they have such an astonishing collection of accents! No two of them speak alike: the burly bearded giant three places off from me at table speaks with a broad Scotch drawl; the handsome, natty little fourth officer with the black eyes and shy red face who sits opposite, in white duck from head to heel, has a bit of a Yorkshire burr on the tip of his tongue; the Ceylon tea planter talks like a New Yorker; and there are fully a dozen variations more between his accent and that of the tall young blond, whose fashionable Eton and Oxford inflections leave one speechless with awe and admiration of their magnificent eccentricities.

Even the menu is of daily interest, for here I become for the first time familiar with food upon which the folk of the English novels are fed. I learn to know and appreciate the Bath bun and the Scotch scone. I make the greatly-to-be-prized acquaintance of the English meat pie, and I recognize touching manifestations of British loyalty in the sweets christened impartially with appellations of royalty: Victoria jellyroll, Alexandra wafers, and Beatrice tarts. Waterloo pudding is one of our favorite desserts, and other British triumphs and glories adorn the bill of fare from time to time.

. . . Sunday the lascar crew, who have contented

themselves all the week with garments of blue cotton check and red turbans, suddenly bloom and burgeon gardenwise. We are lounging in our bamboo chairs on the wide decks, when this startlingly variegated vision bursts upon us: All the brown feet are bare, but the brown nether limbs are clad airily in Swiss muslin trousers, over which falls to the knee a tunic of the same material striped with fine lines of gold, silver, or scarlet thread and girdled with a vivid-hued sash, this again partly covered with a loose silk waistcoat—pink, green, or blue—glittering with spangles. Brimless hats of red and yellow straw, like inverted flat-bottomed baskets, are wrapped with many scarlet folds, and the boat-swains add one more touch of splendor in their great wrought-silver buttons and yards of silver chain, from which hangs suspended the whistle of their office. I am at first inclined to suspect them of having looted the wardrobe of an odalisque [female harem slave] but am assured it is only the muster for the usual Sunday-morning inspection and their accustomed costume for such occasions. A brief but imposing ceremony, this. The officers exchange their white jackets for blue coats. The doctor solemnly confers with the captain, and those in imperfect hygienic condition stand on one foot in apologetic embarrassment as they catch the piercing and reproachful glance of their commander, who passes ceremoniously down the line accompanied by the entire staff, acknowledging with condescending salute the row of brown hands lifted to the brown brows.

The boatswain sounds his whistle, the ranks are broken, and the affair is over.

We sail through the blue days on a level keel. The sea does not even breathe, but it quivers in the terrible splendors of the noon with undreamable peacock radiances.

Every hour brings us nearer the equator, and on the morning of the 23d of December, we sight Singapore, seventy miles only from the center of heat. The waters of the harbor are curiously banded in broad lines of brilliant violet, green, and blue, each quite distinct and with no fusions of color. Against the skyline everywhere are the feathery heads of palms, and the tremendous riot of verdure upon all the hills is of a vivid, dazzling green. The vegetation is enormous, rampant, violent. Seven hundred years has this City of the Lions stood, but the never-ending battle with tropic nature's lust for disintegration has left it with no monuments of its great age, no venerable buildings to testify to its antiquity. In the twelfth century, Singapore was the capital of the Malayan empire, but in 1824 the British purchased it from the sultan of Johore,[2] scarcely more than a heap of ruins.

Only those who travel to these Eastern ports can form any adequate conception of the ability which has directed English conquest in the Orient. When they bullied the Malayan sultan into selling Singapore, they were apparently acquiring a ruinous and unimportant territory. Today this port is the entrepôt [trading cen-

ter] of Asian commerce, a coaling station for vessels of all countries, a deep, safe harbor for England's own ships and men-of-war, and a point from which she can command both seas. The inhabitants of her Straits Settlements number considerably more than half a million, and the exports and imports are each in value something like £10,000,000 yearly. The United States alone buys there every twelvemonth goods worth more than $4,000,000.

. . . It is very hot. The tall blond, who is grandson of one of the world-famous conquerors of the East, arrays himself in snowy silk and linen and dons a terai hat[3] with a floating scarf; but even in this attire, moisture sparkles on his rosy skin, and his yellow curls cling damply to his brow. The Ceylon tea planter, twenty years' resident in the tropics, is garbed in the ordinary costume of civilization, and apparently suffers no discomfort. Accompanied by these two and the lady from Boston, I go ashore.

Queer little square carriages, made for the most part of Venetian blinds, wait for us, drawn by disconsolate ponies the size of sheep. Conveyance in the East is a constant source of unhappiness to me. I was deprecatory with the jinrikisha men in Japan, I humbled myself before the chair bearers of Hong Kong, and now I go and make an elaborate apology to this wretched little beast before I can reconcile it to my conscience to climb into the gharry, or let him drag me about at a gallop.

One is suddenly aware that the sensory nerves

awake in this heat to marvelous acuteness. The eye seems to expand its iris to great size and be capable of receiving undreamed possibilities of luminosity and hue. The skin grows exquisitely sensitive to the slightest touch—the faintest movement of the air. Numberless fine undercurrents of sound reach the ear, and the sense of smell is so strong that the perfumes of fruit and flowers at a great distance are penetrating as if held in the hand. One smells everything . . . delicious hot scents of vegetation . . . the steaming of the earth . . . and the faint acrid odors of the many sweating bodies of workers in the sun. . . .

The water road is full of folk. Tall Hindus go by leading little cream-white bulls with humped necks, who drag rude carts full of merchandise or fruits— pineapples, mangoes, and coconuts. English officials spin past in dogcarts with barefooted muslin-clad grooms up behind, and wealthy unctuous Chinese merchants bowl about in 'rikishas. Nearly all foot passengers are half or three-quarters naked. It is an open-air museum of superb bronzes, who, when they condescend to clothe themselves at all, drape in statuesque folds about their brown limbs and bodies a few yards of white or crimson cloth, which adorns rather than conceals. Everyone has long hair and wears it twisted up at the nape of the neck; this, with the absence of beards and the general indeterminateness of attire, makes it difficult to distinguish sexes. The lower class of work people are black, shining, and polished as Indian idols.

A bullock cart carrying pineapples in Singapore

At work they wear only a breechcloth, but when evening comes, they catch up a square of creamy transparent stuff, and by a twist or two of the wrist, fold it beautifully and loosely about themselves, and with erect heads tread silently away through the dusk—slender, proud, and mysterious-eyed. The Malays are of an exquisite bronze, gleaming in the sun like burnished gold. They have full silken inky hair, very white teeth, and dress much in draperies of dull-red cotton, which makes them objects delicious to contemplate. Mingled with all these is the ubiquitous Chinaman in a pair of short, loose, blue breeches, his handsome muscular body shining as yellow satin.

We reach the hotel at last, its gloom, its cloistered arcades, and great dark rooms pleasant enough as a *refuge from the sun. The dining room, a great vaulted hall through the center of the building, is level with the earth, paved with stone and without doors, opening upon the veranda through three archways.*

Mine is a huge, dim apartment with a stone floor, opening directly upon the lawn and into the dining room, and has only slight jalousies for doors; but no one peers or intrudes. The bed is an iron frame; the single hard mattress is spread with a sheet, and there are no covers at all. Even the pillow is of straw. My bathroom, a lofty flagged chamber, opens into this one, and contains a big earthenware jar which the coolies fill for me three times a day, and into which I plunge to rid me of the burning heat.

. . . That night I have the most terrible adventure. Immediately I get into bed and blow out the candle, I hear what sounds like some great animal stalking about. I am cold enough now—icy, in fact. . . . What can it be? . . .

They tell me tigers come over from the mainland and carry off on an average one person a day. . . . This is probably a tiger. He could easily push open those blind doors and walk in! . . . He is coming towards the bed with heavy stealthy rustlings. There is not even a sheet to draw up over me. The room is hot, utterly black and still, save for the sound of those feet and the loud banging of my heart against my ribs.

. . . The hotel seems to be dead, so horribly silent it is. Has the tiger eaten everyone else already?

. . . The darkness is of no use; he can see all the better for that; so I will strike a match and at least perish in the light.

. . . As the blue flame on the wick's tip broadens, I meet the gaze of a frightfully large, calm, gray rat who is examining my shoes and stockings with care. He regards me with only very faint interest and goes on with his explorations through all my possessions. He climbs the dressing table and smells critically at my hat and gloves. . . . This is almost as bad as the tiger, but as I have no intention of attacking this terrible beast and my notice appears to bore him, I blow out the candle and go to sleep, leaving him to continue those heavy rustlings which so alarmed me.

We secure an open carriage with two fine bronzes in muslin and turbans on the box, and go for a drive. The blond takes us first to call at a great white airy stone bungalow, set on a hill where resides the chief of police, another English officer clad in white and as brown and lean as are all who have seen long service here. He gives a command in Malay to his khidmutgar [waiter, in India], and we are served with tea in the Chinese fashion. No other English official can equal him in his knowledge of the Malay tongue and character, and for this reason, he is sent to conduct negotiations with the sultan of Johore whenever that potentate grows restless.

From his gates the road turns towards the botanical gardens, a great park where wide red ways wind *through shaven lawns and under enormous blossoming trees. Every plant one knows as exotic is here quite at home—the giant pads of the Victoria regia pave the moats with circles of emerald, and the lotus lifts its rose-flushed cups from glassy pools where swans float in shadow. We leave the carriage and pace through the translucent green twilight of the orchid houses built of wire gauze, the plants needing no protection here, where for six thousand years or so the thermometer has been ranging between seventy-five and ninety-five degrees of heat.*

. . . Half-past four! The ship is about to sail. We have wandered through the shops and museums, and have returned once more to our old quarters. Tiny canoes cluster about the vessel, full of beautiful shells of which one can buy a boatload for a dollar. Other canoes hold small Malays ranging from three to seven years of age, all naked save for the merest rag of a breechcloth, all pretty as little bronze curios, and all shouting in shrill chorus for coins. A few shillings changed into the native currency procures a surprising number of small pieces of money, which we fling into the clear water. They plunge over after these with little splashings like frogs, and wiggle down swiftly to the bottom, growing strange and wavering of outline and ghostly green as they sink. They are wonderfully quick to seize the glinting coin before it touches the sands below, and come up wet, shining, and showing their white teeth. We play at this game until the whistle

blows, and then sail away, leaving the blond waving his handkerchief to us from the shore.

An hour later we are still steaming near the palm-fringed coast. There is a sudden cry and struggle forward—a naked yellow body with manacled hands shoots outward from the ship's side and disappears in a boiling circle of foam. A Chinese prisoner, being transported to Penang, has knocked down his guards and taken to the water. The engines are reversed and a life buoy thrown overboard, but he does not appear. After what seems a great lapse of time, a head shows a long distance away and moves rapidly towards the shore. Evidently he has slipped his handcuffs and can swim. A boat is lowered full of lascars very much excited, commanded by the third officer, a ruddy young fellow—calm and dominant. They pursue the head, but it has covered more than half the distance, some two miles, between us and the shore before it is overtaken. There is some doubling back and forth, an oar is raised in menace, and the fugitive submits to be pulled into the boat. I am standing by the gangway when he returns. He is a fine, well-built young fellow. His crime is forgery, and he is to be turned over to the native authorities against whom he has offended. Their punishments are terrible: prisoners receive no food and must depend upon the memories and mercies of the charitable.

. . . One of the lascars holds him by the queue as he mounts the steps. He is wet and chilled, and has a face

of stolid despair. They take him forward, and I see him no more.

. . . *It is Christmas Day—still very hot; and off to our right are to be seen from time to time the bold purple outlines of the coasts of Sumatra. The ship is decorated with much variegated bunting, and the servants assume an air of languid festivity; but most of us suffer from plaintive reminiscences of home, and nostalgia. There is a splendid plum cake for dinner, with a Santa Claus atop, huddled in sugar furs despite the burning heat. We pull Christmas crackers, as in the holidays at home, and from their contents I am loaded with paste jewels and profusely provided with poetry in brief segments and of an enthusiastically amatory nature.*

. . . *Penang.—Its peaks shoot sharply up into the blue air two thousand feet, wrapped in a tangle of prodigious verdure to their very tops, enormous palm forests fringing all the shore. The ship anchors some distance from the docks and will remain but a few hours. We are ferried to land in crazy sampans, the only alternative from outrigger canoes—a narrow trough set on a round log and kept upright by a smaller floating log connected with the boat by bent poles. Only a native, a tightrope walker, or a bicyclist would trust himself to these.*

A gharry and another pitiful little horse take us towards the gardens and the famous waterfall. The road skirts the town and intersects lagoons, where

Malay houses of coconut thatch stand upon piles like ancient lake dwellings. They live over this stagnant water by preference and apparently suffer no harm. Farther on, where the ground rises, are the huge stone bungalows of English officials and rich Chinese merchants, the entrance to the grounds of the latter adorned with ornate doors and guarded by carved monsters, curiously colored.

We overtake a Chinese funeral winding towards the cemetery, all the mourners clad in white. The coffin, of unpainted wood, is so heavy and so large that twenty pallbearers are required to carry it. It is a most cheerful cortège. No one seems in the least downcast or dispirited by this bereavement—death is accepted by that race with the same stolid philosophy as are the checkered incidents of life.

Our guide, a brown lad of ten, stands on the carriage step, clinging to the door, and chatters fluently in tangled and intricate English, of which he is obviously inordinately vain. At the garden entrance he makes us dismount, vehicles not being allowed inside, and leads us along the broad, beautifully tended paths. The garden lies between two very lofty cone-shaped peaks and is as well kept and full of tropical blossoms and verdure as are all the others we have seen. The boy stops to show me in the grass tiny fronds of the sensitive plant, that shudder away from his rude little finger with a voluntary movement startling to see in a plant.

The waterfall in the Botanical Gardens, Penang, Malaya

We hear the rushing speech of waters calling loudly in the hills but see nothing save the mountain's garments of opulent verdure. A path zigzags sharply upward through the trees and vine labyrinth, and by this the boy leads the way with the speed and agility of a goat. We pant along in his wake, barely keeping him in sight.

It is frightfully hot in here among the trees. The atmosphere is a steam bath, and the moisture pours down our faces as we spring from stone to stone and corkscrew back and forth, deafened by the vociferations of the fall but catching no glimpse of it. Exhausted, gasping, streaming with perspiration, we finally emerge upon a plateau high on the peak's side and are suddenly laved in that warm wind that stirred the palm fronds. . . . At our feet is a wide, quivering green pool, crossed by a frail bridge; from far above leaps down to us a flood of glittering silver that dashes the emerald pool into powdery foam, races away under the bridge, and springs again with a shout into the thickets below. We lose sight of it amid the leaves but can hear its voice as it leaps from ledge to ledge down to the valley and is silenced at last in the river.

A tiny shrine built here at the side of this first pool is tended by a thin melancholy-eyed young priest, who lives alone at this great height, his only companions the ceaseless bruit of the waters and the little black elephant-headed god in the shrine. He bears a spot of dried clay upon his forehead—a token of humility. At

243

his morning devotions, he dips his hand in the water, then in the dust, touches it upon his brow, and wears this sign of submission all day. I lay a piece of money upon the altar and in return am given a handful of pale, perfumed pink bells that grow upon the mountainside and are the only sacrifice offered to the little black god. The priest will have me remove my hat and decorate my hair with the flowers in the fashion in which his countrywomen wear them and is pleased when I comply.

. . . Back again through the steaming woods and the palm aisles; then the ship once more, and our faces are turned toward Ceylon.

NOTES

1. Phillips Brooks (1835–93): Episcopal priest, later bishop, and rector of Boston's Trinity Church (1869–91).

2. In 1819, the British East India Company, represented by Sir Stamford Raffles (1781-1826), signed an agreement that paid the sultan of Johore for the right to establish a British trading post on Singapore. In 1824, the Anglo-Dutch Treaty divided the country into two spheres of influence, British and Dutch.

3. Terai hat: a broad-brimmed felt hat with ventilation for use in a tropical climate.

STAGE SIX

BLY: JAPAN

SHORTLY AFTER MY RETURN to Hong Kong, I sailed for Japan on the *Oceanic*. A number of friends, who had contributed so much towards my pleasure and comfort during my stay in British China, came to the ship to say farewell, and most regretfully did I take leave of them. Captain Smith took us into his cabin, where we all touched glasses and wished one another success, happiness, and the other good things of this earth. The last moment having come, the final goodbye being said, we parted, and I was started on my way to the land of the mikado.

The *Oceanic*, on which I traveled from Hong Kong to San Francisco, has quite a history. When it was designed and launched twenty years ago by Mr. Harland, of Belfast, it startled the shipping world. The designer was the first to introduce improvements for the comfort of passengers, such as the saloon amidships, avoiding the noise of the engines and especially the racing of the screw [propeller] in rough weather. Before that time, ships were gloomy and somber in appearance and constructed without a thought of the happiness of passengers. Mr. Harland, in the *Oceanic,* was the first to provide a promenade deck and to give the saloon and staterooms a light and cheerful appearance. In fact, the *Oceanic* was such a new departure that it aroused

245

the jealousy of other ship companies and was actually condemned by them as unseaworthy. It is said that so great was the outcry against the ship that sailors and firemen were given extra prices to induce them to make the first trip.

Instead of being the predicted failure, the *Oceanic* proved a great success. She became the greyhound of the Atlantic, afterwards being transferred to the Pacific in 1875. She is the favorite ship of the O&O line, making her voyages with speed and regularity. She retains a look of positive newness and seems to grow younger with years. In November 1889, she made the fastest trip on record between Yokohama and San Francisco. No expense is spared to make this ship comfortable for the passengers. The catering would be hard to excel by even a first-class hotel. Passengers are accorded every liberty, and the officers do their utmost to make their guests feel at home, so that in the Orient the *Oceanic* is the favorite ship, and people wait for months so as to travel on her.

When I first went to the ship, the monkey had been transferred from the *Oriental*. Meeting the stewardess, I asked how the monkey was, to which she replied dryly: "We have met." She had her arm bandaged from the wrist to the shoulder!

"What did you do?" I asked in consternation.

"I did nothing but scream; the monkey did the rest!" she replied.

I spent New Year's Eve between Hong Kong and Yokohama. The day had been so warm that we wore no wraps. In the forepart of the evening, the passengers sat together in Social Hall talking, telling stories, and laughing at them. The captain owned an organette[1] which he brought into the hall, and he and the doctor took turns at grinding out the music. Later in the evening, we went to the dining hall, where the purser had punch and champagne and oysters for us, a rare treat which he had prepared in America just for this occasion.

When eight bells rang, we rose and sang "Auld Lang Syne" with glasses in hand, and on the last echo of the good old song, toasted the death of the old year and the birth of the new. We shook hands around, each wishing the other a happy New Year; 1889 was ended, and 1890, with its pleasures and pains, began.

* * *

AFTER SEEING HONG KONG with its wharfs crowded with dirty boats manned by still dirtier people, and its streets packed with a filthy crowd, Yokohama has a cleaned-up Sunday appearance. Travelers are taken from the ships, which anchor some distance out in the bay, to the land in small steam launches. The first-class hotels in the different ports have their individual launches, but like American hotel omnibuses, while being run by the hotel to assist in procuring patrons, the traveler pays for them just the same.

An import as well as an export duty is charged in Japan, but we passed the custom inspectors unmolested. I found the Japanese jinricksha men a gratifying improvement upon those I had seen from Ceylon to China. They presented no sight of filthy rags, nor naked bodies, nor smell of grease. Clad in neat navy-blue garments, their little pudgy legs encased in unwrinkled tights; the upper half of their bodies in short jackets with wide flowing sleeves; their clean, good-natured faces, peeping from beneath comical mushroom-shaped hats; their blue-black, wiry locks cropped just above the nape of the neck, they offered a striking contrast to the jinricksha men of other countries. Their crests were embroidered upon the back and sleeves of their top garment as are the crests of every man, woman, and child in Japan.

Rain the night previous had left the streets muddy and the air cool and crisp, but the sun creeping through the mistiness of early morning fell upon us with most gratifying warmth. Wrapping our knees with rugs, the 'ricksha men started off in a lively trot to the Pacific Mail[2] and O&O Companies' office, where I met discourteous people for the first time since I left the P&O *Victoria*. And these were Americans, too. The most generous excuse that can be offered for them is that they have held their positions so long that they feel they are masters, instead of a steamship company's servants.

I stayed at the Grand Hotel while in Japan. It is a large building, with long verandas, wide halls, and airy rooms, commanding an exquisite view of the lake in front. Barring an enormous and monotonous collection of rats, the Grand would be considered a good hotel even in America. The food is splendid and the service excellent. The "Japs," noiseless, swift, anxious to please, stand at the head of all the servants I encountered from New York to New York; and then they look so neat in their blue tights and white linen jackets.

If I loved and married, I would say to my mate: "Come, I know where Eden is," and like Edwin Arnold,[3] desert the land of my birth for Japan, the land of love—beauty—poetry—cleanliness. Japan is beautiful. Its women are charmingly sweet. I know little about the men except that they do not go far as we judge manly beauty, being undersized, dark, and far from prepossessing. They have the reputation of being extremely clever, so I do not speak of them as a whole, only of those I came in contact with. I saw one, a giant in frame, a god in features; but he was a public wrestler.

The majority of the Europeans live on the bluff in low white bungalows, with great rooms and breezy verandas, built in the hearts of Oriental gardens, where one can have an unsurpassed view of the Mississippi Bay,[4] or can play tennis or cricket, or loll in hammocks, guarded from public gaze by luxurious green hedges. The Japanese homes form a great contrast to the bungalows. They are daintily small, like play houses indeed, built of a thin shingle-like board, fine in texture. Chimneys and fireplaces are unknown. The first wall is set back, allowing the upper floor and side walls to extend over the lower flooring, making it a portico built in instead of on the house. Light window frames, with their minute openings covered with fine rice paper instead of glass, are the doors and windows in one. They do not swing open and shut as do our doors, nor do they move up and down like our windows, but slide like rolling doors. They form the partitions of the houses inside and can be removed at any time, throwing the floor into one room.

In the cool of the evening, we went to a house that had been specially engaged, to see the dancing, or geisha, girls. At the door we saw all the wooden shoes of the household, and we were asked to take off our shoes before entering, a proceeding rather disliked by some of the party, who refused absolutely to do as requested. We effected a compromise, however, by putting cloth slippers over our shoes. The second floor had been converted into one room, with nothing in it except the matting covering the floor and a Japanese screen here and

Japanese dancing girls

there. We sat upon the floor, for chairs there are none in Japan, but the exquisite matting is padded until it is as soft as velvet. It was laughable to see us trying to sit down, and yet more so to see us endeavor to find a posture of ease for our limbs. We were about as graceful as an elephant dancing. A smiling woman in a black kimono set several round and square charcoal boxes containing burning charcoal before us. These are the only Japanese stove. Afterwards, she brought a tray containing a number of long-stemmed pipes—Japanese women smoke constantly—a pot of tea and several small cups.

Impatiently I awaited the geisha girls. In the tiny maidens glided at last, clad in exquisite trailing, angel-sleeved kimonos. The girls bow gracefully, bending down until their heads touch their knees, then, kneeling before us, murmur gently a greeting which sounds like "Koinbanwa!," drawing in their breath with a long, hissing suction, which is a token of great honor. The musicians sat down on the floor and began an alarming din upon samisens, drums, and gongs, singing meanwhile through their pretty noses. If the noses were not so pretty, I am sure the music would be unbearable to one who has ever heard a chest note. The geisha girls stand posed with open fan in hand above their heads, ready to begin the dance. They are very short, with the slenderest of slender waists. Their soft and tender eyes are made blacker by painted lashes and brows; their midnight hair, stiffened with a gummy wash, is most wonderfully dressed in large coils and ornamented with gold and silver flowers and gilt paper pompons. The younger the girl, the more gay is her hair. Their kimonos, of the most exquisite material, trail all around them, and are loosely held together at the waist with an obi sash [wide sash with large flat bow in back]; their long flowing sleeves fall back, showing their dimpled arms and baby hands. Upon their tiny feet they wear cunning white linen socks cut with a place for the great toe. When they go out, they wear wooden sandals. The Japanese are the only women I ever saw who could rouge and powder and be not repulsive, but the more charming because of it. They powder their faces and have a way of reddening their under lip just at the tip that gives them a most tempting look. The lips look like two luxurious cherries.

The musicians begin a long chanting strain, and these bits of beauty begin the dance. With a grace, simply enchanting, they twirl their little fans, sway their dainty bodies in a hundred different poses, each one more intoxicating than the other, all the while looking so childish and shy, with an innocent smile lurking about their lips, dimpling their soft cheeks, and their black eyes twinkling with the pleasure of the dance. After the dance the geisha girls made friends with me, examining, with surprised delight, my dress, my bracelets, my rings, my boots—to them the most wonderful and extraordinary things—my hair, my gloves, indeed they missed very little, and they approved of all. They said I was very sweet and urged me to come again, and in honor of the custom of my land—the Japanese never kiss—they pressed their soft, pouting lips to mine in parting.

Japanese women know nothing whatever of bonnets, and may they never! On rainy days they tie white scarfs over their wonderful hairdressing, but at other times they waddle bareheaded, with fan and umbrella, along the streets on their wooden clogs. They have absolutely no furniture. Their bed is a piece of matting; their pillows, narrow blocks of wood, probably six inches in length, two wide and

Geishas playing stringed instruments

six high. They rest the back of the neck on the velvet-covered top so their wonderful hair remains dressed for weeks at a time. Their tea and pipe always stand beside them so they can partake of their comforts the last thing before sleep and the first thing after.

A Japanese reporter from Tokyo came to interview me, his newspaper having translated and published the story of my visit to Jules Verne. Carefully he read the questions which he wished to ask me. They were written at intervals on long rolls of foolscap, the space to be filled in as I answered. I thought it ridiculous until I returned and became an interviewee. Then I concluded it would be humane for us to adopt the Japanese system of interviewing.

I went to Kamakura to see the great bronze god, the image of Buddha, familiarly called Diabutsu. It stands in a verdant valley at the foot of two mountains. It was built in 1250 by Ono Goroyemon, a famous bronze caster, and is 50 feet in height; it is sitting Japanese style, 98 feet being its waist circumference; the face is 8 feet long, the eye is 4 feet, the ear 6 feet 6½ inches, the nose 3 feet 8½ inches, the mouth is 3 feet 2½ inches, the diameter of the lap is 36 feet, and the circumference of the thumb is over 3 feet. I had my photograph taken sitting on its thumb. We also visited a very pretty temple nearby, saw a famous fan tree and a lotus pond, and spent some time at a most delightful tea house, where two

The thirteenth-century bronze Daibutsu, or Giant Buddha, at Kamakura

little "Jap" girls served us with tea and sweets. I also spent one day at Tokyo, where I saw the mikado's Japanese and European castles, which are enclosed by a fifty-foot stone wall and three wide moats. The people in Tokyo are trying to ape the style of the Europeans. I saw several men in native costume riding bicycles. Their roads are superb. There is a street car line in Tokyo, a novelty in the East, and carriages of all descriptions.

It would fill a large book if I attempted to describe all I saw during my stay in Japan. Going to the great Shiba temple, I saw a forest of superb trees. At the carved gate leading to the temple were hundreds of stone and bronze lanterns, which alone were worth a fortune. On either side of the gate were gigantic carved images of ferocious aspect. They were covered with wads of chewed paper. When I remarked that the school children must make very free with the images, a gentleman explained that the Japanese believed if they chewed paper and threw it at these gods and it stuck, their prayers would be answered; if not, their prayers would pass unheeded. A great many prayers must have been answered.

The Japanese are very progressive people. They cling to their religion and their modes of life, which in many ways are superior to ours, but they readily adopt any trade or habit that is an improvement upon their own. Finding the European male attire more serviceable than their native dress for some trades, they promptly adopted it. The women tested the European dress and, finding it barbarously uncomfortable and inartistic, went back to their exquisite kimonos, retaining the use of European underwear, which they found more healthful and comfortable than the utter absence of it, to which they had been accustomed. The best proof of the comfort of kimonos lies in the fact that the European residents have adopted them entirely for indoor wear. Only their long subjection to fashion prevents their wearing them in public.

Japanese patriotism should serve as a model for us careless Americans. No foreigner can go to Japan and monopolize a trade. It is true that a little while ago they were totally ignorant of modern conveniences. They knew nothing of railroads, or streetcars, or engines, or electric lighting. They were too clever though to waste their wits in efforts to rediscover inventions known to other nations, but they had to have them. Straightway they sent to other countries for men who understood the secret of such things and, at fabulous prices and under contracts of three, five, and occasionally ten years' duration, brought them to their land. They were set to work, the work they had been hired to do, and with them toiled steadily and watchfully the cleverest of Japanese. When the contract is up, it is no longer necessary to fill the coffers of a foreigner. The employee was released, and their own man, fully qualified for the work, stepped into the position. And so in this way they command all business in their country.

Kimonos are made in three parts, each part an inch or so longer than the other. I saw a kimono a Japanese woman bought for the holidays. It was a suit, gray silk crepe, with pink peach blossoms dotting it here and there. The whole was lined with the softest pink silk, and the hem, which trails, was thickly padded with a delicate perfume sachet. The underclothing was of the flimsiest white silk. The whole thing cost sixty dollars, a dollar and a half of which paid for the making. Japanese women have mirrors in which they view their numerous charms. Their mirrors are round, highly polished steel plates, and they know nothing whatever of glass mirrors. All the women carry silk card cases in their long sleeves, in which are their own diminutive cards.

English is taught in the Japan schools and so is gracefulness. The girls are taught graceful movements; how to receive, entertain, and part with visitors; how to serve tea and sweets gracefully; and the proper and graceful way to use chopsticks. It is a pretty sight to see a lovely woman use chopsticks. At a tea house or at an ordinary dinner, a long paper laid at one's place contains a pair of chopsticks, probably twelve inches in length, but no thicker than the thinner size of lead pencils. The sticks are

Japanese children

usually whittled in one piece and split only half apart to prove that they have never been used. Every one breaks the sticks apart before eating, and after the meal they are destroyed.

The prettiest sight in Japan, I think, is the native streets in the afternoons. Men, women, and children turn out to play shuttlecock and fly kites. Can you imagine what an enchanting sight it is to see pretty women with cherry lips, black bright eyes, ornamented, glistening hair, exquisitely graceful gowns, tidy white-stockinged feet thrust into wooden sandals, dimpled cheeks, dimpled arms, dimpled baby hands, lovely, innocent, artless, happy, playing shuttlecock in the streets of Yokohama?

Japanese children are unlike any other children I ever saw at play. They always look happy and never seem to quarrel or cry. Little Japanese girls, elevated on wooden sandals and with babies almost as large as themselves tied on their backs, play shuttlecock with an abandon that is terrifying until one grows confident of the fact that they move with as much agility as they could if their little backs were free from nursemaid burdens. Japanese babies are such comical little fellows. They wear such wonderfully padded clothing that they are as shapeless as a feather pillow. Others may think, as I did, that the funny little shaven spots on their heads was a queer style of ornamentation, but it is not. I am assured the spots are shaven to keep their baby heads cool.

The Japanese are not only pretty and artistic but most obliging. A friend of mine who guided us in Japan had a Kodak [camera], and whenever we came upon an interesting group, he was always taking snapshots. No one objected, and especially were the children pleasant about being photographed. When he placed them in position, or asked them to stand as they were, they would pose like little drum majors until he gave them permission to move.

The only regret of my trip, and one I can never cease to deplore, was that in my hasty departure I forgot to take a Kodak. On every ship and at every port I met others—and envied them—with Kodaks. They could photograph everything that pleased them; the light in those lands is excellent, and many were the pleasant mementos of their acquaintances and themselves they carried home on their plates.

The Japanese thoughtfully reserve a trade for their blind. They are all taught massage bathing, and none but the blind are allowed to follow this calling. These people go through the streets uttering to a plaintive melody these words: "I'll give you a bath from head to toe for two cents."

At Uyeno Park, where they point out a tree planted by General Grant when on his tour around the world,[5] I saw a most amusing monkey which belonged to the very interesting menagerie. It was very large and had a scarlet face and gray fur. It was chained to the fence, and when one of the young men in our party went up and talked to him, the monkey looked very sagacious and wise.

In Yokohama, I went to Hundred Steps, at the top of which lives a Japanese belle, Oyuchisan, who is the theme for artist and poet, and the admiration of tourists. One of the pleasant events of my stay was the luncheon given for me on the *Omaha,* the American war vessel lying at Yokohama. I took several drives, enjoying the novelty of having a Japanese running by the horses' heads all the while. I ate rice and eel. I visited the curio shops, one of which is built in imitation of a Japanese house, and was charmed with the exquisite art I saw there; in short, I found nothing but what delighted the finer senses while in Japan.

Bisland: Ceylon

It is a five days' run *from Penang to the island of Ceylon; the ship's company has dwindled to a handful, and time hangs heavily upon us.*

. . . It is eight o'clock in the morning. The ship is anchored off the coast of Ceylon.

We arrived late last night, sailing into the harbor by the light of great tropical stars and the planet gleams of a pharos shining from the tall clock tower of Colombo. Already many ships lie in the narrow roadstead, and it requires the fine art of navigation to slip our boat's huge bulk into her berth between two of these and make her fast to her own particular buoy. The pilot came aboard just outside, and it is his firm hand that jams her nose up to within three hairs' breadth of the vessel in front, holds her there with a grip of iron, and with cautious screw revolutions swings her into line with her heels in the very face of the Australian mail ship—arrived a few hours earlier.

Then the entire passenger list—on deck for the last half-hour, aiding the pilot by holding its breath—sighs relievedly and joyously, and goes below in a body to recuperate on brandy and soda.

. . . I linger a moment in the darkness to smell the fragrance of the night, moved by the vast flowings of a warm, sweet wind. Seafarers of other days told of these perfumes of the Spice Island filling their sails far out at sea, but the coal smoke of the modern ship deadens the

nostril of the modern traveler and fills his heart with naughty doubts of the veracity of the Ancient Mariner.[6]

. . . I am up early to have the first possible view of an island so like to Paradise that Adam was first banished to this place that he might not feel too sharply in the beginning his loss and the contrast. Very like in the early morning looks this island of jewels, of flowers, and palms to the long-lost heavenly gardens. It floats upon a smooth, nacreous waste of waters, under a sky of pale warm violet, veiled in a dawn mist faint and mysterious as dreams. Beyond the massive breakwater of our straitened harbor curve the rims of white beaches frilled with foam, where palms lean over to look at themselves in a sea of green mother-of-pearl. Inland the purple distances rise into lofty outlines deliciously softened and rounded by their enormous garment of verdure. The prospect is very pleasing.

It is very hot. The thermometer even at this hour (it is the last day of December) registers 80°; but it is less oppressive than at Singapore, where one seemed to be breathing tepid water rather than air.

A long wharf juts out into the harbor with a customhouse at its landward end. We pause here to exchange some civilities concerning the weather, and pass on with our luggage unmolested, so soothing and plentiful a lack of curiosity have these officials in British ports.

. . . The soil is red—bright red—the color of ground cinnabar. Not "liver-colored," as the earth seemed to

the ancient Northmen [Norsemen], but deep-tinted as
if soaked with dragon's blood, of which antiquity believed cinnabar to be made. A broad street, fringed
with grass and tulip trees, goes inland, and on either
side are massive white buildings with arched and pil-
lared arcades. . . . The vividness of color here is as-
tounding—brilliant, intense, like the colors of precious
stones. We doubt the evidence of our senses—doubt the
earth can be so red, the sea and sky so blue. . . . It is a
miracle wrought by the ineffable luminosity of the
Eastern day! One's very flesh tingles with an ecstasy of
pleasure in this giant effulgence of color, as might a
musician's who should hear the prodigious vibrations
of some undreamably colossal harp.

   The Grand Oriental Hotel lies to the right of this
road, near the water; big and glaringly white without,
cool and shadowy within. Ships from India, China,
and Australia have just arrived, and the place is
crowded. The clack of many heels rings on the stone
floor of the arcade, which opens upon an inner flowery
court, where also look out the windows of the sleeping-
rooms above, veiled by delicate transparent straw mattings—waving softly in and out in the little hot breezes,
giving treacherous glimpses now and again of a pretty
disheveled head and tumbled white draperies. . . . The
arcade is full of British folk—Australians and Anglo-
Indians, passing to and fro to the dining room, to the
stairs, to the front entrance. Handsome, as an Anglo-
Saxon crowd of the well-to-do is apt to be—tall, florid

*men in crisp white linen and white Indian helmets;
tall, slim, well-poised girls in white muslin, with a
delicious fruit-like pink in their cheeks, brought there
by the heat, which curls their blond hair in damp rings
about their brows and white necks; and tall, imposing
British matrons, with something of the haughtiness of
old Rome in their bearing—the mothers and wives of
conquerors.*

*Our rooms are at the end of a long corridor, looking
on the street. They are carpetless and uncurtained, their
dim twilight being sifted from the burning glare without, through green mattings hung at the windows. Before my door sits my own particular servant, detailed
to wait upon this bedroom. Similar servants are stationed along the corridor in front of their respective
charges. This attendant seems never to go away, for at
whatever hour I need him, he is there. Even at night
he does not desert his post, unrolling a rug and sleeping
where he sat all day. . . . A curious creature—of a sex
not easily to be determined. Mild-browed and woman-
eyed, with long, rippling black hair knotted at the back
and kept smooth with a tortoise-shell band comb, the
brown femininities of his face disappear at the chin in
a short close-curled black beard. He is full-chested as a
budding girl, but clothes himself to the waist in shirt,
coat, and waistcoat, the slender male hips being
wrapped in a white skirt that falls to the ankles.*

*He is, however, an eminently agreeable person. The
gentle and confiding affection of his manner leaves*

The Grand Oriental Hotel, Colombo, Ceylon, exterior

The Grand Oriental Hotel, Colombo, Ceylon, garden and restaurant

speechless with joyful amazement the humbled victim of the harsh and haughty tyranny of the American servant girl. He not only executes orders with noiseless despatch but receives them with a little reverence of the slim fingers to the brow, and a look in his lustrous eyes of such sweet eagerness to serve that my heart is melted within me. I find myself asking for hot water with the coo of a sucking dove; I demand butter at table in the mild tones of a wind harp; and converse with the guide in a manner I might naturally assume to a beloved younger sister. This atmosphere of loving kindness is that of Paradise. It expands the heart with unreflecting happiness, and makes man, even servant man, my brother.

. . . It is the sacred and beautiful hour of tiffin. The dining room is as white, cool, and nobly plain as a Greek temple, long and very lofty—reaching to the roof—the second story opening upon it in an arched and balustraded clerestory. Two punkahs of gold-colored stuff wave above us. On one side we look upon the arcaded court and through the heavy-arched veranda upon the hot gorgeousness of color outside. Bowls of tropical flowers are set on each table, and under the saltcellars and spoons at the corners are laid large leaves of curious lace-like pattern, freaked with splashes of red and yellow. More of the fawn-eyed men with long hair serve us, and the assemblage gathered here for the moment is a remarkable one. Near the door sits a good-looking young man, accompanying a party of blond

girls in smart frocks. It is Wordsworth's[7] *grandson, and
the owner of Rydal Mount. At the table next him is a
stern, lean soldier with a melancholy face—the Lord
Chelmsford in whose African campaign the Prince Imperial was killed and the English suffered a hideous
butchery, surprised by the savages;*[8] *the other side of the
room is a young man with a heavy blond countenance—Dom Leopoldo Agostino and half a dozen
things more, who has just met here, in his voyage round
the world in a Brazilian warship, the news of his
grandfather Dom Pedro's dethronement and exile.*[9] *The
captain of the ship dares not continue the cruise in the
face of peremptory cables from the new government,
and the young man is suddenly marooned here, with
all his luggage and attendants, under the protection of
the British lion, who has always a friendly paw for* les
rois en exil [kings in exile]. *Near us is a man with a
bulging forehead and a badly fitting frock coat of black
broadcloth—a noted mesmerist from America, with a
little Texan wife fantastically gowned; she, poor soul,
having a picturesque instinct, but no technique. Beyond him is a man of middle age, with a fine saturnine
countenance, lean and bold as the head of Caesar, and
an air of great distinction. It is Sir William Robinson,*[10] *an Irishman, a well-known composer, and a colonial governor. Beside him sits Sir Henry Wrenfordsley,*[11]
*a colonial chief justice. At their table is Lady Broome,
a tall, handsome woman with a noble outline of brow
and head. Under the title of Lady Barker, she is the*

author of many well-known and delightful books on life in the Antipodes. Sir Napier Broome[12] *is also tall and handsome and is on his way home from an Australian governorship.*

. . . In the arcade that faces on the street are native shops—tiny cells full of basketwork, wrought brass, laces, jewels; carvings in ivory, ebony, and tortoiseshell; India shawls and silks, Sinhalese silverwork, and such small trinkets and souvenirs best calculated to lure the shy rupee from its lair in the traveler's pocket. Most of these shops are kept by Moormen—large, yellow, unpleasant-looking persons in freckled calico petticoats, heads shaven quite clean and covered with a little red basket too small for the purpose. They inspire carking [troubling] disgust and suspicion by their craven oiliness; their wares for the most part not worth a tenth of the sums asked.

Jewels are to be had at astonishing rates—cat's-eyes and moonstones being sold carelessly by the handful. The arcade is full of itinerant merchants who carry their stock of precious stones—sometimes quite valuable—tied up in a dingy rag, disposing of them by methods of barter quite unique. Twenty times the proper value is demanded, and poignant outcries of bitter astonishment greet the unbelievably meager offer of the sahib,[13] *who should be as father and as mother to the merchant, but who proffers him only an insult. The rag is tied up in wounded amazement half a dozen times before a compromise suggests itself. Innocent joy*

Snake charmers

dawns on the vender's countenance—chance shall settle it. Will the sahib toss to decide whether he shall give for this beautiful cat's-eye two pounds or five? The original sum asked having been twenty, the sahib sees signs of relenting and consents to try the turn of the coin. The toss is fairly conducted, and whether he wins or loses, the importunate merchant appears content, as in any case he makes a profit. This warfare of barter being as the breath of his nostrils, he is reduced to the verge of tears by the heartless conduct of those who pay him his price without protest or haggling.

. . . A snake charmer is squatting in the dust before the hotel, performing feats of juggling: playfully depositing an egg in one ear, and in a moment picking it, with a sweet smile of surprise, out of the other—or seeming to do it.

—He takes off the cover of the snake basket, the reptile within lying sullenly sluggish until a rap over the head induces him to lift himself angrily, puff out his throat, and make ready to strike. But his master is playing a low, monotonous tune on a tiny bamboo flute, with his eyes fastened upon the snake's eyes, and swaying his nude body slowly from side to side.

The serpent stirs restlessly and flickers his wicked, thin red tongue; but the sleepy tune drones on and on, and the brown body moves to and fro—to and fro. Presently, the serpent begins to wave softly, following the movements of the man's body and with his eyes fixed on the man's eyes, and so in time sinks slowly in a languid heap of relaxed folds. . . . The music grows fainter, fainter, dies away to a breath—a whisper—ceases. The man hangs the helpless inert serpent—drunk with the insistent low whine of the flute—about his bare neck and breast, and comes forward to beg a rupee for his pains.

. . . We—the lady from Boston, her son, the Ceylon tea planter, and myself—hire a guide and carriage and go for a drive. Through the town, past the tall clock tower whose flashing light showed our path last night; past the banks and the haunts of the moneychangers—"shroffs"[14]*—with fat, yellow, hook-nosed faces, clad in crisp white buttoned with gold, and with great circles of thin gold wire in their ears and black-and-gold headdresses on their smooth-shaven crowns.—Past the beautiful sickle-shaped beach of Galle Face, and then*

inland along the shadowy dank roads under the heavy green vault of the multitudinous palms—coconut palms (forty millions of these, the guide says); palmyra palms, from which the heady palm wine is made; kitul palms that yield sugar and sago; talipot palms, upon whose papyrus-like leaves were inscribed the sacred writings—Mahawansa[15]—five hundred years before Christ, and preserved twenty-two centuries in wihares [temple containing idols and sacred writings]; and the areca palm, that gives the nuts the natives chew with their betel leaves. We pass banyan trees with roots like huge pythons coiling through the grass, and down-dropped stems from the far-spreading branches, making dim, leafy cloisters. Breadfruit trees, monster ferns, pools full of lotus plants, and orchids growing almost as freely as weeds.

The guide, a gentlemanly person in a skirt, has the usual mane of rippling hair bound in a sleek knot at the nape, and at my request, he untwists this and lets it fall far below his waist in silky black waves—restoring it in a moment by a quick turn of the wrist to its former neat compactness. He has never seen a hairpin, and the gift of one of mine childishly delights and amuses him. He thrusts it in and out of his hair, and finally fastens it upon a string of queer charms and fetishes worn in his bosom.

He wraps for me a bit of areca nut with a paste of wet lime in a leaf of the betel pepper and bids me chew it. Instantly my mouth is full of a liquid red as blood, and tongue and lips are shriveled with a sharp aromatic astringent resembling cloves. I hasten to spit it out, but all day my lips are still hot and acrid from the brief experiment. The entire population of Ceylon are wedded to the betel habit, save the servants of Europeans who object to the unpleasant vampire red of the stained mouth and corroded teeth. It harms no more than tobacco, and the natives prefer it even to food. From time to time along the road we come upon old women sitting upon the earth with little stores of nuts, lime, and betel leaves spread before them for the refreshment of the wayfarer.

. . . "Mem Sahib," says the guide, touching his brow with his fingers, and giving me one of those smiling black glances—"you are my father and my mother. Will you that we go to the cinnamon gardens?". . . And on the way he feeds upon ripe mangoes that have a reddish custard-like pulp, sweetly musky in flavor.

From among the cinnamon bushes growing without order in the white sand, and breathing faint odors in the steaming heat, starts out a lean, naked lad begging for alms. He is not to be shaken off, following in a leaping dance with flying hair and a white-toothed smile, clapping his elbows against his ribs with a noise like castanets and rattling his bones together loudly and merrily as though a skeleton pranced after us through the dust, so that we are fain to end the exhibition of his unique powers with a few coins.

In the museum that stands in the cinnamon gar-

dens, we find Eden's serpents—the reverse side of this painted island paradise. The dull, venomous cobra in his spotted cowl; clammy, strangling folds of long pythons; twenty-foot sharks with horrid semi-circular hedges of teeth—the wolves of these pearl-sown seas— and endless stinging, biting, poisoning creatures wrought into wanton bizarreries by nature in some mood of cynical humorousness. Here are also the uncouthly hideous masks of the old devil dancers; great gold ornaments, splendid robes, and the ingeniously murderous weapons of this mild-mannered race, who count in their history twenty-six kings done treacherously to death. In other rooms are the stuffed skins of beautiful birds, huge mammals, and collections of rich-colored butterflies and moths—all very hardly defended from the ravenous tropical disintegration, as fierce and implacable as the productiveness is profuse. It is a nature that devours her own children, creating with a furious fecundity and consuming all her creations with insatiable, relentless voracity.

. . . A long road among palms. Palm-thatched huts, with idle brown folk, half naked, dreaming in the heat. A door in a ruinous wall—shaven-headed priests in yellow robes—then a dim temple, with tall gods whose heads reach stiffly up to the roof.

Penetrating jasmine odors from altars heaped with stemless pink blossoms, and the Lord Buddha reclining on his elbow, drowsing in the hot semidarkness among the stifling scents. He is forty feet long, painted a coarse vivid crimson and yellow, but his flat wooden face is fixed in the same passive, low-lidded calm that we saw upon it when he sat on his lotus among the Japanese roses or listened in his tiny mountain shrine at Penang to loud voices of the waters. A Nirvana peace, undisturbed by passions or pity . . . dreaming eternal dreams in the hot, perfumed gloom. About the walls are painted in archaic frescoes the pains and toils of his fifty incarnations of Buddhahood, through which he attained at last to this immortal peace. Vishnu and Siva are the tall gods that stand by the doorway, for to these he gives room and shares with them his altar flowers.

A swarm closes about us as we emerge, crying for alms, and not to be ignored or beaten off. Old women hold out the little soft hands of the dimpled naked babies they carry on their hip. They themselves are hideous, repulsive hags—mere wrinkled, disgusting rags of humanity, with red-stained, toothless mouths; and this at forty years. The young women are plump and pretty, with a discontented knot in their brows and hopeless, peevish mouths—femininity being a perplexing and bitter burden in the East. Small brown imps, naked as Adam, save for a heavy silver necklace hung about their fat little stomachs, cling to our knees and use their fine eyes with a coquette's conscious power, smilingly seducing the coin out of our pockets.

. . . It is the last night of the old year, and the dining hall has been converted into a ballroom. The men, all

*in white, with gay sashes about their middle, are cir-
cling languidly with pretty English girls in their arms.
A high, warm wind whirls through the veranda and
flutters the draperies of the lookers-on.*

*. . . Morning!—The new year is coming in a beau-
tiful green dawn. A chrysoberyl sky, translucent golden
green, a misty green sea, and an ocean of feathery green
plumes tossing noiselessly, as with a great silent joy, in
the morning wind.*

*I have sprung out of bed to receive a letter—my first
one from home. A few lines, scrawled on the other side
of the world, that I lean from the window to read in
the faint early light. How beautiful they make the new
year seem!—Whatever this coming year will contain of
grief and rebuffs, at least it has begun with one good
moment, and for that it is well to be grateful.*

NOTES

1. Organette: a mechanical accordion that played music recorded on paper rolls.

2. Pacific Mail Steamship Company (1848–1949): an American company that at this time was operating between San Francisco and Hong Kong and Yokohama.

3. Sir Edwin Arnold (1832–1904) was an English poet, journalist, and travel writer. His best-known work was an epic poem, *The Light of Asia*. In the 1890s he wrote extensively about Japan.

4. Negishi Bay, south of Yokohama, was known to nineteenth-century foreign visitors as "Mississippi Bay," after the U.S. Navy ship on which Commodore Matthew Perry crossed the bay in 1854.

5. Ulysses S. Grant (1822–85) was a Civil War general and the 18th president of the United States. After leaving the presidency, he

and his family made a very public and reported trip around the world from May 1877 through part of December 1879.

6. Ancient Mariner: the main character in the ballad *Rime of the Ancient Mariner* by the English poet Samuel Taylor Coleridge.

7. William Wordsworth (1770–1850) was an English poet.

8. Frederic Augustus Thesiger, second Baron Chelmsford (1827–1905), British army officer, led the campaign against the Zulu in South Africa, 1878–79. Napoleon, Prince Imperial of France (1856–79), and only son of deposed Napoleon III, an observer on Chelmsford's staff, was killed. Although eventually successful, the British suffered heavy losses.

9. Pedro II (1825–91) was the second and last emperor of Brazil (1831–89). He was forced to abdicate by a military coup, November 15, 1889. He and his family went into exile in Europe.

10. Sir William Cleaver Francis Robinson (1834–97) was a British colonial governor and composer. At this time he would have just completed service in Australia.

11. Sir Henry Wrenfordsley (1825–1908) was the second chief justice of the Supreme Court of Western Australia.

12. Mary Anne Stewart Barker, Lady Broome (1831–1911) was a journalist and writer. Born in Trinidad, she spent her adult life in England and many of its colonies, including Australia, New Zealand, and India. Her second husband, Sir Frederick Napier Broome (1842–96) was also a writer and a colonial administrator.

13. Sahib: respectful title used by Indians for European men. The female version for women is "mem sahib."

14. Shroffs: Far Eastern term for bankers or moneychangers.

15. Mahawansa (or Mahavamsa): "The Great Chronicle" or history of the Sri Lankan people.

STAGE SEVEN

Bly: Eastward across the Pacific

I T WAS A BRIGHT SUNNY MORNING when I left Yokohama. A number of new friends in launches escorted me to the *Oceanic*, and when we hoisted anchor, the steam launches blew loud blasts upon their whistles in farewell to me, and the band upon the *Omaha* played "Home, Sweet Home," "Hail Columbia," and "The Girl I Left Behind Me," in my honor; and I waved my handkerchief so long after they were out of sight that my arms were sore for days. My feverish eagerness to be off again on my race around the world was strongly mingled with regret at leaving such charming friends and such a lovely land.

Everything promised well for a pleasant and rapid voyage. Anticipating this, Chief Engineer Allen caused to be written over the engines and throughout the engine room, this date and couplet:

"For Nellie Bly,
We'll win or die.
January 20, 1890."

It was their motto and was all very sweet to me. The runs were marvelous until the third day out, and then a storm came upon us. They tried to cheer me, saying it would only last that day, but the next day found it worse, and it continued, never abating a moment—headwinds, head sea, wild rolling, frightful pitching—until I fretfully waited for noon when I would slip off to the dining room to see the run, hoping that it would have gained a few miles on the day before and always being disappointed. And they were all so good to me! Bless them for it! If possible, they suffered more over the prospect of my failure than I did.

"If I fail, I will never return to New York," I would say despondently; "I would rather go in dead and successful than alive and behind time."

"Don't talk that way, child," Chief Allen would plead; "I would do anything for you in my power. I have worked the engines as they never were worked before; I have sworn at this storm until I have no words left; I have even prayed—I haven't prayed before for years—but I prayed that this storm may pass over and that we may get you in on time."

"I know that I am not a sinner," I laughed hysterically. "Day and night my plea has been, 'Be merciful to me a sinner,' and as the mercy has not been forthcoming, the natural conclusion is that I'm not a sinner. It's hopeless; it's hopeless!"

"Don't think so," the purser would beg; "don't be so disheartened; why, child, if by jumping overboard I could bring you happiness and success, I should do so in a moment."

"Never mind, little girl, you're all right," the jolly, happy-hearted captain would laugh. "I've bet every cent I have in the bank that you'll get in before you are due. Just take my word for it; you'll be in New York at least three days ahead of time."

"Why do you try to cheat me? You know we are way behind time now," I urged, longing to be still farther cheated into fresh hope, to which the doctor would say, dryly: "Look here, Nellie Bly, if you don't stop talking so, I'll make you take some pills for your liver."

"You mean wretch, you know I can't help being blue. It's head sea, and headwinds, and low runs—not liver!"

And then I would laugh, and so would they; and Mr. Allen, who had been pleading for me to "smile just once, give them but one glimpse of my old, jolly smile," would go away content. This is but a repetition of the way in which I was coaxed out of my unhappiness every day, by those great-hearted, strong, tender men.

At last a rumor became current that there was a Jonah on board the ship. It was thought over and talked over and, much to my dismay, I was told that the sailors said monkeys were Jonahs. Monkeys brought bad weather to ships, and as long as the monkey was on board, we would have storms. Someone asked if I would consent to the monkey being thrown overboard. A little struggle between superstition and a feeling of justice for the monkey followed. Just then someone told me that ministers were Jonahs; they always brought bad weather to ships. We had two ministers on board! So I said quietly, if the ministers were thrown overboard, I'd say nothing about the monkey. Thus the monkey's life was saved.

But even with low runs, our trip was bound to come to an end. One night it was announced that the next day we would be in San Francisco. I felt a feverish excitement, and many were the speculations as to whether there would be a snow blockade to hinder my trip across the continent. A hopefulness that had not known me for many days came back, when in rushed the purser, his face a snow-white, crying: "My God, the bill of health was left behind in Yokohama."

"Well—well—what does that mean?" I demanded, fearing some misfortune, I knew not what.

"It means," he said, dropping nerveless into a chair, "that no one will be permitted to land until the next ship arrives from Japan. That will be two weeks."

The thought of being held two weeks in sight of San Francisco, in sight of New York almost, and the goal for which I had been striving and powerless to move, was maddening.

"I would cut my throat, for I could not live and endure it," I said quietly, and that spurred him on to make another search, which resulted in finding the report safely lodged in the doctor's desk.

Tugboat and steamers in San Francisco Bay

Later came a scare about a smallpox case on board, but it proved to be only a rumor, and early in the morning the revenue officers came aboard bringing the newspapers. I read of the impassable snow blockade which for a week had put a stop to all railroad traffic, and my despair knew no bounds. While the *Oceanic* was waiting for the quarantine doctor, some men came out on a tug to take me ashore. There was no time for farewells. The monkey was taken on the tug with me, and my baggage, which had increased by gifts from friends, was thrown after me. Just as the tug steamed off, the quarantine doctor called to me that he had forgotten to examine my tongue, and I could not land until he did. I stuck it out, he called out "all right"; the others laugh, I wave farewell, and in another moment I was parted from my good friends on the *Oceanic.*

Bisland: Middle East

A T CEYLON THE AUSTRALIAN MAIL SHIP *Britania waits for us. She is one of the enormous Peninsular and Oriental vessels built in the Jubilee year and is on her way home to England.*

. . . Here again farewells: to the dear little old lady from Boston and to my kind and charming friend the Ceylon tea planter, who has placed me under an endless debt of gratitude by his many courtesies. It is four o'clock in the afternoon of the 1st of January when we swing out of the harbor and direct our course towards Africa.

The height of luxury is achieved on these Peninsular and Oriental steamships. No steerage travel being provided for, space is not stinted to first-class passengers, and saloons, decks, and bedrooms are ample and handsome. The ship's company, Australians on their way home to England, have made themselves thoroughly at home for the six weeks' cruise. Their rooms they have hung with photographs and drapery and bits of bric-à-brac, and on deck each one has a long bamboo lounging chair, a little table, and a tea service for that beautiful ceremony of five-o'clock tea—all being made possible by the fact that the sea is smooth as glass and the decks level as a drawing-room floor. Courtesies are exchanged in the form of invitations to this afternoon tea. Three times a week the band plays for dancing on deck; tableaux, private theatricals, and fancy balls fill the evenings, and in the afternoons the after-part of the ship is lively with games of cricket.

. . . Always above and below us it is intensely blue, hot, and calm. Flights of film-winged fishes rise from our path and flit away like flocks of sea sparrows. Sometimes a whale blows up a column of shining spray and leaves a green wake to show his hidden path. But nothing marks the passing of the hours save the coming and going of light.

Time goes by in lotus dreams that have no memory of a past or reckoning of a future till we wake suddenly, and find anchor cast in the Gulf of Aden.

. . . Red barren masses of stone, broken and jagged like "An old lion's cheek teeth."[1]

. . . An astonishing aridity everywhere, all the more startling by contrast with the fierce verdure of the lands we have last seen.

Not a drop of rain has fallen here in three years, and no green thing lives in the place. Even the tawny hills rot and fall to dust in the terrible desiccation. The earth is an impalpable dun powder that no roots could grasp; the rocks are seamed, cracked, and withered to the heart—the dust and bones of a dead land.

. . . As a coaling station and harbor from which warships may guard the entrance of the Red Sea, Aden is valuable; and, therefore, like Hong Kong, Singapore, Penang, Ceylon—like everything much worth having in this part of the world—it is an English possession. There are wharves of heavy masonry; the governor's

residence, a verandaed bungalow shut in with green *persiennes* [louvered shutters], standing on a little eminence some distance back from the water; and one narrow street of heavy white stone houses with flat roofs, fringing the shore.

A carriage is hired to convey us to the Tanks [cisterns]—the only bit of sightseeing to be done at Aden. These Tanks are of unknown antiquity and are variously attributed to Solomon, the Queen of Sheba, the Arabs, and—as a last guess—to the Phoenicians. Historians, when in doubt, always accuse the Phoenicians. In this rainless region, where water falls only at intervals of years, it was necessary to collect and preserve it all, and someone built among the hills huge stone basins with capacity of hundreds of thousands of gallons. These basins are quite perfect still, though the name of the faithful builder thereof has long ago perished.

The road winds upward from the sea to a barrier of rocks and pierces them with a black echoing pass two hundred feet high and fifteen wide, where the English fortifications lie—a place to be held by twenty men against an army. Here we find Tommy Atkins again, still clad in white linen from top to toe and still rosily swaggering.

On the other side of the wall of hills is the town, a motley assemblage of more flat-topped stone dwellings, all lime-washed as white as snow. In the midst is a well where women in flowing drapery, with tall jars, draw water as if posing for Bible illustrations, and a camel *market in which fifty or more of the brown, ungainly beasts have been relieved of their burdens and lain down for the night—doubled into uncomfortable heaps and bubbling and moaning with querulous discontent.*

Night is coming on. There is a crystalline luminosity in this dry air that the vanished sun leaves faintly golden-green. Every fold and crevice of the red rock wall overflows with intense violet shadows that still are full of light. There is no evening mistiness of vision; the little flat white town, the shore, the turbaned figures moving to and fro in the streets, the ships afloat on the glassy sea, the tawny outline of the rocks—all standing out with keen clearness through the deepening of the twilight.

. . . Later by the silver fire of a full moon, by whose light one can read and see colors, we go again to the Tanks, passing on the route a loaded train of camels lurching away to the desert through the black shadows of the pass, and, stepping beside them, lean, swarthy Arabs, draped statelily in white—such a caravan as might have gone down into Egypt to buy corn from pharaoh four thousand years ago—nothing in the interval changed in any way.

Our footsteps and our voices echo in hollow whispers from the empty Tanks and the mysterious shadows of the hills, though we walk lightly and speak softly, awed by the vast calm radiance of the African night.

Other than this, it is very silent in this dead and

The water tanks at Aden

A camel caravan crossing the desert

*desert spot, not a leaf to rustle, not an insect to cry—
and even the sea has no speech.*

. . . Our way home lies through a reverberant tunnel beneath the fort, where we meet more camels still with that same lounging stride, still with that air of evangelical superiority to a wicked world, and still making, with closed mouths, those suppressed moans of wounded feeling.

The port is fast asleep. In the distance a man-of-war is slowly steaming out of the harbor on its way to the lower coast to over-awe the Portuguese making futile protests against English domination in the neighborhood of Delagoa Bay.[2]

. . . Quite in a moment it seems, it is tomorrow—our last day in the tropics—and I go up on deck before the sun has risen, into the delicious moist warmth of the equatorial morning. Every moment I have spent in the tropics is to me just as vivid as this. I see everything. Not a beauty, not a touch of color, escapes me. Every moment of the day means intense delight, beauty, life. . . . And now, after six months, not a line has faded or grown dim. I can live back in it in every emotion, every impression, as though not an hour divided me from it. . . . It is well to have thus once really lived.

. . . The deck swarms with native merchants selling ostrich feathers, grass mats and baskets from Zanzibar, ornaments of shells, boxes of Turkish Delight [candy], embroideries, photographs, and a three-months-old lion cub in a wooden cage.

Port Said and the Suez Canal

The Bombay mail, for which we waited, has arrived, and new passengers come ashore with mountains of luggage. There is some stir among us because Mr. Stanley[3] *has just arrived on the coast from the interior of Africa, and there is talk of his going home in our ship; but the government sends down a special convoy to take him to Egypt, and we steam away without him.*

A cold west wind meets us in the Red Sea; the passengers get out their furs, and there is no more lounging on deck—one must walk briskly or sit in the sun wrapped in rugs.

I wake one night missing the throbbings of the screw and find that we are going at a snail's pace in smooth water. The moon is very dim behind the clouds, and from the porthole it would appear that we are sailing across endless expanses of sand; nothing else is to be seen. Morning shows a narrow ditch in a desert, half full of green water—so narrow and so shallow apparently that nothing would convince us our great ship could pass through save the actual proof of its doing so.

At one of the wider parts made for this purpose, we pass a French troop ship which dips her colors and sends a ringing cheer from the throats of the red-trousered soldiers on their way to Tonquin.[4]

Later a dead Arab floats by in the green water but is regarded with indifference as a common episode and merely suggestive of an imprudent quarrel overnight.

Nothing is to be seen save stones and sand to the very horizon.

A dim and lurid sunset ends the day, and when night comes, we are anchored off the town of Port Said—a wretched little place, dusty, dirty, and flaring with cheap vice—all the flotsam of four nations whirling about in an eddy of coarse pleasures. The shopkeepers are wolfish-looking and bargain vociferously. Almost every other door opens into a gambling hell and concert hall. One of these gambling places boasts an opera.

In the concert hall, Traviata⁵ is being sung by a fourth-rate French troupe, and the audience sit about at little tables, drinking and eating ices. I ask for something native—Turkish—to drink, and they bring me a stuff that to all the evidences of sight, taste, and smell cries out that it is a mixture of paregoric and water, and one sip contents me. We are glad to go away.

The Mediterranean is cold and not smooth, but here there comes upon one a sense of historical association.

In India nature is so tremendous she swallows up all memory of man; in Aden one remembers only the Bible; but nearing Greece, the past takes shape and meaning, and history begins to have a new vividness and significance. Here man has been "lord of the visible earth," has dominated and adorned her. She has been but the stage and background against which he played out the tragedies and comedies of humanity.

One morning at sunrise the stewardess taps at the door: "The first officer's compliments, miss, and will you please get up and look out of the scuttle."

I wrap myself in my kimono—treasure-trove from Japan—and thrust head and shoulders through the wide porthole. Directly before me is Candia—abrupt mountains rising sharply from the sea and crowned with snow. Among them are trailing clouds looping long scarfs of mist from peak to peak; at their feet Homer's "wine-dark sea," furrowed by a thousand keels . . . Greek galleys; Roman triremes [galleys with three sets of oars]; fighting vessels from Carthage; merchant and battleships from Venice, Genoa, and Turkey; the fleets of Spain; men-o'-war with the English lions at the peak; and, lastly, the world's peaceful commerce, sailing serenely over the bones and rotting hulls that lie below.

. . . The sun comes up gloriously out of the sea, deepening it to a winy purple in its light. Suddenly the mountaintops take fire; the snow flushes softly, deepens rosily in hue, grows crimson with splendor; the sleeping mists begin to stir and heave, to lighten into gold, to float and rise into the warming blue above. Once more the splendors of a new day—such a sunrise as Cervantes may have seen; as glad Greek eyes may have witnessed bowing in prayer to the sun god; as the galley slave may have watched dully as a signal for new labors; and admirals gazed upon with tightening lip, not knowing whether the new sun should look upon defeat or victory, glory or death.

Then the dressing-gong clangs noisily through the ship, and the colors pale into the common day.

Next morning, the 16th of January, we are fast to

295

*the docks at Brindisi, and but one more stage of the
journey remains to be made.*

NOTES

1. Bisland quotes a line from "An Epistle Containing the Strange
Medical Experience of Karshish, the Arab Physician" by Robert
Browning (1812–89), English poet.

2. Delagoa Bay is today known as Maputo Bay in Mozambique.
In June of 1889, Portugal seized a British railway that connected
Delagoa Bay to the Transvaal in South Africa.

3. Sir Henry Morton Stanley (1841–1904) was a journalist and
African explorer, best known for locating the missionary David
Livingstone on the shores of Lake Tanganyika in 1871. In 1890, he
would have been returning to Europe from Cairo.

4. Tonquin, or Tonkin, was the European name for the region
around Hanoi, Vietnam, during the French colonial period (1883–
1945).

5. *La Traviata* is an opera by Giuseppe Verde.

THE LAST STAGE

BLY: EASTWARD ACROSS THE CONTINENT

I ONLY REMEMBER my trip across the continent as one maze of happy greetings, happy wishes, congratulating telegrams, fruit, flowers, loud cheers, wild hurrahs, rapid hand-shaking, and a beautiful car filled with fragrant flowers attached to a swift engine that was tearing like mad through flower-dotted valley and over snow-tipped mountain, on—on—on! It was glorious! A ride worthy a queen. They say no man or woman in America ever received ovations like those given me during my flying trip across the continent. The Americans turned out to do honor to an American girl who had been the first to make a record of a flying trip around the world, and I rejoiced with them that it was an American girl who had done it. It seemed as if my greatest success was the personal interest of everyone who greeted me. They were all so kind and as anxious that I should finish the trip in time as if their personal reputations were at stake.

The special train had been waiting for my arrival in readiness to start the moment I boarded it. The deputy collector of the port of San Francisco, the inspector of customs, the quarantine officer, and the superintendent of the O&O steamers sat up all the night preceding my arrival so there should be no delay in my transfer from the *Oceanic* to the special train. Nor were they the only ones to wait for me. One poor little newspaper woman did not see bed that night so anxious was she for an interview which she did not get. I was so entirely ignorant about what was to be done with me on landing that I thought I was someone's guest until I was many miles away from San Francisco. Had I known in advance the special train was mine, every newspaper man and woman who cared to should have been my guest.

My train consisted of one handsome sleeping car, the San Lorenzo; and the engine, *The Queen*, was one of the fastest on the Southern Pacific.

"What time do you want to reach New York, Miss Bly?" Mr. Bissell, general passenger agent of the Atlantic and Pacific system, asked me.

"Not later than Saturday evening," I said, never thinking they could get me there in that time.

"Very well, we will put you there on time," he said quietly, and I rested satisfied that he would keep his word.

It did not seem long after we left Oakland Mole until we reached the great San Joaquin Valley, a level green plain through which the railroad track ran for probably three hundred miles as straight as a sunbeam. The roadbed was so perfect that though we were traveling a mile a minute, the car was as easy as if it were traveling over a bed of velvet.

At Merced, our second stop, I saw a great crowd

of people dressed in their best Sunday clothes gathered about the station. I supposed they were having a picnic and made some such remark, to be told in reply that the people had come there to see me. Amazed at this information, I got up, in answer to calls for me, and went out on the back platform. A loud cheer, which almost frightened me to death, greeted my appearance, and the band began to play "By Nellie's Blue Eyes."[1] A large tray of fruit and candy and nuts, the tribute of a dear little newsboy, was passed to me, for which I was more grateful than had it been the gift of a king.

We started on again, and the three of us on the train had nothing to do but admire the beautiful country through which we were passing as swiftly as cloud along the sky, to read, or count telegraph poles, or pamper and pet the monkey. I felt little inclination to do anything but to sit quietly and rest, bodily and mentally. There was nothing left for me to do now. I could hurry nothing, I could change nothing; I could only sit and wait until the train landed me at the end of my journey. I enjoyed the rapid motion of the train so much that I dreaded to think of the end. At Fresno, the next station, the town turned out to do me honor, and I was the happy recipient of exquisite fruits, wines, and flowers, all the product of Fresno County, California.

The men who spoke to me were interested in my sunburnt nose, the delays I had experienced, the number of miles I had traveled. The women wanted to examine my one dress in which I had traveled around, the cloak and cap I had worn, were anxious to know what was in the bag, and all about the monkey.

While we were doing some fine running the first day, I heard the whistle blow wildly, and then I felt the train strike something. Brakes were put on, and we went out to see what had occurred. It was hailing just then, and we saw two men coming up the track. The conductor came back to tell us that we had struck a hand-car, and pointed to a piece of twisted iron and a bit of splintered board—all that remained of it—lying alongside. When the men came up, one remarked, with a mingled expression of wonder and disgust upon his face: "Well, you ARE running like h—!"

"Thank you; I am glad to hear it," I said, and then we all laughed. I inquired if they had been hurt; they assured me not, and good humor being restored all around, we said goodbye, the engineer pulled the lever, and we were off again.

At one station where we stopped, there was a large crowd, and when I appeared on the platform, one yell went up from them. There was one man on the outskirts of the crowd who shouted: "Nellie Bly, I must get up close to you!"

The crowd evidently felt as much curiosity as I did about the man's object, for they made a way and he came up to the platform. "Nellie Bly, you must touch my hand," he said, excitedly. Anything to please the man. I reached over and touched his hand, and then he shouted: "Now you will be successful. I have in my hand the left hind foot of a rabbit!"

Well, I don't know anything about the left hind foot of a rabbit, but when I knew that my train had run safely across a bridge which was held in place only by jackscrews, and which fell the moment we were across, and when I heard that in another place the engine had just switched off from us when it lost a wheel, then I thought of the left hind foot of a rabbit and wondered if there was anything in it.

"Come out here, and we'll elect you governor," a Kansas man said, and I believe they would have done it, if the splendid welcomes they gave me are any criterion. Telegrams addressed merely to "Nellie Bly, Nellie Bly's Train," came from all parts of the country filled with words of cheer and praise at all hours of the day and night. I could not mention one place that was kinder than another. Over ten thousand people greeted me at Topeka. The mayor of Dodge City presented me, in behalf of the citizens, with resolutions of praise. I was very anxious to go to Kansas City, but we only went to the station outside of the limits, in order to save thirty minutes.

I was up until four o'clock, talking first with a little newspaper girl from Kearney, Nebraska, who had traveled six hundred miles to meet and interview me, and later dictating an account of my trip to a stenographer, who was seasick from the motion of the train. I had probably slept two hours when the porter called me, saying we would soon be in Chicago. I dressed myself leisurely and drank the last drop of coffee there was left on our train, for we had been liberally entertaining everybody who cared to travel any distance with us. I was surprised, on opening the door of my stateroom, to see the car quite filled with good-looking men. They were newspaper men, members of the Chicago Press Club, I found a moment later, who had come out to Joliet to meet me and to escort me to their city. Mr. Cornelius Gardener, the vice president of the club, in the absence of the president, took charge of our little party. Before we were in, I had answered all their questions, and we joked about my sunburnt nose and discussed the merits of my one dress, the cleverness of the monkey, and I was feeling happy and at home and wishing I could stay all day in Chicago.

Carriages were waiting to take us to the rooms of the Press Club. In the beautiful rooms of the Press Club, I met the president, Stanley Waterloo, and a number of clever newspaper men. I had not been expected in Chicago until noon, and the club had arranged an informal reception for me, and when they were notified of my speedy trip and consequently earlier arrival, it was too late to notify the members. After a most delightfully informal reception, I was escorted to Kinsley's, where the club had a breakfast prepared. And then I learned that, owing to some misunderstanding, none of the men had had anything to eat since the night before. After breakfast the members of the Press Club, acting as my escort, took me to visit the Chicago Board of Trade. When we went in, the pandemonium which seems to reign during business hours was at its height. My escorts took me to the gallery, and just as we got there, a man raised his arm to yell something to the roaring crowd, when he saw me, and yelled instead: "There's Nellie Bly!"

In one instant the crowd that had been yelling like mad became so silent that a pin could have been heard fall to the floor. Every face, bright and eager, was turned up towards us, instantly every hat came off, and then a burst of applause resounded through the immense hall. People can say what they please about Chicago, but I do not believe that anywhere else in the United States a woman can get a greeting which will equal that given by the Chicago Board of Trade. The applause was followed by cheer after cheer and cries of "Speech!," but I took off my little cap and shook my head at them, which only served to increase their cheers.

Shortly afterwards, the Press Club escorted me to the Pennsylvania Station, where I reluctantly bade

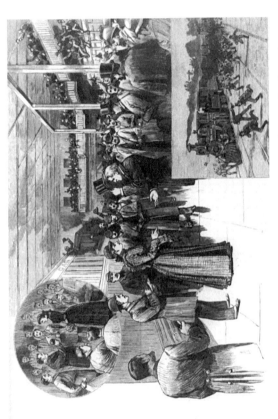

Nellie Bly's reception at Jersey City with vignettes of presentation of an award and arrival at Philadelphia from Leslie's Illustrated Newspaper

them goodbye, unable to thank them heartily enough for the royal manner in which they had treated a little sunburnt stranger.

Now I was on a regular train which seemed to creep, so noticeable was the difference in the speed of traveling. Instead of a fine sleeping car at my disposal, I had but a stateroom, and my space was so limited that floral and fruit offerings had to be left behind. In Chicago, a cable which afforded me much pleasure reached me, having missed me at San Francisco.

"Mr. Verne wishes the following message to be handed to Nellie Bly the moment she touches American soil: M. and Mme. Jules Verne address their sincere felicitations to Miss Nellie Bly at the moment when that intrepid young lady sets foot on the soil of America."

It was after dark when we reached Columbus, where the depot was packed with men and women waiting for me. A delegation of railroad men waited upon me and presented me with beautiful flowers and candy, as did a number of private people. I did not go to bed until after we had passed Pittsburgh, and only got up in the morning in time to greet the thousands of good people who welcomed me at Harrisburg, where the Harrisburg Wheelman's Club sent a floral offering in remembrance of my being a wheelman.[2] A number of Philadelphia newspaper men joined me there, and at Lancaster I received an enthusiastic reception.

Almost before I knew it, I was at Philadelphia, and all too soon to please me, for my trip was so pleasant I dreaded the finish of it. A number of newspaper men and a few friends joined me at Philadelphia to escort me to New York. Speechmaking was the order from Philadelphia on to Jersey City. I was told when we were almost home to jump to the platform the moment the train stopped at Jersey City, for that made my time around the world. The station was packed with thousands of people, and the moment I landed on the platform, one yell went up from them, and the cannons at the Battery and Fort Greene boomed out the news of my arrival. I took off my cap and wanted to yell with the crowd, not because I had gone around the world in seventy-two days, but because I was home again.

*   *   *

To so many people this wide world over am I indebted for kindnesses that I cannot, in a little book like this, thank them all individually. They form a chain around the earth. To each and all of you, men, women, and children, in my land and in the lands I visited, I am most truly grateful. Every kind act and thought, if but an unuttered wish, a cheer, a tiny flower, is imbedded in my memory as one of the pleasant things of my novel tour.

I T IS A VIVIDLY BRIGHT DAY *in January, 1890—the 16th. There is a tingling crispness in the air as if it were early autumn—a slight frostiness that chills the skin but does not penetrate the veins. Rather the deep breaths of this keen, pure sea ozone make the blood pulse with a swift, delicious warmth, like a plunge into cold water.*

. . . We are anchored at Brindisi—the ancient Brundisium of the Romans—a town more than twenty-five centuries old, but which does not by any means look its age. It does not appear particularly attractive either from the wharves. The Britannia *goes on and around to Portsmouth, but the English government runs a train down through France and Italy to meet the P&O steamers, and thus gain five days in the arrival of the Indian and Australian mails. This mail train carries one passenger coach for the benefit of personages from the colonies who may be in haste to reach home; and if there are not a sufficient number of these distinguished servants of the empire to fill the car, more ordinary travelers can occupy the vacant berths by cabling ahead and securing them. I have taken this precaution at Ceylon and find there will be no difficulty in the matter, provided I can get my luggage through the customs in time.*

It is almost impossible to get anything done. The whole ship is in an uproar. Mails and luggage are being disembarked. My luggage is finally marked as passed; a porter is hired to transport it; I go off to attend to the visé of tickets [visa], dispatching of cables, and other minor matters, and arrive ten minutes before the advertised departure of the train.

. . . No luggage! I fling out of the car, rush back again to the ship, and discover the missing possessions in the hands of a pig-headed Italian who insists they have not been properly examined and demands the keys.

Various necessary additions to my wardrobe during the voyage have so enlarged the contents of my little box that only careful packing and the emphatic sitting down upon it of the stewardess and myself have induced it to shut at all. Now this amiable official insists, despite the fact that it goes under seal and bond straight through to England, upon opening it and strewing my garments about the deck.

I hope I did not forget the dignity a gentlewoman should preserve under the most trying of circumstances, but I fancy that my tones, while low, were concentrated and that the little American I used was "frequent and fluent and free," for the man turned pale and wavered.

I snatched up my belongings, flung them in pell-mell, jumped upon the box, snapped to the hasp, and ran off with a porter towards the train, blank despair in my heart. Happily, Italian trains are not bound down by narrow interpretations of timetables, and I do succeed in catching it, with the luggage and some few tattered remnants of a once nice temper.

It is very destructive of the mental equilibrium to lose the temper so thoroughly, especially if one is out of practice, and it is fully an hour before the exceeding beauty of the country through which we are passing begins to have its soothing effect and to make me fain to forgive the Italians because of Italy! On our right is the Adriatic, blue as lapis lazuli and gay with flocking sails. Here and there lie little snow-white towns along its shores, and between are the gray olive orchards, that have something strangely human in their gnarled grotesqueness.

. . . The English government pays the Italian government a large subsidy for this train and the swift passage of the mails, but the ubiquitous person who attends to all our needs—is porter, guard, steward, cook, and brakeman in one—has his own ideas on the subject of haste, and acts accordingly. When we reach a town where he has friends, he goes out, quietly winds us up like a Waterbury watch,[3] dismounts, and is received with affectionate enthusiasm by a little crowd on the platform. He inquires solicitously after each one's kin unto the fourth and fifth generation, gives his careful attention to all the local gossip, and retails the news he has been gathering all along the line. When he can no longer hear or tell some new thing, he remembers our existence, climbs once more upon his perch, lets us run down with a sudden whir, and we go on our way. At mealtimes he retires into a tiny den amidships, and from a space but little larger than a matchbox

produces delightful soups and salads, excellent coffee, well-cooked game, baskets of twisted Italian bread, wine, and oranges. At night he arranges our sleeping berths, and I think would perform barber duties and assist with our toilets if called upon to do so. He is a fatigued and blasé personage who looks as if chronically deprived of his due allowance of sleep, and he evidently regards the traveling public as a helpless, nervous creature always in a peevishly ridiculous hurry.

We begin to climb into the mountains, and it grows very cold. Oddly angled vineyards hang precariously to the steep sides of the heights, propped into place by dams of stone that keep the soil from sliding downhill. Queer villages are tucked into clefts, with streets that are merely narrow stairs. Now and again we flash by the bold outlines of a ruined castle crowning a crag: the site always chosen with so much discretion that one wonders not only how enemies ever got in, but how the owners themselves ever emerged—unless they fell out.

. . . A film of snow appears here and there, and the cold intensifies. Suddenly we catch a glimpse of white heights outlined against the blue—we are among the Alps, and the Mount Cenis Tunnel is not far away.

. . . A space of darkness, of thundering, clattering echoes—and then France!

. . . Everything is quite different all at once. A fine new fortress commands the tunnel; the station is better built, larger, and in better repair than those we have seen in Italy. The customs officer, a well-set-up and

good-looking Frenchman in a smart uniform, inquires politely if we have anything to declare, and when we answer in the negative, sets his heels together, gives a profound salutation, and vexes us no more.

Everywhere is an air of greater prosperity, thrift, and alertness. The train does not stop to admit of gossiping and goes at added speed.

Telegrams have been following me along the route concerning the possibility of catching a ship at Le Havre. The train is rather behind time, and unless the Transatlantique *will consent to delay her departure for an hour or two, it will be useless to attempt to cover the space between Villeneuve, Paris, and Le Havre before tomorrow at seven. There is hope, however, that she will wait, and Friday night, some two hours after midnight, the guard rouses me to deliver a telegram which says I must be ready at four to change cars for Paris. This means leaving my box—it is under seal for London—and crossing the ocean with the few belongings in a traveling bag. I rise and dress quietly, scribble a few notes of farewell to such of my fellow passengers as have been especially courteous, and am all ready when we halt at Villeneuve. A young Frenchman, agent for Cook's tourist bureau in Paris, has come to meet me but brings the discouraging intelligence that the ship has refused to wait and that there is no chance of catching her. It is not until reaching America that I discover this is a mistake and that the* Transatlantique *waited several hours, not only in the harbor, but when the tide* made it necessary to cross the bar, lingering outside for another half-hour in hopes I might still come, for the French captain was interested in my endeavor and had received official permission for the delay.

This change subjected me to inconvenience and to suffering, from the effects of which it took much time to entirely recover. For then began a most trying experience, from the strain of which not even the most vigorous constitution could escape unharmed. The cause of this false information was never satisfactorily ascertained. It, however, succeeded in lengthening the voyage four days.

. . . It is too late—half-past four—to return to bed, so I throw myself on the couch and wait for day. A faint rime clouds the window when dawn breaks, but a breath dispels it, and outside are lovely Corot-like visions—pale, shadowy, gray—worth the lost sleep to have seen. Here and there a thin plume of smoke curls up against the dull frosty sky from the chimney of a thatched lime-washed cottage set amid barns and stacks.

As the day grows, peasants such as Millet pictures come out of the cottages and follow the road, carrying fagots [twig bundles] or baskets of potatoes and turnips. Two legs and a pair of sabots [wooden shoes] appear under a perambulating heap of hay. A big dog drags a small cart full of milk cans, and a woman with a cap and tucked-up skirts trudges along beside, blowing on her fingers to warm them.

All this, just as did Italy, seems very familiar. I know it quite well from pictures and books. It gives one the sensation—reversed—awakened by reading a realistic novel in which all the little details of daily life are minutely and accurately reproduced.

It is ten o'clock when we reach Calais, and the Dover boat has gone, so there is time for a bath and breakfast—luckily, as I shall not have another meal for forty-eight hours; but of this I have no prevision.

The Channel is gray and stormy when we start, and a gout of rain splashes now and then upon the deck. Later the sun struggles through the clouds and turns the gloom to a stormy gray-green and shifting silver—and there looms slowly through the mists the white cliffs of England!

For me this keen windy sea is thick with phantom sails . . . the high-beaked galleys of the Conqueror, the silken wings of the White Ship, Henry's fleet carrying victorious armies into France, Drake's and Raleigh's prows, galleons from the East, certain small sailing craft going swiftly and furtively by dusk, carrying fugitive monarchs—the myriad wings of a nation of sea birds, spread for pleasure or for prey. . . .

Starting two months ago from a vast continent which the English race have made their own, where the English tongue, English laws, customs, and manners reign from sea to sea, in my whole course around the globe I have heard that same tongue, seen the same laws and manners, found the same race. Have had

The White Cliffs of Dover, England

proof with my own eyes of the splendor of their empire, of their power, their wealth, of their dominance and orgulousness [pride], of their superb armies, their un- dreamable commerce, their magnificent possessions, their own unrivaled physical beauty and force—and lo! now at last I find from a tiny island ringed with gray seas has sprung this race of kings. It fills my soul with a passion of pride that I, too, am an Anglo-Saxon. In my veins, too, runs that virile tide that pulses through the heart of this Lord of the Earth—the blood of this clean, fair, noble English race! . . .

. . . Dover—and one sets foot at last on the mother soil. (We are, by the way, the only people who call our land a mother.)

. . . the blue boudoir of a first-class carriage—then English landscapes under the level rays of a setting sun.

Certain characteristics here are very reminiscent of Japan. The neatness and completeness of everything; the due allowance of trees dispersed in ornamental fashion; nature so thoroughly tamed and domesticated; the picturesque railway stations; and a certain moist softness in the air. But where everything there is light, fragile, and fantastic, here it is solid, compact, and durable.

. . . Darkness falls. A dull glare is reflected from the heavens that speaks the presence of a great gaslit city. A myriad sparks twinkle in the distance—the "Lights o' London!"

. . . Miles and miles and miles of houses. A huge,

shadowy half-globe looming against the sky—the dome of St. Paul's.

. . . Towers and delicate spires, and lights shining through many lance-like windows—Parliament Houses, where lords and commons sit in debate.

. . . Long gleams quivering serpent-like across a wavering black flood—we have passed over the Thames, and here is Charing Cross.

. . . Clatter, hurry, and confusion—everyone giving different suggestions and directions. I had meant to remain overnight in London and take the North German Lloyd steamer at Southampton the next day, but here the news meets me that this ship has been suddenly withdrawn and will not sail till late in the week. My one chance is the night mail to Holyhead and to catch the Bothnia, *which touches at Queenstown next morning. This train leaves in an hour and a half. I have not slept since two o'clock the night before, nor eaten since breakfast, and my courage is nearly at an end. One of my fellow travelers, who has been most kind to me all the way from Ceylon, comes to my rescue and assumes all responsibilities. I am sent off to the hotel to dine in company with two kind and charming fellow voyagers, Sir William Lewis and his daughter, while he arranges my difficulties. I am far too tired and disturbed, however, to eat, and can only crumble my bread and taste my wine. At half-past eight my friend appears and carries me off to the Euston station. He has snatched his dinner, got rid of the dust of travel, and into evening*

clothes. He has brought rugs and cushions that I may have some rest during the night, a little cake in case I grow hungry, and heaps of books and papers. My foot warmer is filled with hot water, the guard is induced to give me his best care and attention, and then I go away alone again, somewhat comforted by the chivalrous goodness of the traveling man to the uncared-for woman.

. . . I fall asleep from fatigue, am shaken by horrible dreams, and start awake with a cry. The train is thundering through a wild storm. I try to read, but the words dance up and down the page. The guard comes now and then to see if I need anything, and deep in the night I reach Holyhead. Gathering up my multitudinous belongings, I run through the rain and sleet to the little vessel quivering and straining at the pier. The night is a wild one, the wind in our teeth, and the journey rough and very tedious. The cold and tempestuous day has dawned before we touch Kingstown and are hurried—wretched for lack of sleep and the means of making a fresh toilet—into the train for Dublin. The Irish capital is still unawake when I rattle across it from station to station this Sunday morning, and immediately I am off again at full speed through a land swept with flying mists and showers—a beautiful land, green even in January.

Later I see ruddy-cheeked peasants going along the roads to church—a type I am familiar with in America. I gaze contemplatively at these sturdy young men *and wonder how soon they will be New York aldermen and mayors of Chicago; how soon those rosy girls, in their queer, bunchy, provincial gowns, will be leaders of society in Washington and dressed by Worth.*

. . . I am growing frightfully hungry, having eaten nothing since yesterday morning in Calais. There is the spice cake, but with no liquid save a little brandy in a flask, I soon choke upon the cake and abandon it. The train is behind time, owing to the late arrival of the Channel boat, and stops only for the briefest moments. At noon we reach Queenstown, having curved around a fair space of water and past the beautiful city of Cork. The ship has not yet arrived but will doubtless be here in a few moments, the bad weather having delayed her; and my luggage is all hurried down to the tender, where I should be sent, too, did I not wail with hunger.

The Queen's Hotel is not far from the station, but the evil luck which has pursued me for the last two days ordains that the kitchen of this hostelry should be undergoing repairs at this particular moment, and no food is to be had. By dint of perseverance, in frantic protest and reckless objurgation, I finally secure a cup of rather cold and bitter tea and a bit of dingy bread that looks as if it had been used to scrub the floor with before being presented to me as a substitute for breakfast. I am warned to hold myself in readiness for an instantaneous summons to the tender, for when the steamer is signaled, there is no time to waste. So hastily

I make such toilet as is possible with my dressing bag aboard the tender and sit alone in the waiting room, attendant on the summons.

Hour after hour goes by, but no summons comes. I dare not move lest the call come during my absence, and sit there hopeless, helpless, overwhelmed with hunger, lack of sleep, and fatigue. At six o'clock my patience is at end, and I am clamorously demanding more food, when they bring the long-expected notice. The ship has been signaled, and the tender must be off.

It rains in torrents, mingled with sleet, and the wind blows a tempest. The tender puts out from shore and is whirled about like an eggshell. The wind drives us back, and over and over again we essay the passage before we can make head against the wild weather. It is two hours and a half later when we get alongside the ship, and I am chilled to the bone, sick and dizzy for want of food and sleep, and climb stumblingly across the narrow, slippery, plunging path that leads from one ship to the other. No sooner have I set foot on the glassy deck than the push of an impatient passenger sends me with a smashing fall into the scuppers, where I gather bruises that last a week. A compassionate stewardess comes to the rescue and puts me to bed—speechless and on the verge of tears.

. . . The weather is terrible—a season long to be remembered for the January storms of the north Atlantic. The waves toss our ship back and forth among them like a football. Even were I not too miserable to move,

the plunging of the vessel would make it impossible to keep one's feet. The ship laboriously climbs a howling green mountain, pauses irresolute a moment on the crest, and then toboggans madly down the farther side, her screw out of water, and kicking both heels madly in the air to the utter dislocation of one's every tooth and joint. Down, down she goes, as if boring for bottom, and when it is perfectly certain that she can never by any chance right herself, she comes nose upmost with a jerk, shakes off the water, and attacks a new mountain, to repeat the same performance on the farther side.

Two-thirds of the passengers are very seasick, and I quite as wretched and prostrate from my late painful experiences as if still subject to the malady. It is the third or fourth day out, and I am beginning to take heart of grace and to long to leave my stuffy little cabin. The ship is rolling frightfully still, and while revolving in my mind an attempt to rise, a sudden lurch sends the heavy jug full of water flying out of its basin into the berth, where it smashes into twenty pieces upon my face and chest, and drenches me with icy water. The doors of the gangway are left open lest they freeze together, and therefore a bitter wind sweeps through the cabin, so that when hauled from my dripping bed, and it is discovered that the key of my box, where are the only dry changes of garment, is mislaid, I am stabbed through and through my wet and clinging clothes by this terrible cold.

Passengers crowd the railing as an ocean liner approaches New York

Thus suppressed again for another three days, it is only towards the end of the week—the storm being abated—that I am able once more to stand on my feet. It is a most amiable and friendly little company that finally assembles in the cabin; the recent woes we have all passed through having made us sympathetic and considerate. We even get up in time a concert for the seamen's orphans and play shuffleboard on the still uncertain deck for prizes. But this crossing of the zone of storms has greatly delayed us, and it is late in the evening of the eleventh day when we take our pilot aboard. The morning of the twelfth day is cold but evidently has some thought of clearing, and the sea is less rough.

. . . A rim of opaque film grows on the horizon that the emigrants on the forward deck regard with eager interest and hope. The passengers stand about in furs, pinched and shivering, their noses red, but their eyes full of pleased anticipation. Any land would be dear and desirable after near a fortnight of this cold and frantic sea—but when it is one's own—!

The film thickens and darkens, and suddenly resolves itself into Coney Island, where, as we swiftly near the shore, the plaintive reproachful eyes of the great wooden elephant are turned upon us as if to deprecate our late coming.[4]

The water has smoothed itself into a bay, and a huge gray woman, holding an uplifted torch, awaits our coming; the emigrants regard her wonderingly—the symbol of liberty held aloft, and a benignant counte-

nance turned towards all the outer world. We are by the shores of Staten Island. A pretty English girl who has braved the winter storms to follow her new husband to a foreign country remarks surprisedly that all this looks much like England—evidently having expected log cabins and a country town. But I have no time to be amused at her ignorance—I am saying joyously to myself

> *"Is this the hill, is this the kirk,*
> *Is this mine own countree?"[5]*

Suddenly a great flood of familiarity washes away the memory of the strange lands and people I have seen and blots out all sense of time that has elapsed since I last saw all this. I know how everything—the streets, the houses, the passersby—are looking at this moment. It is as if I had turned away my head for an instant and now looked back again. My duties, my cares, my interests, which had grown dim and shadowy in these last two months, suddenly take on sharp outlines and become alive and real once more. I feel as if I had but sailed down the bay for an hour and was now returning.

. . . The ship slides into dock. I can see the glad faces of my friends upon the pier. My journey is done. I have been around the world in seventy-six days.

NOTES

1. "By Nellie's. . .": The title of the song, written by William J. Scanlan, published in London in 1886, was actually "My Nellie's Blue Eyes."

2. Wheelman: a Victorian term for a bicycle rider. In June of 1889, Bly had written a column for *The World* in which she reported on her efforts to learn how to ride a bicycle.

3. In 1888, the Waterbury Watch Company of Connecticut was the largest-volume watch producer in the world.

4. In 1884, a massive structure known as the Elephantine Colossus opened on Coney Island in Brooklyn. One hundred fifty feet high, the structure contained stores, galleries, an amusement arcade, and a concert hall in the elephant's body, and telescopes in its eyes. Built of wood and tin, the Elephantine Colossus burned down in 1896.

5. These lines are taken from *The Rime of the Ancient Mariner*, by the English poet Samuel Taylor Coleridge.

EPILOGUE

At the close of her race around the world, Nellie Bly was, in the estimation of *The World,* "the best-known and most widely talked-of young woman on earth today." Shortly after her triumphant return, Bly took a leave of absence to undertake a forty-city lecture tour. Though the tour began auspiciously (her first audience gave her a triple ovation), public opinion soon began to turn. It was one thing for a young woman to go around the world and apparently quite another for her to profit from it; there seemed also to be something distasteful in the notion of a woman presuming to speak, uninterrupted, for an entire evening. Newspapers across the country editorialized against her. Halls in Chicago and Philadelphia were scarcely half filled, and the tour was soon abandoned. Nellie Bly, observed a Cincinnati newspaper, "has discovered that a successful lecture tour in the United States is a far more difficult undertaking than a tour around the world in seventy-three [sic] days."

Soon after, Bly refused to testify in a libel suit that had been filed against *The World* by a victim of one of her exposés. She was bitter over what she perceived as mistreatment by her employer. "*The World* never even said 'thank you' to me after my return," she complained to a fellow journalist, though they had "made thousands of dollars clear on their increased circulation during my absence and immediately after my return." At the close of her lecture tour, Bly quit *The World*, vowing never to return.

Instead, she signed a three-year contract to write serial fiction for a popular New York weekly magazine. She had no real talent for this type of writing, however, and only a single story of hers ever appeared in the paper. Of course, there was another kind of writing at which Nellie Bly genuinely excelled—but she could never go back to the undercover reportage that had launched her career in the first place. She was now too famous.

Unlike Nellie Bly, Elizabeth Bisland was not comfortable with fame, but she had acquired a taste for travel. In May 1890, she boarded another ocean-crossing steamship. She would spend the following year—when the American public's interest in her was at its height—in England.

While there, she collaborated with Rhoda Broughton[1] on a novel, *A Widower Indeed*. She attended balls and dinners, and a garden party hosted by the Prince of Wales. In England she also met a wealthy American attorney named Charles Wetmore,[2] and at the end of the year the two returned to New York to get married. Shortly afterward they moved into a Tudor mansion called Applegarth that they had built on Long Island, where in the next few years Bisland would write an autobiographical novel, *A Candle for Understanding*, as well as two highly regarded essay collections, the last published shortly before her death at the age of sixty-seven. She was buried in Woodlawn Cemetery in the Bronx, beside her husband.

In 1893, three years after her triumphal arrival in New Jersey (and having long since lost any other sources of income), Nellie Bly finally returned to *The World*. For the next year her work comprised an uncomfortable mix of big-name interviews—including jailhouse interviews with labor leader Eugene V. Debs[3] and the anarchist Emma Goldman[4] —and follies, such as a night spent inside a "haunted" house. In July of 1894, Bly traveled to Chicago to report on a strike among the workers in the company town of Pullman,[5] Illinois. Aboard the train she met a man named Robert Seaman,[6] and within the week the two had eloped. Not only was Seaman seventy years old (forty years older than Bly), he was the owner of the Iron Clad Manufacturing Company of Brooklyn and was said to be worth $5 million. As the years went along, Bly became increasingly involved in the company's operations, and when Seaman died in 1904, she assumed control of the business; she was, as she liked to say, "the only woman in the world personally managing industries of such a magnitude."

It turned out that Bly had a talent for industrial design—at one time there were twenty-five patents with Nellie Bly's name on them, including one for the first steel barrel made in the United States—but she was not at all interested in finances, and she made the critical mistake of giving her husband's accountants complete control of the company's books. Some of the employees took advantage of her, embezzling hundreds of thousands of dollars. Eventually Bly was forced to declare bankruptcy; several creditors sued her for breach of contract, followed by years of suits and countersuits. In 1914, when the court demanded that she open the company's books, Bly refused the order; as a result, charges were filed against her for obstruction of justice and nonpayment of legal fees. Four days later Bly fled the country for Austria.

For five years Nellie Bly lived in exile, traveling through war-torn Central Europe, filing occasional dispatches for William Randoph Hearst's *Evening Journal*. When World War I was over, she returned to the United States, where she was cleared of all the earlier charges. Now almost penniless, she began writing a regular column for the *Evening Journal*. Her work at the *Journal* was primarily charitable in nature; most often she wrote columns about people in need and solicited help from her readers. Week after week, donations came in to Bly, who redistributed them to the poor, the ill, the suffering. She seemed to have regained the enthusiasm of her youth, the satisfaction that came from using her influence to provide help to those who needed it. By now, though, the hard condition of her later years was taking its toll. She had put on a lot of weight, and much of the time she was tired and ill. Still, she persisted in her work; she slept little, ate poorly, and went out in all kinds of weather. In January of 1922, Bly caught pneumonia, and within two weeks she was dead. She was fifty-seven years old.

By sheer coincidence, Nellie Bly was also buried in Woodlawn Cemetery—no more than a quarter-mile from the gravesite of Elizabeth Bisland. It was just one of many things the two women had in common. Although one had come from Pennsylvania, the other from Louisiana, both were laid to rest in Woodlawn; both married wealthy men, both were childless, both lived in Europe during the First World War, both were widowed, and both died of pneumonia.

Both women, too, were writers right up to the very end.

Notes

1. Rhoda Broughton (1840–1920) was a popular novelist and the host of Oxford's Browning Society, where the guests occasionally included Robert Browning himself.

2. Charles Whitman Wetmore (1854–1919) was an Ohio-born, Harvard-educated lawyer, financier, and businessman.

3. Eugene V. Debs (1855–1926) was a railroad labor leader and Socialist Party candidate for president in 1908, 1912, and 1920. He served jail terms for his activities in the Pullman Strike and during World War I for sedition. A founder of the International Workers of the World (IWW), he later found the group too radical and withdrew.

4. Emma Goldman (1869–1940) was born in Lithuania and immigrated to the United States in 1885. While working in clothing factories, she became active in the socialist and anarchist movements. Her opposition to World War I led to a jail term and then in 1919 deportation to the Soviet Union. She quickly became disillusioned there and spent the rest of her life lecturing and writing in western Europe.

5. Pullman Strike: On May 11, 1894, workers in the Pullman Palace Car Company in Illinois walked off the job in protest against wage cuts. By June 30, 125,000 sympathetic rail workers refused to handle Pullman cars, thus tying up rail traffic west of Chicago. Violence soon broke out. President Cleveland obtained an injunction against the workers and sent federal troops to quell disorder. The strike dwindled, Pullman agreed to rehire workers if they signed an agreement not to join a union, and the plant reopened on August 2.

6. Robert Livingston Seaman (1822–1904). His first career was in the wholesale grocery business, but recognizing the need for milk cans, he moved into the sheet metal trade and founded the Iron Clad Manufacturing Company, which, at his death, was the largest supplier of cans in the country.

Index

Index

Note: Page numbers in italics refer to illustrations. Numbers after *n* refer to notes. EB and NB refer to Elizabeth Bisland and Nellie Bly, respectively.

Index

List of the Lakeside Classics

The Lakeside Classics

The Lakeside Classics

The Lakeside Classics

The Lakeside Classics

IMAGE CREDITS

Courtesy of Matthew Goodman: xxxix

The Internet Archive: from *A Trip around the World*, George Moerlein (Cincinnati: M. & R. Bergheim, 1888): 154, 292

Library of Congress: xxvii, 2, 7, 19, 30, 96, 102, 114, 123, 176, 221, 235, 242, 283, 290, 304, 314, 321

Property of the publisher: postcards: 63, 146, 169, 171, 180, 187, 206, 210, 216, 267, 271

University of Chicago Library: from *Autour du monde: Aquarelles souvenirs de voyages (Paris: L. Boulanger, 189-):* 260, 289; from *Cosmopolitan Magazine,* May 1890: 81; from *Japan, described and illustrated by the Japanese,* F. Brinkley (Boston: J. B. Millet Company, 1897): 86, 127, 129, 251, 256; from *Surface Japan*, Don C. Seitz (New York: Harper & Brothers, 1891) 254

University of Chicago, Special Collections Research Center: from *Dans l'intimité de personnages illustres*, Maurice Devriès (Paris: Éditions M.D.): 49; from *A Flying Trip around the World,* Elizabeth Bisland (New York: Harper Brothers, 1891): xlii, 2; from *Le Tour du monde en quatre-vingts jours*, Jules Verne (Paris: J. Hetzel et Cie, 1900): ii, xvii, 56

Courtesy of University of Iowa Library, Special Collections Department: xl

DESIGNED, TYPESET, PRINTED, BOUND, AND DISTRIBUTED BY
R. R. DONNELLEY & SONS COMPANY

COMPOSITION:
ALLENTOWN, PENNSYLVANIA
CHENNAI, INDIA

SCANNING AND IMAGE PROOFING:
RR DONNELLEY
PREMEDIA TECHNOLOGIES
ELGIN, ILLINOIS

COMPUTER TO PLATES, PRINTING, AND BINDING:
CRAWFORDSVILLE, INDIANA

ADDRESSING AND MAILING:
RR DONNELLEY
RESPONSE MARKETING SERVICES

WORLDWIDE DISTRIBUTION:
RR DONNELLEY LOGISTICS

BODY TYPEFACE:
11/12.85 POINT ADOBE GARAMOND PRO

CLOTH:
ARRESTOX VELLUM, LAKESIDE GREEN,
BY HOLLISTON MILLS, INC.

PAPER STOCK:
50-POUND WHITE LAKESIDE CLASSIC
FROM LINDENMYER
BY GLATFELTER

LAKESIDE CLASSICS ARE PRINTED
ON A PERMANENT PAPER
FOR ENDURING QUALITY